ROOM'S DICTIONARY OF CONFUSIBLES

ROOM'S DICTIONARY OF CONFUSIBLES

Adrian Room

ROUTLEDGE & KEGAN PAUL
London, Boston and Henley

First published in 1979
by Routledge & Kegan Paul Ltd
39 Store Street, London WC1E 7DD,
Broadway House, Newtown Road,
Henley-on-Thames, Oxon RG9 1EN and
9 Park Street, Boston, Mass. 02108, USA
Reprinted in 1979
Set in 9 on 10 pt Imprint
and printed in Great Britain by
Ebenezer Baylis & Son Ltd,
The Trinity Press, Worcester, and London
© Adrian Room 1979

British Library Cataloguing in Publication Data

Room, Adrian

Room's dictionary of confusibles.
1. English language – Glossaries, vocabularies, etc.
I. Dictionary of confusibles
423'.1   PE1680   78-40970

ISBN 0 7100 0120 7

CONTENTS

'Take care of the sense, and the sounds will take care of themselves'

(maxim offered by the Duchess for the edification of Alice in Wonderland)

INTRODUCTION

'Let thy words be few', counsels the unknown author of the Book of Ecclesiastes. Sound advice, too. In everyday life, however, it is an injunction not so easy to obey. Words are *not* few. We are obliged to use words plentifully, even prolifically, if we are to communicate. So round the clock we speak words, hear words, read words, think words and dream words. And it is hardly surprising, therefore, that when communicating we get our wires crossed occasionally. We say one word when we mean another, half-comprehend or misunderstand words, and encounter unfamiliar and 'hard' words daily.

In short, we confuse words.

This dictionary contains a selection of words that are frequently confused, either mentally, and so in unexpressed form, or in our speech and writing. The selection is necessarily a personal one and, of course, it is far from comprehensive. We all have our pet 'confusibles', our own 'I-always-mix-those-up' syndrome. 'Progeny', we read – and half think of 'prodigy'. 'Meaningful dialogue', someone says – and we wonder how meaningful 'duologue' would be in the same context. 'Ostensibly', we write – and reflect that possibly we should have said 'ostentatiously'. Or perhaps even 'ostensively'? It's not just excited children who exclaim: 'She's brought my present!' when they mean 'bought'.

There seem to be two main categories of words that get mixed up. The first type of word is one that is fairly specialised, erudite or bookish. Occasionally it is a rather more familiar word. Either way, it has a knack of involuntarily conjuring up an ordinary, everyday word unrelated to it in origin or meaning, and so produces an incongruous but frequently apt mental association. 'Fatuous', for example. Say, hear or read 'fatuous', and 'fat' will spring to mind. One has the image of a rotund, rather low-grade comic or a portly but not over-witty uncle – an agreeable link. Or how about 'guerrilla'? A corny one, of course, but the association with 'gorilla' is strong enough, and the overtone – common to both words – of hidden danger in the jungle appeals to the whimsical in us.

Such conjured-up words I think of as 'suggestibles'. And a 'suggestible' I would define as 'a word which is involuntarily evoked by another, although unrelated to it in origin or even in meaning'.

Since the germ of 'confusibles' lies in 'suggestibles', it might be interesting to instance one or two more. Here are twenty further examples. For the first ten I indicate what will be, I imagine, the association in most people's minds; for the second ten the reader is left to determine and define his own link, which will probably be both involuntary and spontaneous.

word	suggestible	association
wainscot	waistcoat	something encircling or surrounding
bombast	bomb	force, power, vigour
latent	late	delayed appearance or materialisation
ambush	bush	concealed snare in the countryside
viking	king	noble ruler or conqueror
jubilee	jubilant	rejoicing, celebration
capstan	captain	symbol of naval strength and authority*
whet	wet	aperitif (which is wet and whets the appetite)
tapir	taper	animal with tapering nose
haggard	hag	wild and ugly looking
hallow	halo	
brackish	bracken	
shrift	shift	
calvary	cavalry	
absinthe	absent	
brunt	blunt	
lemon sole	lemon	
belfry	bells	
greyhound	grey	
walnut	wall	

* Advertising provides another association: that of tobacco and cigarettes.

The last four in this list are vintage suggestibles: words that have come to be firmly yet originally incorrectly associated. 'Lemon sole' has nothing to do with lemons but is derived from a thirteenth-century French word *limande* of unknown meaning. Similarly, 'belfry' has its origin in an old German word *bervrit* or *bercvrit* meaning 'siege-tower' – which the structure once was. 'Greyhound' comes from a conjectured Old English word *grieg*, whose meaning is uncertain, plus 'hound'. (Dog experts claim that greyhounds, moreover, are any colour but grey!) A 'walnut' is not a 'wall nut' but a 'foreign nut'. The Old English word for it was *walh-hnutu*: the first half of this gives Wales and the Welsh their name, since to the Anglo-Saxon invaders they were 'foreigners' in their own land.

If clarification of the linking concepts of the remaining six words is needed, it will be found at the end of the book, Appendix II, page 153.

So much for a suggestible.

What, then, is a confusible?

Obviously, the term is not a linguistic one. It may make some purists flinch, indeed, but it seems a handy word to describe the phenomenon dealt with by the present dictionary, although itself not found in most standard dictionaries of English.

A confusible, basically, is *a word that not only resembles another in spelling and pronunciation, but one that additionally has a similar or associated meaning.* Put rather more formally, it is a word having a lexical and semantic (but not necessarily etymological) affinity with another. It is thus rather more than a malapropism – as in Mrs Malaprop's famous 'nice derangement of epitaphs' – and closer, perhaps, to a paronym, although linguists are not fully agreed as to what a paronym really is. One definition runs: 'Paronyms are words with an identical root that sound the same but are different in meaning; they are accented on the same syllable, belong to the same part of speech, and express concepts whose distinctions consist in particular additional shades of meaning that serve to define the concept more precisely' (O. V. Vishnyakova, *Paronyms in Russian*, 'Higher School' Publishing House, Moscow, 1974, pp. 8–9). ('Paronym' has the literal meaning of 'beside name'.)

Whereas, however, a suggestible is a fairly common word conjured up by a rarer one, a confusible can be either narrow (or 'specialist'), or ordinary and everyday. Thus confusibles, like misfortunes, never come singly. They are often as not found in pairs, but – as a glance through the headwords of the dictionary will show – also exist in larger groups, so that one has at times quite sizeable 'confusible clusters'. A is confused with B, which is also mixed up with C and sometimes with D . . . and so on.

Simply on the grounds of space, the field of confusible candidates for this selection had to be narrowed in some way. I did this by applying six fairly well defined criteria. If the confusibles met the criteria, and also, of course, conformed to the overall definition above, they were short-listed. A final selection was arrived at rather more subjectively: if the confusibles seemed to be particularly common, or particularly interesting in some way, they were in. Even in cases where one confusible of a pair turns out, after all, not to be a confusible – that is, the two words mean the same after all – the pair was included, if only to show that the supposed *faux amis* are really *vrais* (see, for example, **daring**, **inflammable**, and **resource**).

The criteria were established by putting each confusible through six paces:

1 Do the words in the pair or larger group resemble each other closely in spelling? Do they in fact contain a high proportion of identical letters (not necessarily in the same order)? Do the words, in particular, begin with the same letters? Most confusibles meet this requirement.
2 Do the words sound alike – are they, that is, homophones or near-homophones? Examples would be **flair/flare**, **cord/chord**, **fraction/faction**.
3 Do the confusibles have the same number of syllables? See, for example, **effective/effectual** (the latter usually being pronounced with three rather than four syllables), **flamenco/fandango**, **sensitivity/sensibility**.
4 Are the confusibles accented on the same syllable? Examples: **discomfort/discomfit**, **treacherous/traitorous**.
5 Do the confusibles belong to the same part of speech, i.e. are they both verbs, adverbs, adjectives, etc.? Examples: **triumphant/triumphal** (both adjectives), **ostentatiously/ostensibly** (both adverbs), **undoubted/redoubted** (both verbs – in this case both past participles used as adjectives).

3

6 Can the confusibles be classified under the same stylistic label, i.e. are they both foreign words, technical jargon, scientific terms, slang expressions or the like? This factor can increase the degree of confusibility considerably. Examples: **ménage/manège** (both French words), **malachite/marcasite** (terms from mineralogy), **kinky/kooky** (slang words), **bear/bull** (financial jargon), **e.g./i.e.** (abbreviations – both foreign).

If the answer is 'yes' to one or more of these, and if the confusibles match up to the basic sight-sound-sense criterion, they are likely to find their place in these pages. In some cases, indeed, confusibles exist that conform to all six criteria. Let us check the pair **fraction/faction**, for instance, through all six steps. They look alike (1), sound alike (2), have the same number of syllables (3), are identically stressed (4), are both nouns (5) and both political terms (6). In addition they share a common meaning – 'militant group'. Confusibles, therefore, *par excellence*.

The proportion of everyday confusibles, however, is greater than is perhaps expected. But to confuse 'fuggy' with 'fusty' or 'scamp' with 'scrimp' is not entirely just a matter of a slip of the tongue or of an inadequate mental 'vetting'. Often there is another influence at work. This is the phenomenon known as phonaesthesia – a word as linguistically impressive as 'confusible' is non-technical and general. In the Addenda to the second edition of his *Changing English* (André Deutsch, 1975), the late Professor Simeon Potter defined phonaesthesia thus: 'sound-meaning associations which would seem to be not merely echoic or onomatopoeic but rather linguistically innate and universal'.

Such a definition ties in closely with the nature of a confusible. In practice, phonaesthesia implies that words sounding alike suggest a common general meaning. This is particularly noticeable of many very ordinary words beginning with the same consonant grouping. A number of words starting with 'st-', for example, denote a fixed or rigid state, such as stable, stand, state, static, station, stay, steady, steep, step, stereotype, sterile, stick, still, stone, stop, stout. Several words, again, beginning with 'sl-' express the general notion of a downward gliding motion, such as slack, sledge, sleek, sleep, sleeve, slender, slide, sling, slip, slither, slobber, slope, slow, slumber, slump. The reader may like to apply the idea to other consonants. Try, for example, the dullness and tediousness expressed by 'dr-' words (drag, dreary, dregs, drizzle, droop, drudge), the lightness and superficial rapidity of 'fl-' words (flake, flap, flee, flick, flirt, float, flounce), or the conciseness and precision evoked by 'cl-' words (clasp, class, clean, clench, clever, clinic, clock, cluster). Many words with phonaesthetic properties turn out to be confusibles – see, for instance, **babble, clang, encumber, scamp** and **solid**.

The sixth and last of the criteria, however, is far from being the least important. It is possible, in fact, to consign many pairs or groups of confusibles to the same specific subject category. Words familiar to us because they fall within our own 'speciality' – we are all specialists these days – will not of course confuse. Words outside our own range of subjects or specialities, though, may well turn out to be confusibles. The dictionary includes confusibles from a fairly wide range of subject categories. Here is a bird's eye preview of some of the more common ones to be represented:

Animals: **crayfish, draught horse, gerbil, macaw, swordfish**
Architecture: **bay window, conduit, pagoda, plaza, suburbia**
Art: **amber, Art Nouveau, baroque, op-art, passe-partout**
Diplomacy: **honourable, mufti, nabob, signor**
Entertainment: **Cinerama, Emmy, flamenco, Gaiety girls, razzmatazz**
Ethnology: **ayah, kraal, Mohawk, mulatto, Scottish**
Fashion: **cashmere, magenta, nylon, organdie, sari**
Food and drink: **amontillado, burgundy, chive, gourmand, viniculture**
Geography: **Arctic, leeward, Micronesia, prairie, tundra**
History: **czarevitch, Gestapo, Ming, rajah, Renaissance**
Linguistics: **Celtic, epsilon, phoneme, umlaut**
Literature: **dialogue, epic, euphemism, preface**
Mathematics: **million, numerator, ordinal, perimeter, rhombus**
Medicine: **bacteria, bile, larynx, orthopaedic, typhoid**
Military: **ammunition, Bren gun, corvette, strategy**
Music: **clavichord, largo, meistersingers, solfeggio, zither**
Mythology: **augury, dryad, jinn, Minotaur, nymph**
Religion: **Buddha, Capuchin, hoodoo, miracle play, sexton**
Science and technology: **albumen, carbon monoxide, cyclotron, quasar**
Sport: **judo, marathon, matador, veteran car**

As well as 'ordinary' words, a certain leavening of proper names has been included. I would have liked to add a seasoning of abbreviations, but confusible abbreviations are legion and really demand a dictionary of their own. A thin representation of abbreviations will nevertheless be found.

The arrangement of the dictionary is straightforward. In the headwords of the entries, confusibles are normally given in the order 'familiar→unfamiliar' or 'general→specific'. This is because in many cases it is the second word that is regarded as a confusible of the first. In some instances, however, this order is not observed, notably where there are more than two confusibles. The order, too, is an arbitrary one where the confusibles are equally current. Confusibles that are not the first headword in an entry are cross-indexed in their appropriate alphabetical place.

The definition in brackets after the headwords is the 'common factor' that unites the confusibles in meaning. It is naturally not a dictionary definition in the accepted sense, but simply a pointer to the association between the words that will occur to most people when they encounter either word of the pair. The definition will show that in many cases the associative link is a limited one: not all senses of a given word are dealt with in the entry. See, for example, the specific confusible sense of **let**, **move** and **vacant**.

The main entry usually treats the words in the same order as they appear in the heading. In some cases, too, pronunciation and alternative spelling is indicated, and a few entries mention confusibles that, since they do not conform to the basic

5

criterion, do not appear in their own right (for example 'compliment' in the entry on **supplement**). The main task of each entry, however, is to define and distinguish the words, and this is done mostly by means of brief definitions and examples of usage. The origin of several confusibles is given, especially when it is unexpected. The etymology of a word, in fact, can sometimes give a clue as to *why* the word has come to be a confusible.

Prefixes and suffixes present a particular hazard in the world of confusibles, and they are dealt with separately in Appendix 1, p. 147.

Finally, the dictionary, in its limited and modest scope, aims to be, like its older and wiser brother, the *Concise Oxford Dictionary*, 'essentially descriptive rather than prescriptive'. I have tried to show how a given word is actually used – and confused – rather than point to its 'correct' usage. Only rarely is this objective departed from, and then usually in connection with a definition cited by a particular dictionary (see, for example, 'rangy' at **randy**).

References in the text to specific sources or dictionaries indicate the provenance of the confusibles themselves and the authorities consulted concerning them. *Chambers*, for example, is *Chambers Twentieth Century Dictionary* (revised edition with new supplement, 1977), and *SOED* the *Shorter Oxford English Dictionary* (third edition with corrections, 1975).

Many of the confusibles were extracted from the pages of the *Concise Oxford Dictionary* (sixth edition, 1976) where one word and its definition conjured up another or where pairs of confusibles were found lying in reasonably close proximity to each other on the same page. Others were taken from the columns of *Roget's Thesaurus of English Words and Phrases* (Longmans, 1962) and Martin Lehnert's *Reverse Dictionary of Present-Day English* (VEB Verlag Enzyklopädie, Leipzig, 1973), where over 100,000 words are listed in alphabetical order starting with their final letters. Combing these three works for confusibles was a time-consuming but intriguing operation, which in fact yielded far more candidates than could be accepted.

Other dictionaries consulted apart from *Chambers* and the *SOED* were the first two volumes of the *Supplement to the Oxford English Dictionary* (A–G, 1972 and H–N, 1976), the Hamlyn *Encyclopedic World Dictionary* edited by Patrick Hanks (1971), and the great doyen of American dictionaries, *Webster's Third New International Dictionary* (1971 edition, with addenda). This last work's treatment of etymologies is unrivalled.

Partridge invariably refers to Eric Partridge's useful, if now rather dated, *Usage and Abusage* (Penguin Books, 1970), which itself has several entries disentangling confusibles. Another source of a smallish but very valid group of confusibles was the *Associated Press Stylebook* edited by Howard Angione (The Associated Press, New York, 1977). Confusibles can plague a journalist more than most, perhaps.

Specialized words and their meanings I checked in the *Encyclopaedia Britannica* (fifteenth edition, 1976), and in a number of specific authorities ranging from L. P. Bloodgood and P. Santini's *The Horseman's Dictionary* (Pelham Books, 1963) to J. A. Cuddon's superb *Dictionary of Literary Terms* (André Deutsch, 1977).

I owe, too, a debt to Philip Howard's stimulating little book *New Words for Old*

6

(Hamish Hamilton, 1977) and Kenneth Hudson's unusual *Dictionary of Diseased English* (Macmillan, 1977). May works such as these, and the BBC's two printed collections of broadcast talks, *Words* (1975) and *More Words* (1977), continue to guard and guide the course of the English language. May they encourage, too, more of us to be word-watchers.

Last of all, but of course not least of all, I must thank my unassuming but most competent secretary, Nicola Village, for watching my own words and setting them all out so well for the printer.

Stamford, Lincolnshire   Adrian Room

DICTIONARY

abaft/abeam (not ahead – of a ship at sea)
Draw an imaginary line through the centre of a ship at right angles to it. Anything behind this line will be 'abaft' – as distinct from 'astern', when it will be to the rear of the stern. Anything actually on this imaginary line, to left or right – port or starboard – will be 'abeam'.

abdicate/abrogate/arrogate/derogate
(cancel or alter a person's status)
To 'abdicate' is to renounce formally, as most commonly by a monarch of the throne. The verb can also apply to other kinds of authority or standing, so that one can 'abdicate' one's power, office, duties or rights. To 'abrogate' a law is to cancel or annul it. To 'arrogate' something is to seize or claim it without right, as when a person 'arrogates' certain privileges to himself. To 'derogate' is to lessen or detract from in some way: to 'derogate' a person's authority, for example, is to undermine it, and to 'derogate' someone's rights is to restrict them. The 'ar-' prefix in 'arrogate' is a form of 'ad-', that is, 'to', with the '-rogate' root of three of the verbs meaning 'ask'.

abeam see **abaft**

ability see **capability**

ablaut see **umlaut**

abrogate see **abdicate**

abrupt/brusque/brisk (peremptory)
'Abrupt' has the basic sense of 'sudden', and referring to someone's manner can suggest rudeness, and imply a discourteous interruption. An 'abrupt' manner can, of course, actually be a sign of shyness, but it tends to be more the hall-mark of extroverts than of introverts. 'Brusque' suggests a businesslike manner, not necessarily a discourteous one. Here, too, brusqueness can indicate the introvert, especially if it takes the form of a kind of gruffness. If 'brush-off' suggests 'brusque' so much the better: the word ultimately goes back to the Latin *brucum* (broom). 'Brisk' is the most extrovert of the three, with no suggestion of shyness. The word implies a lively efficiency and frequently connotes an almost hale and hearty state, as when one walks at a 'brisk' pace in a 'brisk' wind.

abstruse see **obscure**

abuse/misuse (as verb: use improperly; as noun: improper use)
To 'abuse' something is to use it wrongly or badly, as when 'abusing' a privilege or one's authority. To 'abuse' a person is to malign him. To 'misuse' something, on the other hand, is simply to use it for a purpose for which it was not intended, as one's knife for putting cheese into one's mouth. All too often a rarish word gets 'misused' – but hardly ever 'abused'.

Abwehr see **Bundeswehr**

abyss see **crevice**

accidental see **incidental**

accord/account (independently, in the phrases 'of one's own accord', 'on one's own account')
The two phrases are sometimes confused both in meaning and formation ('on' for

9

'of', and vice versa). To do something 'on one's own account' is to do it with some kind of initiative, whether by oneself or for oneself. Something done 'of one's own accord', however, is done voluntarily, without prompting. Here, too, a measure of initiative is suggested.

account see **accord**

acerbic see **acid**

acid/acrid/acerbic (sharp, stinging)
Apart from its use as a chemical term, 'acid' basically denotes a sharpness or sourness of taste, as of a lemon or an 'acid' drop. Applied to a person it implies a sharp temper or kind of caustic hostility, as seen in an 'acid' remark or an 'acid' tongue. In addition to sharpness, 'acrid' suggests a stinging or smarting quality; an 'acrid' remark is a biting one, and stronger than an 'acid' one. In its literal sense, 'acrid' is often used for smoke and fumes that sting the eyes and nose. 'Acerbic' is less often used as an adjective than 'acid' or 'acrid', but as a noun ('acerbity') is quite often used of words spoken bitterly and usually snappily, as when one is stung into making some kind of retort. The literal sense of 'acerbic' is 'sour-tasting'.

acrid see **acid**

act see **action**

action/act (thing done)
As *Partridge* points out, an 'action' applies in particular to the doing of something, whereas an 'act' refers to the thing done. One can thus take avoiding 'action' – the thing one does is to avoid – as the result of a deliberate 'act' – one that is intentional and thus has a definite consequence. An 'act', too, is usually of short duration, while an 'action' may take some time and indeed consist of several individual 'acts'. This temporal difference is illustrated by such legal terms as 'Act of God' and 'civil action'.

activate/actuate (set working)
'Activate' has the basic sense 'make active' and as such is used mainly in scientific expressions, as to 'activate' sewage (aerate it) and 'activate' carbon (make it more active). 'Actuate' is a more general word whether used in a literal sense of things – to 'actuate' a switch is to operate it – or in a figurative sense of people, where it is usually passive, as when one is 'actuated' by selfish motives. It is in fact close in meaning to 'motivated'.

actuate see **activate**

acuity/acumen (sharpness of mind)
'Acuity' – related to 'acute' with its sense of sharpness – is used of any human faculty and applied to any of the five senses as well as the mind. 'Acumen', however – sometimes wrongly accented on the first syllable instead of the second – is applied to mental sharpness only, suggesting a penetrating mind or a discerning one. It is therefore a virtual synonym for 'perspicacity' – itself a confusible (see **perceptive**).

acumen see **acuity**

addled see **muddled**

adjacent/adjoining (close to, next to)
If one thing is 'adjacent' to another, it borders it or is next to it, without necessarily touching, as a field that is 'adjacent' to the road and 'adjacent' angles in geometry. An 'adjoining' object, however, has a common point with some other object, as an 'adjoining' room or yard, which leads off or into some other part of the premises.

adjoining see **adjacent**

adjure/conjure (entreat)
Both these verbs – each accented on the second syllable – have the general sense of making an earnest request. To 'adjure', however, as implied in its origin from Latin *adjurare* (swear), suggests that the person entreated is put under some kind of oath, whereas to 'conjure', with its origin in Latin *conjurare* (swear together), is properly better applied to more than one person. The verbs are very bookish, though, and can be easily avoided by means of such alternatives as 'implore', 'urge' or 'beg'.

admission/admittance (right to enter)
The difference is between physically entering a place – as in the familiar notice 'No admittance except on business' – and the granting of the right to join a particular group of people, as the 'admission' of a guest to one's club, a patient to hospital, or an immigrant into a foreign country. *Partridge* points out that when these two factors are combined, as when one goes to the cinema or enters a sporting contest, 'admission' is used, often referring to the price demanded – 'Admission 50p'.

admittance see **admission**

ado see **to-do**

adventuresome see **adventurous**

adventurous/adventuresome/venturesome/venturous (bold)
An 'adventurous' person is one who seeks adventure, with the implication that a risk is being taken or that courage is needed. Such a person may well have an 'adventurous' spirit, and enjoy trips that for one reason or another are 'adventurous'. An 'adventuresome' youth, however, takes more of a risk than a purely 'adventurous' one – his involvements may well be foolhardy ones. Rasher still is a 'venturesome' youth, who constantly takes risks and whose exploits are usually hazardous. The word is frequently used to describe a mood or inclination. 'Venturous' is close to 'venturesome' in meaning but describes more the nature of the enterprise than the attitude that prompted it. If a prisoner, one would make a 'venturous' bid for freedom rather than a 'venturesome' one.

adverse to see **averse to**

aeon see **era**

aesthetic/ascetic (refined – of taste)
The basic meaning of 'aesthetic' is appreciating what is beautiful. If one has a well developed 'aesthetic' sense one is, by implication, more artistic than practical. But in their different ways both an athlete and an artisan will have an 'aesthetic' sense if they are aware of the beauty of what they create, in spite of the fact that the artisan, at least, is involved in a practical craft. Someone whose outlook is 'ascetic' is also aware of the finer things of life, but in his case his aims are usually harshly idealistic, with the implication that abstention is the best means of achieving the end. The word has religious connotations – it is therefore not surprising to find its origin in the Greek *asketes* (monk).

affect/effect (exert influence on)
To 'affect' something is to have an 'effect' on it. Smoking thus 'affects' your health. If something 'affects' you it concerns you. The possible harm caused by smoking thus 'affects' all of us. To 'effect' something – the verb cannot apply to people – is to bring it about. Heavy smoking may well 'effect' a deterioration in your health, therefore. The difference lies in the prefixes: 'affect' has *ad-* (towards); 'effect' has *ex-* (out). The first of these denotes a cause; the second . . . an 'effect'.

afflicted see **inflicted**

aggravate/exacerbate/exasperate (irritate)
To 'aggravate' something is to make it worse, as by scratching a mosquito bite. To 'aggravate' a person is to annoy him – a use of the word that some people deplore. To 'exacerbate' a thing – the word is related to 'acerbic' (see **acid**) – is to increase its bitterness or harshness, especially of a disease or someone's bad mood. To 'exasperate' someone is to irritate him in the extreme, usually to a degree of frustration. The root of the word is Latin *asper* (rough).

agnostic see **atheist**

albumen/albumin (substance found in the white of an egg)
Both words derive from Latin *albus* (white). 'Albumen' actually *is* the white of an egg – as a general scientific term – or else the nutritive matter, called the endosperm, round the embryo of a seed. 'Albumin', a narrower chemical term, is the name of a class of proteins soluble in

water. Some biochemists, however, equate 'albumin' with 'albumen', and dictionary definitions of both words vary considerably.

albumin see **albumen**

allegory see **analogy**

Allhallows see **All Saints' Day**

allies/Axis (united forces in Second World War)
Both words denote an alliance of countries. The 'allies' were the armed forces of the allies of Britain, in particular the Americans, French and Russians. These fought against the 'Axis', the name used for the alliance of Germany, Italy and Japan and originating historically from the Rome–Berlin Axis of 1936. The idea was that the 'axis' was the line joining Rome and Berlin – and later extended to Tokyo – with the alliance being the pivot on which the countries revolved. But there was also a London–Washington 'axis', and subsequently a Moscow–Peking one.

allocate/allot (appoint as one's due or share)
To 'allocate' something is to set it aside for a specific purpose. One can thus be 'allocated' a place to park one's car, or a room in a hotel or hostel. To 'allot' something is to give it, but with an implied restriction, and the understanding that one is sharing something. If you are 'allotted' five minutes to make your speech, you must thus share the overall time with everyone else. There's no choice; that will – quite literally – be your lot.

allot see **allocate**

All Saints' Day/All Souls' Day/ Allhallows/Hallowe'en (late autumn festival of religious origin)
'Hallow' means 'holy', so that 'Allhallows' is another name for 'All Saints' Day' on 1 November, when the Anglican and Roman Catholic churches commemorate all the saints thus including all those who have no day of their own at any other time in the year. The day after this is 'All Souls'

Day', dedicated by the church to the memory of the faithful departed. These are strictly religious festivals. 'Hallowe'en', originally 'All-hallow-even', is thus the eve of, or day before, 'All Saints' Day', 31 October, which in the old Celtic calendar was the last night of the year. The pagan ceremonies of the day were not very successfully transformed by the church into the eve of a major religious festival. They survive quite healthily in the form of 'Hallowe'en' parties and other traditional customs smacking romantically of witchcraft and general black magic.

All Souls' Day see **All Saints' Day**

allure see **lure**

alternately/alternatively (relating to one of two)
'Alternately' means one after the other, in time or space; 'alternatively' means one *instead* of the other. It's as simple as that.

alternatively see **alternately**

amah see **ayah**

amatory see **amorous**

amber/umber/ochre (shade of yellow or brown)
'Amber', deriving ultimately from an Arabic word meaning 'ambergris', is the colour of the fossil resin, pale yellow, or of the resin itself, which is yellowish brown. Conventionally it is the colour of the 'caution' traffic light and urine. 'Umber' is a type of earth, perhaps originally from Umbria, in Italy, that produces a reddish brown pigment, known also as burnt 'umber'. 'Ochre' is also an earth – a metallic oxide of iron ranging in colour from pale yellow to orange and red and, like 'umber', used as a pigment.

amend/emend (change, alter)
To 'amend' something is to improve it. A bill 'amended' in Parliament is thus altered for the better. The very common verb 'mend' is in fact derived from it, with the improving sense still clear in such an expression as 'mending' one's ways. To

'emend' something, on the other hand, is to correct it, remove the errors from it. The word is most often used with reference to a text of some kind that has been corrected. The noun of 'amend' is 'amendment'; of 'emend' it is 'emendation'.

amiable/amicable (friendly)
'Amiable' is used of a person or his nature or facial expression, so that an 'amiable' workmate might well have an 'amiable' smile to indicate his 'amiable' disposition. 'Amicable' refers to something done with goodwill, in particular an agreement or combined undertaking such as an exchange of views. It is always pleasant when differences can be settled in an 'amicable' way, which can happen when one of the sides is, for once, in an 'amiable' mood.

amicable see **amiable**

ammunition/munitions (offensive weapons)
'Ammunition' comprises virtually all missiles and means of attack fired from weapons of all kinds and includes weapons that are their own means of attack such as bombs, mines and chemical agents. The 'am-' is not a prefix, as the word derives from French *la munition*, which was originally taken as *l'amunition*. 'Munitions' widens the offensive to embrace both 'ammunition' and weapons of all kinds. A 'munitions' factory may thus produce not only shells but the guns that fire them.

amok see **berserk**

amontillado/Montilla/manzanilla/ marsala (type of sherry)
Only two of these are true sherries. 'Montilla' is a dry, sherry-type wine made in the region around Montilla, in southern Spain, and 'marsala' is a light-coloured wine resembling sherry shipped from the Sicilian port of Marsala. 'Amontillado', like 'Montilla', comes from the Montilla district, but is a real sherry, a medium dry one, its dry equivalent being called 'fino', and the sweet variety 'oloroso'. 'Manzanilla' is a very dry pale sherry, with its name not deriving from a place but from the Spanish word for 'camomile' (see

calamine). The sherry itself comes from the vineyards at the mouth of the Guadalquivir in southern Spain – properly from the town of Sanlucar, eight miles west of Seville, near which, intriguingly, there is in fact the small village of Manzanilla.

amoral see **immoral**

amorous/amatory (loving)
An 'amorous' poem could, if the writer chose, be an erotic or even lewd one. An 'amatory' poem, however, is simply one written by a lover. Similarly an 'amorous' look could mean business, but an 'amatory' look is just one given by someone in love. Put another way, 'amorous' may imply the physical aspect of love; 'amatory' pertains to love in the abstract.

anaesthetic/analgesic (as noun: deadener of pain or bodily sensation)
The prime purpose of an 'anaesthetic' is to deaden sensation locally or generally, the latter resulting in unconsciousness. An 'analgesic' may also deaden sensation, but its basic aim is to relieve or remove pain by blocking the transmission of nerve impulses. A mild 'analgesic' is aspirin, a strong one is morphine. Both words have the Greek prefix *an-* denoting absence of, respectively, feeling and pain.

analgesic see **anaesthetic**

analogy/allegory (artistic device whereby one thing is compared to another, unlike it)
The essential feature of an 'analogy' is that although two things may partially resemble each other, or be alike, they are basically of quite a different nature. Compare death to sleep and you have an 'analogy'. You also have a metaphor if you say death *is* sleep, and it's an extended metaphor that is the basis of an 'allegory', which is a story told in symbolic terms. Examples of an 'allegory' are, in literature, *Pilgrim's Progress*, and, in art, Holman Hunt's *The Scapegoat*.

Anderson shelter/Morrison shelter (type of air-raid shelter in Second World War)
The 'Anderson shelter', named after Sir John Anderson, British Home Secretary

at the outbreak of the war, was a smallish prefabricated shelter, usually half buried in the back garden. The 'Morrison shelter' was essentially an indoor construction, made of steel and shaped like a table. It was designed to give protection if the house collapsed, and was named after Herbert Morrison, British Secretary of State for Home Affairs from 1940 to the end of the war.

announce/pronounce/proclaim
(declare publicly)
'Announce' is the general word – to say what is going to happen. One thus 'announces' one's plans for the future or the time of the proposed next meeting. To 'pronounce' something is to declare it solemnly or authoritatively, frequently in public. The key point in the Anglican marriage service is when the priest 'pronounces' that the man and woman 'be Man and Wife together'. To 'proclaim' something is to 'announce' it – but widely, so that it is generally known, as the results of an election. Something 'proclaimed', such as a holiday, may result from a decision of some kind.

annual/perennial (occurring every year)
If something is 'annual' it happens every year, once a year. We are all familiar with 'annual' visits to the dentist, tax returns and Christmas parties. The literal meaning of 'perennial', from Latin *per* (through) and *annus* (year) is 'lasting right through the year', i.e. continuous. The word is often used, though, to mean 'recurrent', as a 'perennial' problem. The noun 'perennial', meaning the plant, is technically regarded as one that lasts more than two years, as distinct from the 'annual', which lasts one year, and the 'biennial' (see **biannual**).

antagonist/protagonist (leader of a cause or campaign)
A 'protagonist' is, properly, the leading character in a novel or play. Possibly under the influence of the better known 'antagonist' it has come to acquire the popular meaning of one who champions or supports a cause. But an 'antagonist' is really someone opposed to someone else, an opponent.

Confusion over 'protagonist', too, has occurred through Greek *protos* (first) being misunderstood as the prefix 'pro-' (for).

Antarctic see **Arctic**

antiquarian/antiquary (one dealing in old or historical objects)
Basically, an 'antiquarian' is a person who is interested in old objects and an expert on them. An 'antiquary' – the accent is on the first syllable – is by contrast someone who tends to concentrate more on old objects that are curiosities rather than, say, the findings of an archaeological expedition. This is not to say that an 'antiquary' is not an expert; he can in fact be a real professional or specialist, even if his occupation seems more of a hobby than a full-time occupation. The two words can overlap, though, since they have a common link with antiquities and antiques. As an adjective, 'antiquarian' can apply to antiquities or to 'antiquary', hence, referring to the latter, an 'antiquarian' bookshop.

antiquary see **antiquarian**

antiseptic/aseptic (preventing disease)
It's a matter of prefixes: an 'antiseptic' agent is directed against (Latin *anti*) sepsis, whereas something that is 'aseptic' is free (Greek *a-*) from the germs of disease. One thus applies 'antiseptic' ointment to a wound and then covers it with an 'aseptic' dressing.

aphorism see **maxim**

apogee/perigee (extreme point)
The two are opposites. The 'apogee' of one's career is the highest point of it, its climax. The terms are from astronomy, the 'apogee' being the point in the orbit of a heavenly body when it is farthest from the earth, and the 'perigee' – not used much figuratively – when it is nearest to it. A possible false association with 'peroration' may be a factor in the confusion that sometimes occurs. The '-gee' is 'earth', as in 'geology'.

arbiter/arbitrator (judge)
An 'arbiter' is a person who has the power

to judge, or who thinks he has. 'I'll be arbiter of that, thank you', says someone who feels his authority or standing is being challenged. An 'arbitrator' is someone called upon to settle some kind of dispute, with the implication that he will examine the background of the point at issue. The word has a legal or political ring about it. Both an 'arbiter' and an 'arbitrator' arbitrate, with 'arbitration' being the official word to describe what an 'arbitrator' does. An 'arbiter' can get away with making an arbitrary decision; an 'arbitrator' certainly cannot.

arbitrator see **arbiter**

arcane see **arch**

arch/arcane (secretive)
'Arch' is usually used to mean 'knowing', 'sly', with the implication that a secret is being withheld. The *SOED* says the word is usually used of women and children, but there is no need for this qualification since anyone can give an 'arch' smile or an 'arch' look. The word is nothing to do with arching one's eyebrows; its origin is the prefix 'arch-' used as an independent adjective by association with such cunning characters as archknaves and archrogues. 'Arcane', deriving from Latin *arca* (chest) – which also gave Noah his Ark – means 'secret' in the sense of 'obscure' or 'mysterious'. From the 1960s it became something of a vogue word, and itself rather 'arcane'.

Arctic/Antarctic (polar region)
Which is which? The 'Arctic' is the region round the North Pole, which lies under the constellation of the Great Bear – Greek *arktos* (bear) – while the 'Antarctic' is 'anti' it, round the South Pole. The occasional confusion between the two may be caused by the fact that although Britain and the USA are geographically close to the 'Arctic', it is the feats of British and American explorers in the 'Antarctic' that remain prominent in the mind, boosted by the history books and films such as *Scott of the Antarctic*.

arise see **rise**

armoury/arsenal (weapon store)
An 'armoury' is a store for weapons and other military equipment but not, in general, for ammunition. By contrast, an 'arsenal' is a repository of weapons and military equipment of all kinds, as well as ammunition. It is also the word for a building of this kind where troops are trained, such as Woolwich Arsenal (now transferred to Sandhurst), London, which was also the training ground of the soccer team Woolwich Arsenal (now transferred to Highbury). A less common meaning of 'arsenal' is that of the building where military equipment of all kinds is manufactured. The word goes back via the Italian *arsenale* (dock) to the Arabic *dar-sina'a* (workshop), whose initial 'd' disappeared somewhere along the line.

arouse see **rouse**

arpeggio see **solfeggio**

arrogate see **abdicate**

arsenal see **armoury**

Art Deco see **Art Nouveau**

artful see **arty**

artist/artiste (artistic performer)
An 'artist' need not be just someone who practises one of the fine arts, such as a painter or sculptor; in a more general sense it is someone who shows skill or cleverness, that is, art, in what he does, as an angler or orator. The word 'artiste' was introduced into English from the French in the nineteenth century as a consequence of the limited sense of 'artist'. Today it is used mainly of actors and singers, of either sex, but can be readily extended to include such creative experts as stylists and chefs, especially to suggest a professional excellence. It retains its near-French pronunciation of 'arteest'.

artiste see **artist**

Art Nouveau/Art Deco (style of art in fashion in the early twentieth century)
'Art Nouveau' (new art) came first. It

flourished between about 1890 and 1910 throughout Europe and the USA and was characterised by the use of long, flowing lines and curves. Germany called it the *Jugendstil* (youth style) and Italy the *stile Liberty*, after the London drapery firm started by Arthur Liberty in 1875. 'Art Deco', with name derived from the 1925 exhibition in Paris of the 'Arts décoratifs et industriels modernes', is the term that came to be used in the 1960s for the style that developed in the 1920s and became prominent in the 1930s. It had the aim of adapting the application of the 'Art Nouveau' style to the design of mass-produced furniture, posters, plastic ornaments and the like. A revived interest in the style and its objects developed in the 1970s.

arty/crafty/artful/arty-crafty (skilfully artistic)
An 'arty' person is not so much skilfully artistic as ostentatiously so, wearing 'arty' clothes or sporting an 'arty' tie. 'Crafty' originally meant skilful but is now used to mean sly, cunning – indeed, even 'devious'. 'Artful', too, means cunning, but with a certain ingenuity. Dickens's 'Artful Dodger' picked pockets with a nice combination of slyness and artistry. 'Arty-crafty', now a rather dated word, denotes a kind of earnest but trivial artistic interest. Its origin lies in the Arts and Crafts Exhibition Society, founded in London in 1888. Devotees of the arts and crafts movement were regarded by some with the same degree of suspicion or disparagement as displayed today in some quarters for champions of hydroponics, macrobiotics and numerology.

arty-crafty see **arty**

ascetic see **aesthetic**

aseptic see **antiseptic**

assail see **assault**

assault/assail (attack)
To 'assault' someone usually implies physical violence, often criminal in nature. This is reflected in the legal term 'assault and battery' where 'assault' is an 'attempt

or offer to beat another' and 'battery' the actual beating. To 'assault' a person's sense of decency is to shock or scandalise him. To 'assail' a person is usually figurative, meaning to attack him violently with abuse, pleas, arguments and the like. You can 'assail' the lawn, however, if the grass is overlong, by making a determined attack on it with a mower, just as you yourself can be 'assailed' by doubts – bombarded by them.

assay see **essay**

assent/consent (as verb: agree)
The difference is really that between active and passive. If you 'assent' to someone's view or suggestion, you need little persuading. The word is almost a synonym of 'accede' or 'acquiesce'. To 'consent' to something, however, is to give it your positive agreement, often having weighed up the matter before making a decision. A father may readily 'assent' to his daughter's marriage, or reluctantly 'consent' to it.

assert/asseverate (state as being true)
Both verbs have the sense of declaring something, with 'asseverate' implying a formal or solemn declaration. 'Asseverate' suggests 'severe', and correctly so, as the two words are related.

asseverate see **assert**

assiduous/sedulous (conscientious, determined)
To be 'assiduous' in one's work or a particular task is to be steadfast in one's application. In spite of the fact that the word derives from the Latin *assiduus* (sitting down to) it could well apply to an athlete training for a contest. If the persistence is there, so is the assiduousness – or assiduity. 'Sedulous' means very much the same, but implies that attention is paid to detail. A proof-reader should 'sedulously' study the text for misprints, for example. The noun is 'sedulity' or 'sedulousness'.

assignation see **assignment**

assignment/assignation (set task)
An 'assignment' is a task or piece of work

that has been specially allotted to a particular person or group of people. The term is used in American education to denote a pupil's or student's task, as an 'assignment' of ten arithmetic problems or an essay on the Boston Tea Party. 'Assignation' is more the actual act of assigning, and in America has the additional connotation of the arranging of an illicit meeting between lovers.

assume see **presume**

assure/ensure/insure (make sure or certain)
In the commercial sense, 'assure' strictly speaking applies to the arrangement of insurance against something that is certain to happen as, in particular, death (life 'assurance'), so that one can 'insure' against other occurrences that may or may not happen, such as floods or accidents. 'Assure' in this specifically defined sense still exists in the names of some insurance companies, as that of the London Assurance, one of Britain's oldest. In a different sense, both 'assure' and 'ensure' are close in meaning: 'make safe or sure', 'guarantee'. The distinction can be seen in a phrase such as 'success is assured', meaning simply that it is certain. 'Success is ensured' means that particular steps or actions have been taken to guarantee it. In American usage 'ensure', in the commercial sense, is sometimes used as a variant of 'insure'.

astonished/astounded/dumbfounded
(amazed, greatly surprised)
'Astonished' suggests a reaction to something unexpected or remarkable or inexplicable, as an actor's superb – or abysmal – performance or one's first chemistry experiment at school. One would be 'astounded' if the surprise made one unable to think or act, as when one is lost for words at a friend's generosity. The word is more forceful than 'astonished'. 'Dumbfounded', as it suggests, implies a striking dumb with amazement. A forthright female 'no' to a popped question must have caused many a would-be husband to be 'dumbfounded'.

astounded see **astonished**

astronaut/cosmonaut (spaceman)
Both perform essentially the same task: the difference is in nationality – an 'astronaut' tends to be American and a 'cosmonaut' Russian. The Russians themselves make a similar distinction – a Soviet spaceman is a *kosmonavt*. Both derive from Greek: respectively 'star sailor' and 'space sailor'.

atheist/agnostic (one not inclined to believe in God)
Everyone knows what an 'atheist' is: his Greek privative prefix a- (without) marks him as someone who denies the existence of God or of divine beings. An 'agnostic', with the same prefix, is not, as often held, someone who doesn't know whether there is a God or not, but someone who believes it is impossible to know or prove anything about the existence of God. An 'agnostic', therefore, says that the existence of God cannot be proved – or disproved. The word was invented by T. H. Huxley in his *Science and Christian Tradition*, published in 1870, from the Greek *agnostos* (unknowable), as the opposite of 'gnostic'.

atmosphere/stratosphere/ionosphere/ troposphere/tropopause (layer of gas surrounding the earth)
The 'atmosphere' is properly the envelope of gas, in the shape of a sphere, that surrounds the earth. It comprises, going outwards, the 'troposphere', which extends from sea level up to about seven miles, the 'stratosphere' – seven to fifty miles in altitude – and the 'ionosphere' – the upper region of the 'atmosphere' extending from around fifty miles in a succession of ionised layers – the first called the Heaviside layer – to a distance of several hundred miles. Between the 'troposphere' and the 'stratosphere' is the 'tropopause', a boundary layer. Most aircraft fly somewhere in the 'stratosphere', while clouds and 'weather' are in the 'troposphere'.

attest see **testify**

au courant see **au fait**

au fait/au courant (informed)
If you are 'au fait' with something you have a practical knowledge of it, you know how

it works or is arranged. The French phrase *mettre au fait* means to give someone information about something, acquaint him with it. To be 'au courant', on the other hand, means to be up to date with news or recent developments, literally 'in the course' of things.

auger see **awl**

augury/auspice (omen)
Originally 'augury' was the practice of an augur, the Roman official who interpreted omens. It now simply refers to any sign or indication, as an 'augury' of success – or equally of failure. An 'auspice', by contrast, is a good omen, one that occurs in favourable circumstances, or circumstances seen as boding well for the future. The divining of such omens was carried out by the watching of birds, the classical bird-watcher being called an *auspex*. In the plural, the word means patronage, of course, as when work is done under the 'auspices' of some organisation or sponsor. The adjective can be a confusible: see **auspicious**.

aura/aurora (unnatural emanation)
The word 'aura' has passed from a medical term – the sensation like a cold current of air experienced before an attack of epilepsy or hysteria – to the subtle emanation said by spiritualists to surround a person like an atmosphere. From this latter sense it has come to be used of the special air or character of a person, such as an 'aura' of wisdom or simplicity. 'Aurora' originally meant the dawn (it is the Roman name of the goddess of the dawn), then later something suggesting the dawn. Today the word is used for the phenomenon known as the aurora borealis or northern lights, the luminous display seen in or near the region of the North Pole. 'Aura' may occasionally be half-associated (wrongly) with 'aroma', since this, too, is a type of emanation with a figurative as well as a literal meaning.

aurora see **aura**

auspice see **augury**

auspicious/propitious (favourable)
'Auspicious' indicates that the time or moment is right for success in the future. It has an overtone, too, of importance, so than an 'auspicious' occasion or an 'auspicious' moment is one that not just points to a good future but is memorable in itself. 'Propitious' – which sometimes acquires a false association with 'prosperous' – indicates favourable conditions not so much in the future as at the moment. One can thus talk of 'propitious' weather, or of meeting in 'propitious' circumstances.

authoritarian see **authoritative**

authoritative/authoritarian (having authority)
An 'authoritative' manner implies that the person in question has authority – speaks or acts as one who knows, or is in a position to know. An 'authoritarian' manner suggests that subjection to authority is favoured – usually that of the person possessing such a manner.

avenge/revenge (inflict pain or harm in return for pain or harm)
The two words were once interchangeable. Today 'avenge', a more objective and impersonal verb, suggests a legitimate vindication, as of a wrong or an offence against oneself. A murder might be 'avenged', but not 'revenged'. With 'revenge' the pain or harm inflicted might in fact be imaginary or non-existent. A worker who wants to 'revenge' himself on the way his boss treats him may have an axe to grind rather than the wish to right a manifest wrong. The noun of 'avenge' is 'vengeance'; of 'revenge' it is . . . 'revenge'.

averse to/adverse to (opposed to)
To be 'averse to' something is to be disinclined towards it. If you are 'not averse to' an alcoholic nightcap, you are really saying you are in favour of it. To be 'adverse to' a thing – the word is used more of things than of people, as conditions 'adverse to' one's interests – is to be opposed or unfavourable towards it. The difference is in the prefixes, with 'averse' having a reduced 'ab-' (away) and 'adverse' having 'ad-' (towards).

avid/rabid (greedy)
'Avid' implies a general greediness: an 'avid' interest is a keen one, a person 'avid' for success desperately desires it. 'Rabid' suggests a furious intensity, so that a 'rabid' hunger is almost a morbid one. The words derive respectively from Latin *avidus* (eager) and *rabidus* (raving), with the second related to 'rabies'. 'Rabid' is sometimes half-confused with 'ravage': see **ravishing**.

avoid/evade/elude (escape from, keep out of the way of)
To 'avoid' a thing or a person is to steer clear of him, shun him. To 'evade' someone or something is to escape him/it by cunning or trickery, as when one 'evades' the taxman or a question. To 'elude', as when one 'eludes' one's creditors or 'eludes' pursuit, is to escape not just by cunning but by real artifice. A word that 'eludes' you has, for the moment, fallen into oblivion. For another confusible of 'elude', see **escape**.

awake see **wake**

awaken see **wake**

award see **reward**

awl/bradawl/auger (instrument for boring holes)
An 'awl' is used for piercing small holes, mainly in leather or wood. A 'bradawl' is an awl used for boring holes in wood specifically for brads – small nails with small heads. An 'auger' is a carpenter's tool larger than a gimlet with a spiral groove, also for boring holes in wood. It's a word that like 'apple' and 'apron' originally had an initial 'n' ('a nauger'). (Its spelling must be distinguished from 'augur' – see **augury**.)

axiom see **maxim**

Axis see **allies**

ayah/amah (nurse or maid in the East)
An 'ayah' is an Indian nurse or lady's maid. Although in fact a Hindi word it derives from the Portuguese *aia*, the feminine of

aio (tutor). An 'amah' is similar – though possibly more amahs are wetnurses – and also from the Portuguese (*ama*, nurse), but the word is used mainly by Europeans in the Far East, not in India.

babble/rabble/gabble/rabbit/burble/blather (talk rapidly or incoherently)
A nice case of phonaesthesia (see Introduction, p. 4). The degree of rapidity, incoherence, or general wordiness can perhaps be best expressed by associations: for 'babble' – 'baby', for 'rabble' – 'rapid', for 'gabble' – 'gab' (gift of the), for 'rabbit' – 'ramble', for 'burble' – 'bubble', for 'blather' – 'baloney' (which has its own confusible, **blarney**). All can be followed by 'on'; 'rabbit' virtually always is.

babel see **bedlam**

bacilli see **bacteria**

bacteria/bacilli (disease-producing organisms)
'Bacilli' *are* 'bacteria', in fact – only 'bacilli' produce spores and 'bacteria' do not. They are the simplest group of non-green vegetable organisms and are involved in fermentation and putrefaction as well as the production of disease. They are rod-shaped (Greek *bakterion* and Latin *bacillus* both mean 'little stick') as distinct from *cocci* which are spherical and *spirilla* which are spiral, among others. The singular of 'bacteria' is 'bacterium'; of 'bacilli' it is 'bacillus'.

badinage see **banter**

baleful/baneful (evil)
Strictly speaking, 'baleful' means 'full of

bale', an old-fashioned word for evil. The most common sense of the word today, though, is 'lugubrious' or 'dismal', as a 'baleful' look or expression, sometimes seen on the faces of bored monkeys in zoos and elderly judges in courtrooms. 'Baneful' – literally 'full of bane' – is even stronger, since 'bane' is an old word for murder or death. It now means 'destructive' or 'poisonous'. One might thus talk of the 'baneful' effect of alcohol or a 'baneful' habit. The modern sense of 'bane', as in 'He/She is the bane of my life', is considerably toned down from the original.

balmy see **barmy**

baloney see **blarney**

baluster see **banister**

baneful see **baleful**

banister/baluster (one of a series of pillars supporting a rail)
The main difference is that 'banisters' – the word in the plural can refer to the pillars or the rail itself – are usually indoors, running down a stairway, and that 'balusters' are normally outside and are the stone pillars supporting a parapet across a bridge, say, or along the edge of a terrace. A whole row of 'balusters' complete with rails forms a balustrade. Both 'banister' and 'baluster' ultimately derive from the Greek *balaustion* (pomegranate flower). The reference is to the ornamental shape of many pillars.

banter/badinage (teasing talk)
'Banter' is good-humoured chaffing, often on a particular topic. Stag nights and wedding receptions are frequently noted for the 'banter' directed at the groom. 'Badinage', as its French origin suggests (from *badiner*, to jest, joke), is more stylish, and on the whole also lighter and more delicate. The origin of the word 'banter' is not known.

bar/barrier (obstruction, obstacle)
When used figuratively, 'bar' suggests an acceptable or reasonable obstacle or condition, as a 'bar' to promotion after a certain age. A 'barrier' has the connotation of something stronger, more of an impediment, but nevertheless an obstacle that can be overcome with an effort or patience. In the summer of 1977 *The Times* had the triumphant headline: 'Shares break through the 500 barrier', the figure itself representing a psychological 'barrier' in the FT Index that, once passed, indicated a healthier economy.

barbarian see **barbarous**

barbaric see **barbarous**

barbarous/barbaric/barbarian (savage, uncivilised)
The Greek word *barbaros*, possibly related to **babble**, and also the Latin derivative *barbarus*, was used to designate a foreigner or stranger, someone who 'babbled' in another tongue. The word resulted in the name of the Barbary Coast in north west Africa and earlier, the people known as Berbers who lived there. Such 'barbarians' were, to the Greeks and Romans, uncivilised folk, and this is the general sense of the word today. 'He is a real barbarian', means that he is uncouth, ill-mannered, discourteous or whatever. 'Barbarous' means 'like the barbarians' – cruel and inhuman, so that one can talk of 'barbarous' customs, laws or treatment. 'Barbaric' is a milder word, often meaning little more than 'in bad taste' or, of something impressive, 'crude'. Thus yelling football fans can, to some ears, make a 'barbaric' noise, and baroque architecture, to some eyes, has a 'barbaric' splendour.

barmy/balmy/palmy (crazy, carefree)
Both 'barmy' and 'balmy' mean 'silly' or 'crazy'. Dictionaries disagree as to which spelling came first or indeed as to the origin of the words. Barm is actually the froth on fermenting malt liquor, but it is hard to see how this means 'crazy'. 'Balmy', however, could literally mean 'like balm', that is (punningly) 'soft'. Yet another explanation is that 'barmy' has its origin in the former Barming Asylum, near Maidstone, Kent: someone destined or fit for the establishment was said to be 'barmy'. So the confusion lies more in the spelling and the origin than the meaning. 'Palmy', however,

means prosperous and flourishing, and no irresponsibility is implied in the phrase 'the palmy days of youth'. The reference is a literal one, to palm trees, and 'bearing the palm'. ('Do you allow dates?' a distinguished visitor asked the headmistress of a girls' school while waiting to present the prizes. 'Oh yes,' replied the good lady, 'so long as they don't eat too many.')

baroque/rococo (florid style in architecture and painting)
'Baroque', derived from the Portuguese *barroco* (irregular) via the French, is a style that was developed in sixteenth century Italy. Its hall-marks were lack of symmetry, bold and convoluted forms, and exaggerated pictorial and ornamental effects. It can be seen today in the churches of Roman Catholic countries such as Spain and Austria and as echoed in the paintings of such artists as Rubens, Caravaggio and Murillo. 'Rococo', said to be derived from French *rocaille* (shellwork, rockwork), was the final stage of the 'baroque' period, in roughly the first half of the eighteenth century. Different materials were used, such as stucco, wood, metal, and tapestries, the key feature of the style being the use of ornamentation in the form of shellwork, scrolls and the like.

barque/barquentine/brigantine/brig
(type of sailing ship)
A 'barque' has three or more masts, all of them square-rigged (with sails set at right angles) except the aftermost, which is fore-and-aft. A 'barquentine' also has three or more masts, but the foremast is square-rigged and all the others fore-and-aft. A 'brigantine' has two masts, with the foremast square-rigged and the mainmast having a fore-and-aft mainsail and square topsails. The 'brig' is also two-masted, but both masts are square-rigged. All very ship-shape.

barquentine see **barque**

barrier see **bar**

base/basis (foundation)
'Base' is normally used literally, with a number of technical and scientific mean-

ings, although 'to base' can mean 'to put on a basis'. 'Basis', by contrast, is usually a figurative word meaning 'determining principle'. The plural of 'base' is 'bases', and of 'basis' – 'bases' (pronounced 'baseez').

basis see **base**

bastard/dastard (cruel or brutal person)
Literally, of course, a 'bastard' is an illegitimate child, hence (formerly) one to be despised, and hence (in common use today) a term of abuse, especially for a violent or cruel person. Oddly, 'dastard' has come to have the same application – a term of abuse for a person who commits a brutal act, especially when the victim is not given a chance. Originally the word meant 'coward' – specifically a mean or sneaking one.

bathos see **pathos**

bay window/bow window (projecting window)
A 'bay window' is often curved, but can also be rectangular or polygonal. A 'bow window' is curved only. 'Bow windows' have something of a historical or stylish ring to them. Mr Micawber went to bed planning to add 'bow windows' to the house 'in case anything turned up'.

bear/bull (type of share on the stock exchange which can be profitable)
The terms really apply to the speculators: a 'bear' reckons that conditions are unfavourable, so he sells his shares hoping to buy them in later (assuming they go on falling) and make a profit. A 'bull' does the opposite: buys hoping to sell later at a profit, on a rising market. An old proverb talked of 'selling the skin before you have the bear'. The story behind 'bull' is obscure, although both the animal and the shareholder are headstrong.

beast/brute (wild animal; savage person)
'Beast' suggests a large animal such as a lion ('King of Beasts'), tiger or elephant, and a coarse (in any sense), cruel or filthy person. 'Brute' is used less often of animals. Of a person it suggests stupidity, lack of

intelligence, or want of reasoning. The words are frequently accompanied by adjectives reflecting these attributes, such as 'dirty beast', 'drunken brute', 'wicked beast', 'callous brute'.

bedlam/babel (noise and confusion)
The words can be traced back to, respectively, the biblical towns of Bethlehem and Babylon, with 'bedlam' directly originating from the Royal Bethlehem (or Bethlem) Hospital in south east London – a lunatic asylum that in 1930 was transferred to new premises at Shirley, near Croydon, Surrey. As a common noun it implies noise and disorder as well as confusion. 'Babel' has its immediate derivation in the Tower of Babel (with 'Babel' the Hebrew name of Babylon) in Genesis 11, where the confounding of language took place. It suggests an uproar or hubbub, or incoherent speech as at a rowdy meeting. The resemblance of 'babel' to **babble** is fortuitous.

beefcake see **cheesecake**

begrudge/grudge (give or grant unwillingly)
To 'begrudge' someone something is to be envious of their possession of it. To 'grudge' a thing to a person, however, is to give it or grant it to him reluctantly. One friend can 'grudge' you a loan of £20, and another can then 'begrudge' you this loan since he could have done with it himself.

bellicose see **belligerent**

belligerent/bellicose (militant, warlike)
'Belligerent', used literally or – frequently – figuratively, means 'warlike', 'pertaining to war', as a 'belligerent' tone of voice or a 'belligerent' code of conduct. 'Bellicose' implies seeking to wage war or actually doing so, so that of people it often means something close to 'pugnacious', as a 'bellicose' old man.

belly see **billow**

Benedicite see **Benedictus**

Benedictus/Benedicite (canticle in Book of Common Prayer)
Both words are from the Latin *benedicere*

(to bless), with 'Benedictus' the past participle (blessed) and 'Benedicite' the imperative (bless!). They are the first words of Latin texts. The 'Benedictus' occurs twice in the Anglican liturgy: the first time as a canticle in the service of Morning Prayer (as an alternative to the *Jubilate*), the second in the new alternative Order of Communion, into which it was introduced from the Roman Mass. The first 'Benedictus' begins the sentence translated 'Blessed be the Lord God of Israel'; the second has the English version 'Blessed is He that cometh in the name of the Lord' (found in the Book of Common Prayer only, Psalm 118,v.26, l.1 where the second word is 'be', not 'is'). The 'Benedicite', whose opening words in English are 'O All ye Works of the Lord, bless ye the Lord', is a canticle preceding the 'Benedictus' in the order of Morning Prayer, and is an alternative to the *Te Deum*. It is an extract from the apocryphal Book of Daniel, where it was purported to be sung by the 'Three Holy Children' in Nebuchadnezzar's burning fiery furnace.

beneficent see **benevolent**

benevolent/beneficent (well disposed)
Strictly, 'benevolent' is *wishing* to do good for others, or being generally amiably disposed, while 'beneficent' is *doing* good for others by conferring gifts on them. An ideal Father Christmas is presumably as 'benevolent' as he is 'beneficent'.

berserk/amok (frenziedly out of control)
The words are sometimes confused, although people 'go berserk' but 'run amok'. To go 'berserk' is to become suddenly violent and destructive, as reputedly were the berserkers or berserks, the giant warriors in Scandinavian legend who were filled with wild frenzy in battle. To run 'amok' – not related to 'muck' – is to become violently murderous or homicidal, as Malays are claimed to. (The word is of Malay origin.) The word has a quite acceptable alternative spelling 'amuck'.

biannual/biennial (twice a year – or once every two years)
'Biannual' means 'happening twice a year';

'biennial' means 'happening every other year'. As a noun, 'biennial' is used of plants that live for two years. These confusibles can be easily avoided by using 'half-yearly' and 'two-yearly'. The Latin prefix *bi-* (two) is even more ambiguous in 'bi-monthly', which can mean either 'twice a month' or 'every two months'. Here, too, Anglo-Saxon alternatives are preferable – 'twice-monthly', 'two-monthly'.

biathlon see **marathon**

bicentenary/bicentennial (200th anniversary)
A 'bicentenary' is a 200th anniversary, with the word as an adjective meaning 'pertaining to a 200th anniversary'. A 'bicentennial' is preferred American usage with the same meaning: the word became familiar to Britons in this spelling in 1976 with the celebration of the 200th anniversary of the US Declaration of Independence. As an adjective, 'bicentennial' means 'lasting 200 years' or 'recurring every 200 years'. See also **centenary**.

bicentennial see **bicentenary**

biennial see **biannual**

bile/gall/spleen (bitter liquid secreted in the body or organ secreting this)
Both 'bile' and 'gall' are terms used for the liquid which is bitter and yellowish and secreted in fact by the liver. One of the main functions of 'bile' is to aid digestion, but it was formerly known as 'choler' and regarded as one of the four so-called humours (the others being blood, phlegm and melancholy). Figuratively it has the sense of 'peevishness'. The connection with 'gall' – itself having the figurative sense 'bitterness of spirit' or 'rancour' – is that 'bile' proceeds from the liver into the 'gall' bladder, where it is concentrated and from which it is discharged after meals. 'Spleen', like 'bile', also means 'peevishness' – as when one 'vents one's spleen' on someone, although it is not a liquid but an organ near the heart end of the stomach in which the blood undergoes certain corpuscular changes. It was formerly thought to be

the seat of courage, melancholy, ill humour and the like.

billion see **million**

billow/belly (swell out)
The words are related in origin, with 'billow' used mainly of the swelling of large waves at sea or the surging of a mass of smoke or fog. 'Belly' – also related to 'bellows' – is used mainly of something that stays swelled out, such as sails on a ship. Curtains in the wind, however usually 'billow'.

blanch see **blench**

blare see **blast**

blarney/baloney/boloney (nonsense)
'Blarney' is used to mean flattering or cajoling talk. 'Let's have none of your blarney, now!' If that sounds Irish, it's because the gift of talk of this kind, especially wheedling flattery, is said to be given to whoever kisses the Blarney Stone, in the village of the same name near Cork in southern Ireland. 'Baloney', and its alternative spelling 'boloney' means at the most 'nonsense', 'rubbish', and at the least, 'waffle'. The word is said to be linked with the 'polony', or Bologna sausage, from the eponymous town in Italy. This is conjectural, however, and may well itself be 'baloney'.

blast/blare/bray (raucous noise)
A 'blast' is essentially loud and piercing, as of trumpets, whistles, horns or sirens. A 'blare' is more loud and raucous, as of a radio playing at maximum volume, a loud-speaker, or brass instrument played *cuivré*. A 'bray' is first and foremost the harsh and breathy cry of a donkey, but can also be used of trumpets, especially when the sound is discordant, or of a loud, human, asinine laugh. The three words are frequently used as verbs.

blatant/flagrant (undisguisedly offensive)
'Blatant', delightfully defined by *Chambers* as 'calumniously clamorous; egregiously vulgar', can be used of things and persons. Of things it has the sense 'shamelessly

obvious', as a 'blatant' lie or error. Of a person, it implies a lack of concern over his bad behaviour by the offender, as is shown by a 'blatant' liar or plagiarist. 'Flagrant', glossed by Johnson in his *Dictionary* as 'flaming into notice', has a similar sense to 'blatant' but is a stronger word. 'Flagrant' disregard for rules suggests that one not only flouts them, but does so with relish. *Partridge* quotes Anthony Eden, in a speech made in 1936, as using the wrong word of the pair when he spoke of a 'blatant breach of good faith'.

blather see **babble**

blaze/blazon (vividly exhibit)
There are three meanings to 'blaze': to burn brightly, as of a fire; to proclaim, as with a trumpet; to mark trees by chipping off the bark, as when indicating a trail. The third of these meanings in fact derives from the 'blaze', or white mark, on a horse's head, which in turn has its origin in the first sense. To 'blazon', from an Old French word *blason* (shield), of unknown origin and not related to any form of 'blaze', is to show something or display it conspicuously or publicly, as, literally, heraldic arms on a shield. It is difficult to believe, though, that one of the two words does not influence the meaning of the other.

blazon see **blaze**

blench/blanch (turn pale or white)
'Blench' is the more general word, meaning to make, or go, pale or white. But when used with such words as 'fear' – 'She blenched with fear' – it also acquires the other sense of 'blench': to shrink or quail. 'Blanch' is confined more to a literal use, as of 'blanching' almonds by peeling them. Here the influence is of 'bleach', so that the two in some senses are virtually synonymous: linen can be either 'blanched' or 'bleached' on the grass.

bloom/blossom (come into flower)
The difference is a delicate one: to 'bloom' is to be in the *first* stage of full flower, as literally or, when used of a person, to be in a state of health and vigour and beauty

(or handsomeness). One thus talks of the 'bloom' of youth: youth itself may last several years, but it is the first full attainment of it that is the 'bloom'. To 'blossom' is to flower, but at the same time to give promise of fruit to come. One can thus say of someone that he is 'blossoming' into a talented writer, or that she is 'blossoming' into a gifted actress.

blossom see **bloom**

bludgeon see **cudgel**

blush/flush (of person: redden with embarrassment or other emotion)
One usually 'blushes' from embarrassment, shame, modesty or shyness. One 'flushes' from something stronger, from any sharp, sudden emotion, in fact, such as pride, anger, joy or great shame. Often, however, the cause of a 'flush' is a good one such as success or victory. The word seems to derive from a combination of 'flash' and 'gush' under the influence of 'blush'. Occasionally, too, there is confusion between 'first flush', the initial elation of victory, etc. and 'at (the) first blush', meaning 'at (the) first glance'.

blusterous see **boisterous**

blustery see **boisterous**

boiled/broiled (cooked)
'Boiled' means cooked in water (normally), as eggs, vegetables, potatoes and some kinds of meat such as beef, mutton and lamb. 'Broiled' means 'cooked by direct heat', as in an oven or under a grill, of fish or poultry. A 'broiler' is a young chicken ready for 'broiling'. The word is related to French *brûlé* (burned).

boisterous/blustery/blusterous (rough and buffeting)
'Boisterous' is usually applied to violent natural forces such as the wind or the sea. Of behaviour it suggests roughness and rowdiness, as of noisy boys – which two words evoke the adjective – while of a mood it hints at a rough playfulness. 'Blustery' and 'blusterous' suggest more a temporary roughness, and they lack the playfulness

that 'boisterous' can imply. A 'blustery' wind is rather a threatening one, and a 'blusterous' mood is a boastful or bragging one.

bollard see **bulwark**

boloney see **blarney**

bon vivant/bon viveur (one who enjoys wining and dining)
'Bon vivant' is the older term, from the French meaning literally 'good liver' (i.e. one who lives well). It is close to the sense of **gourmand**, with overtones of one who wines and dines unwisely, and rather too well. 'Bon viveur', which is also French for 'good liver' – although the French itself is spurious, and a concocted phrase – has a sense similar to 'bon vivant' but with an air of respectability, of a 'man about town'. The term, too, is applied not merely to one who is an expert on food and drink but who is knowledgeable on such gentlemanly pursuits as touring and travel. Fanny Cradock and her husband adopted the joint nom de plume 'Bon Viveur' for their reports of hotel and restaurant meals around Britain in the *Daily Telegraph*.

bon viveur see **bon vivant**

bordeaux see **burgundy**

border/boundary (frontier, limiting line)
'Border' implies the area or tract on the edge of territory, such as the 'Border Country' which lies close to the dividing line between England and Scotland. 'Boundary' suggests the limit or extent of a territory, the actual line marking the furthest extent reached by a country or administrative region, such as a county 'boundary' or a stream that forms the 'boundary' between two estates.

boundary see **border**

bourbon see **burgundy**

bow window see **bay window**

bradawl see **awl**

Brahma see **Buddha**

brandish see **flourish**

bravado see **bravery**

bravery/bravado/bravura (show of courage)
'Bravery' is courage or valour in general. 'Bravado', from Spanish *bravada*, is a specific act of bravery or daring designed to impress or intimidate – or to conceal timidity. 'Bravura', an Italian word (spirit), is mainly associated with music, in which it denotes a passage, usually a difficult one, played or sung with skill and gusto. More generally it is a display of daring, or simply a brilliant performance or attempt at one.

bravura see **bravery**

bray see **blast**

Bren gun/Sten gun (type of machine-gun)
The 'Bren gun' came first. It was manufactured at Brno, Czechoslovakia in 1937 and its construction was perfected at a small-arms factory at Enfield, Middlesex. Thus 'Bren' is an acronym of the first two letters of each place. The 'Sten gun' first saw the light of day in 1942. Like the 'Bren', it is a light machine-gun fired from the shoulder or hip. It, too, was produced at Enfield, but its first two letters are those of the initials of the inventors, Major S. Sheppard and Mr T. Turpin, a Civil Servant. (Although according to one authority, the '-en' is borrowed from 'England'.)

brig see **barque**

brigantine see **barque**

Bri-Nylon see **nylon**

brisk see **abrupt**

broiled see **boiled**

brush see **bush**

brusque see **abrupt**

brute see **beast**

bucentaur see **Minotaur**

Buddha/Brahma (Indian god)
'Buddha' ('The Enlightened One') is the
title given by Buddhists to the founder of
their faith, who flourished in the fifth
century BC. Buddha's real name was
actually Sayyamuni, and he is the latest of
a series of Buddhas who will continue, it is
thought, indefinitely. 'Brahma' ('Creator')
is the supreme god of Hinduism. Later
Hinduism has a trinity in which 'Brahma'
is the personal Creator, Vishnu the
Preserver, and Siva the Destroyer.
Buddhism arose as a reaction to Brahman-
ism and in particular to its caste system:
Buddhists believe that all people are equal.

bull see **bear**

bulwark/bollard (solidly built structure
on a ship)
The 'bulwark' – not connected with bulls
but, apparently, 'bole' (of a tree) and 'work'
– is the solid part of the ship's side that
extends above the deck. A 'bollard',
possibly also deriving from 'bole', is a
vertical post on which hawsers are made
fast, both on a ship and on the quayside.
'Bulwark', but not 'bollard', can be used
figuratively to indicate a protecting force or
agent: 'He's been a real bulwark in my
trials and tribulations.'

Bundesrat see **Bundeswehr**

Bundestag see **Bundeswehr**

**Bundeswehr/Bundestag/Bundesrat/
Reichswehr/Reichstag/Reichsrat/
Abwehr** (German state department)
Those titles which incorporate the word
'Bund' (German for 'Federation', i.e. of
West Germany) are all post-war and the
'Reich' equivalents (literally 'realm',
'empire') all existed between 1919 and
1945. The 'Bundeswehr' is the West
German Army, while the 'Bundestag' and
'Bundesrat' are, respectively, the upper
and lower houses of the West German
parliament. Those words incorporating
'Reich' apply to the earlier equivalents,

with the 'Reichstag' also being the building
where the house met in Berlin. (It was destroyed by fire in 1933.) The 'Abwehr'
('Resistance') was the German counter-
intelligence section in the Second World
War. The second elements of the names
derive from *Wehr* (defence), *tagen* (to meet,
sit in conference) and *Rat* (council).

burble see **babble**

burgundy/bordeaux/bourbon (type of
wine)
There are many varieties of 'burgundy',
both red and white. It is a full, dry wine
produced in the Burgundy region of
France. 'Bordeaux' wines, from the region
of the same name in the south of France,
include red wines such as Médoc and St
Emilion, and white wines such as the sweet
Sauternes and dry varieties of Graves.
'Bourbon', as no American will need to be
told, is not a wine but a type of whisky
distilled in the USA and popular with both
goodies and baddies in novels and movies –
and in real life. It was originally produced
in Bourbon county, Kentucky: it's a nice
quirk that the county name was imported
from France.

bush/shrub/scrub/brush (single low,
woody plant, or a stretch of such plants)
'Bush' is both the familiar small tree
(botanically a small cluster of 'shrubs'
growing as a single plant) and a stretch of
wild, uncultivated land in Australia or
Africa with – or even without – such
'bushes'. A 'shrub' is usually regarded as
larger than a 'bush' but smaller than a tree,
a collection of them forming a 'shrubbery'.
'Scrub', not used often in the plural, is a
collective term for 'shrubs' or low trees,
especially as in the Australian 'bush'.
'Brush' or 'brushwood' more or less equals
'scrub', that is, it is densely growing
'bushes' and 'shrubs'. (The word is probably related to 'brush' in the sense of
'implement with bristles for sweeping'.)
This quadruple set of confusibles can
prove rather thorny.

bustle/hustle/hassle (as verb: hasten,
harass)
To 'bustle' is to hurry with a great show of

energy. The word is probably influenced by 'busy' and 'bundle'. To 'hustle', in turn no doubt influenced by 'hurry' and 'bustle' and perhaps 'jostle', is to force (someone) hurriedly or roughly, as when someone is 'hustled' into a car or through a door. The verb 'hassle' is of American origin and suggests 'harass', which it basically means. All three verbs are used as nouns.

by heart/by rote (from memory)
Something learned 'by heart' has been consciously or unconsciously committed to memory and can be recited at recall, as a poem, the procedure for operating a machine and the like. A thing learned 'by rote' has been learned mechanically, parrot-fashion, with no real thought for the meaning. The origin of the latter is not too clear – it does not seem to be connected with Latin *rota* (wheel).

by rote see **by heart**

cachou see **cashew**

calamine/camomile/calomel (medical or medicinal preparation)
'Calamine' is a soothing liquid for the skin, especially to offset the effects of sunburn, rash, etc. It contains zinc oxide and is in origin related to the Latin word *Cadmia* (Cadmian earth) which gives cadmium. 'Camomile' is a medicinal preparation from the strong scented foliage and flowers of the herb of the same name. The herb itself derives its name from the Greek *chamai-melon* (earth apple). 'Calomel' is a tasteless solid – actually mercurous oxide – used in purgative medicines. Its origin is said to be in the Greek words *kalos* (beautiful) and *melas* (black), which seems odd since the substance itself is white.

callow see **shallow**

calomel see **calamine**

camomile see **calamine**

Campari see **Cinzano**

candelabra see **chandelier**

canopy/panoply (protective covering)
The Greeks had a special word for a bed with mosquito curtains – *konopeion* (in turn from *konops*, 'mosquito'). This is the origin of 'canopy', which is now any suspended or supported overhead covering for anything or anyone from a bed to a bishop. A 'panoply', from a Greek word meaning literally 'all arms', is technically a complete suit of armour but can also be used, in a more stylish or poetic sense, for a complete covering of anything, especially if it is protective or impressive, such as the 'panoply' of a Red Indian chief or the weaponry and electronic gadgetry of a modern fighter aircraft.

capability/capacity/ability (quality of being able to do or act)
'Capability' is basically the quality of being 'capable' in any way, as physically, intellectually or emotionally. 'Capacity' suggests power, often of the mind, as when someone has the 'capacity' for hard work. 'Ability' usually implies the possession of a particular attribute that enables one to do a particular thing. One person thus might have the 'ability' to run very fast (he will do this when he has to), another the 'ability' to overcome her blushing (she will do so when the occasion demands it). All three words, however, overlap somewhat in their meanings.

capacity see **capability**

capital punishment see **corporal punishment**

Capuchin/Carmelite/Carthusian/Cistercian (member of a religious order)
All four are Roman Catholic orders. The 'Capuchins' are Franciscan friars who wear a long cowl, their name derived from the

Italian *cappuccio* (hood). The 'Carmelites' are monks or nuns who now exist in several orders. Their original order, however, was founded on Mount Carmel in Palestine in the twelfth century. The 'Carthusians' are monks whose order was founded in 1086 near the town of Grenoble in the French Alps, with their first monastery called La Grande Chartreuse – a name that in its turn has given us 'chartreuse', the liqueur made by the monks there, and 'Charterhouse'. (Charterhouse public school was founded, together with a hospital, on the site of a 'charterhouse' or 'Carthusian' monastery in London. The school transferred to Godalming in Surrey in 1872 and took its name with it.) The 'Cistercian' order of monks and nuns was founded in the south of France near Cîteaux in 1098.

carabineers see **carabinieri**

carabinieri/car(a)bineers/Carbonari (special armed force)
The Italian Army Corps who serve as the police are called the 'carabinieri'. They are armed with rifles ('carbines'). 'Carbineers' or 'carabineers' were armed soldiers. In England the name was preserved in the regiment known as the 3rd Carabineers, now incorporated in the Royal Scots Dragoon Guards. The 'Carbonari' (literally 'charcoal-burners') were a nineteenth century secret political society active in southern Italy and also France and Spain whose aim was to bring about a republican government. They are said to have evolved from medieval charcoal-burners, and went to the extent of calling their meeting-place a 'hut', the outside area the 'forest' and their opponents the 'wolves'.

carbineers see **carabinieri**

Carbonari see **carabinieri**

carbon dioxide see **carbon monoxide**

carbon monoxide/carbon dioxide (poisonous gas)
'Carbon monoxide' (CO) is a gas formed when carbon burns with an insufficient supply of air, hence its latent presence in car exhaust fumes. 'Carbon dioxide' (CO_2) or 'dry ice' is the gas in fizzy drinks and fire extinguishers and is basically what we breathe out, having breathed in mainly oxygen. Its danger as a poisonous gas lies in its presence as 'choke damp' in mines.

carborundum/corundum (hard abrasive substance)
'Carborundum' – properly a trade name formed from 'carbon' and 'corundum' – comes in powder or blocks and is used for such purposes as grinding tools and refractory lining in furnaces. 'Corundum', a word which ultimately goes back to the Sanskrit for 'ruby', is a mineral aluminium oxide used both as a precious gem and for the manufacture of bearings in such fine machinery as watches and motors. Mixed with iron oxides and spinel (another hard mineral) it becomes emery.

carcajou see **cockatoo**

cardinal see **crimson** (shade of red) or **ordinal** (class of numbers)

careen see **career**

career/careen (move rapidly)
To 'career' – the word is related to 'car' – is to run or move at speed, so that a vehicle can 'career' round a corner or down a hill. In the USA the word is often used synonymously for 'careen', which properly is to turn a ship onto its side for cleaning or caulking. The derivation here is Latin *carina* (keel): when a ship is on her side the keel will be exposed. See also the related confusible **keel over**.

caribou see **cockatoo**

Carmelite see **Capuchin**

carmine see **crimson**

carnation see **crimson**

carnelian see **crimson**

carp see **cavil**

carpus see **tarsus**

Carthusian see **Capuchin**

cashew/cachou/jujube (small lozenge or sweetmeat)
'Cashew' is the nut, from the tree growing in tropical America. 'Cachou' is the pill or pastille for sweetening the breath, especially after smoking. Confusion is increased since it used to contain, among other condiments, 'cashew' nut. Trees of the botanical genus Zizyphus gave their name to the 'jujube', which properly is the fruit, resembling a small plum, of these trees. By extension it came to mean a small, sweet lozenge. Winston Churchill used to suck them, and drop them, when sitting in the Commons.

cashmere/kerseymere/cassimere
(type of woollen cloth)
'Cashmere' is a fine, downy wool from Kashmir goats and often popular for making shawls. It is also a wool fabric of twill weave, in imitation of the real thing. 'Kerseymere', by contrast, is a coarse woollen cloth, a ribbed twill. Its name is a variant of 'cassimere', which became altered by association with Kersey, a village in Suffolk formerly a wool-making centre. 'Cassimere', which in turn is a variant of 'cashmere', is a plain or twilled woollen cloth usually used for men's clothes. All three words are thus quite closely inter-woven.

cassimere see **cashmere**

castigate see **chastise**

cat see **reach**

cataclasm see **catastrophe**

cataclysm see **catastrophe**

catacomb/hecatomb/catafalque/cenotaph (place for preserving dead bodies or for commemorating the dead)
Historically, 'catacomb', or in its Latin form *catacumbas*, was the name of the cemetery of St Sebastian on the Appian Way, with the word itself of unknown origin. The term came to be applied to an underground cemetery, especially one with tunnels and recesses for the coffins and tombs such as those around Rome or in Paris. A 'hecatomb' is nothing to do, except indirectly, with 'tomb'; it is a great mass killing or slaughter – originally the public sacrifice of a hundred oxen, from the Greek *hekaton* (hundred) and *bous* (ox). A 'catafalque' is an elevated structure on which a dead body lies in state or is carried. The word is related to 'scaffold'. A 'cata-falque' is usually in the form of a tomb or a 'cenotaph', which literally means 'empty tomb', such as the memorial to the dead of both World Wars in Whitehall, London.

catafalque see **catacomb**

catastrophe/cataclysm/cataclasm
(disaster or violent upheaval)
'Catastrophe' is the general term, from the Greek word meaning 'overturning'. A 'cataclysm', literally a 'washing down', is usually reserved for a social or political upheaval, although the term is also used by geographers to refer to a physical action which produces a change in the earth's surface and causes flooding. A 'cataclasm', literally 'breaking down', is a disruption of the normal order of things. Here too the word has a scientific use: in geology it refers to a breaking down process of rocks.

cavil/carp (find fault with in an irritating manner)
To 'cavil' is to raise irritating, often trivial, objections. To 'carp' means almost the same, but in addition suggests that the objections are unreasonable. 'He's always carping at the way she dresses.' It has a suggestion of persistent nagging – perhaps because of a suggestion of 'harp'. There's some basis for this, as Latin *carpere* (to pluck) lies behind both 'carp' and 'harp'. 'Cavil' derives from Latin *cavillari* (to make captious objections) and is related to 'calumny'.

Celtic/Gaelic (native language of Scotland or Ireland)
Properly, 'Celtic' is a whole group of Indo-European languages, including Irish, Scottish (or 'Gaelic'), Welsh, Breton, Manx and, until it died out, Cornish. All these tongues are spoken by the descendants of

the Celts, a west European race that included the Gauls and the Ancient Britons. 'Gaelic' is commonly used to denote the language spoken by the Scottish branch of the Celtic family. Linguists also use it, however, to apply to the language of the Scottish *and* Irish and Manx Celts, as well as the language of ancient Ireland. With other terms such as 'Goidelic' and 'Brythonic' the plethora of words relating to the languages of the British Isles borders on the babelic.

cembalo see **clavichord**

cement see **concrete**

cenotaph see **catacomb**

censor/censure (as verb: to condemn, ban)
To 'censor' something is to act as a censor by cutting, toning down, editing, blue-pencilling or whatever. To 'censure' a thing or a person is to criticise it or him severely. One thus 'censures' a person's behaviour or one's current unfavourite fashion or art form. The adjective of 'censor' is 'censorial' and of 'censure', 'censorious'. The respective nouns are 'censorship' and 'censure'.

censure see **censor**

centaur see **Minotaur**

centenary/centennial (hundredth anniversary)
A 'centenary' is a hundredth anniversary, with the adjective the same as the noun. The American equivalent term is 'centennial', although the identical adjective is also used in British English to mean 'lasting or occurring every hundred years'. Colorado is nicknamed the 'Centennial State' as it was admitted as a state in the 'centennial' year of the existence of the USA (1876). For similar distinctions see **bicentenary**.

centennial see **centenary**

centipede/millipede (insect with hundreds of legs)
The 'centipede' does not have a hundred legs, but anything from 14 to 177 *pairs*.

There are around 2,800 species, and they belong to the even less aptly named class *Chilopoda* (thousand legs). 'Millipedes' belong to the class *Diplopoda* (double legs). There are about 8,000 species and they have not a thousand legs as their name suggests, but up to 400, i.e. 200 pairs.

cerebellum see **cerebrum**

cerebrum/cerebellum (part of the brain)
Both are anatomical terms. The 'cerebrum' is the front and upper part of the brain, with the 'cerebellum' lying behind it and below it. The second word is a diminutive of the first, which is the Latin for 'brain', in turn giving the English word 'cerebral'.

ceremonial/ceremonious (pertaining to, or showing, ceremony)
'Ceremonial' serves as an adjective for both 'ceremony' and 'ceremonial', so that ceremonial' dress is the formal dress worn for either. 'Ceremonious' means 'full of ceremony' in the showy or fussy sense, as a 'ceremonious' occasion (a grand one) or a 'ceremonious' gesture of the hand (a rather snooty one).

ceremonious see **ceremonial**

cesarevitch see **czarevitch**

chancel see **choir**

chandelier/candelabra (branched support for several lights)
Most 'chandeliers' hang from the ceiling. Originally they all held candles, hence the word's origin in French *chandelle*. A 'candelabra', strictly 'candelabrum', is really an ornamental branched candlestick, from the Latin word for 'candle'. It doubles up as a 'chandelier', however, in actual usage, although the French word seems more popular.

chantry see **choir**

chaperone/cicerone/chatelaine (female in authority)
A 'chaperone' is a 'mature' woman who accompanies, escorts or otherwise monitors

a younger woman in public. The original 'chaperone' wore a 'chape' or cape. A 'cicerone' is not necessarily a woman. The term is used of a guide who explains the curiosities or antiquities of a place, such as a museum or historical site. Cicero was one of the world's record speakers, many guides emulate him; hence the title. A 'chatelaine' could not be male: she was the lady of the castle, and is now the mistress of a household, especially an elegant or fashionable one. All three words are rather mannered, but by no means obsolete.

charger/courser (war horse)
The aim of a 'charger' was not to charge in battle but to carry (from this now secondary meaning of 'charge'). A 'courser' was also a 'charger' but since the seventeenth century the word has come to be used of a race horse rather than a war horse, one that 'courses'.

chary see **wary**

chasm see **crevice**

chasten see **chastise**

chastise/chasten/castigate (punish)
'Chastise' is a variant of 'chasten' with the basic meaning 'inflict corporal punishment'. 'Chasten', which is related to 'chaste' and 'castigate', means 'inflict suffering on, in order to improve morally'. Its past participle is in common use as an adjective, as a 'chastened' look. 'Castigate' has a meaning close to 'chasten', except that the punishment inflicted is often verbal and the aim is not to improve but to correct. It has a secondary meaning, 'severely criticise'. All three words are close in meaning, with perhaps 'chastise' and 'castigate' the closest, and all are ultimately derived from Latin *castus* (pure).

chatelaine see **chaperone**

cheesecake/beefcake (picture or pose of the human form designed to emphasize its attractiveness)
Unlike the genesis of Adam and Eve, 'cheesecake' came first, ex the USA. The word's earliest recording is in 1934, and it

soon came to be used of pin-ups and pictures of attractive women in general, especially ones that emphasised their sex appeal. The idea is that 'cheesecake' is rich and sweet and tasty – compare 'crumpet' in its popular sense. 'Beefcake' appeared after the war as a not-too-serious rival, when photos of husky film stars with fine physiques became popular. 'Cheesecake' can also indicate the quality of the subject portrayed – the 'luscious legs look' – while 'beefcake' may also imply, as *Chambers* puts it, 'brawn as distinct from brain'. 'Beefcake' as a comestible is unknown.

cherish see **nurse**

cherubic see **chubby**

Chianti see **Cinzano**

chilli see **pickles**

Ch'ing see **Ming**

chive/endive (salad plant)
The 'chive' is related to the leek and onion and has long slender leaves used as seasoning. The leaves of the 'endive', a species of chicory, are finely divided and curled and, when blanched, used for salad.

chlorate see **chlorine**

chloride see **chlorine**

chlorine/chloride/chlorite/chlorate
(poisonous gas or related compound)
'Chlorine', so named by Sir Humphrey Davy from its colour – the Greek for 'green' is *chloros* – is a greenish-yellow poisonous gas (Cl) that is irritating to breathe. With the other words it's a matter of suffixes: a 'chloride' is a chemical compound of two substances, one of which is 'chlorine'; 'chlorite' is a salt of chlor*ous* acid; 'chlorate' is a salt of chlor*ic* acid. For these suffixes, and those of 'chlorous' and 'chloric' see Appendix I, Table 2, page 149.

chlorite see **chlorine**

choir/chancel/chantry (area surrounding the altar in a church)
The 'choir' in a church extends from the

crossing (the intersection of the nave and the transepts) to the east or altar end; in a cathedral it is the area between the nave and the main altar. In both it houses the choir in their choirstalls. The 'chancel', which is not related to 'chant', is the space round the altar, usually enclosed, for the clergy. Its origin is in the Latin *cancelli* (bars, lattice) which originally enclosed it. 'Chantry' is, however, related to 'chant'. It is a small chapel or altar in a church or cathedral endowed for priests to sing masses, usually for the soul of the endower.

chord see **cord**

chortle see **chuckle**

chrome/chromium (shiny metallic substance)
'Chrome' is, in fact, 'chromium', of which it is the French form. The word is used especially to apply to the various coloured pigments such as 'chrome' yellow or 'chrome' oxide which are compounds of the shiny metallic element 'chromium'. (The yellow 'chrome' is lead chromate, and the green, chromic oxide.) Both words derive from Greek *chroma* (colour).

chromium see **chrome**

chubby/cherubic/seraphic (baby-faced or sweet-expressioned)
'Chubby' is really 'round and plump', though when applied to cheeks can suggest an endearing, baby-like nature or appearance. 'Cherubic', of course, is 'cherub-like'. Cherubs were often portrayed in art as beautiful, winged children with 'chubby' innocent faces. 'Seraphic' is, similarly, 'seraph-like'. Whereas cherubs form the second order of angels, seraphs belong to the highest order. They, too, are represented in art as pretty children – more often simply as a child's head with wings. 'Seraphic' suggests more 'blissful' than 'chubby', especially when applied to a smile.

chuckle/chortle (as verb: laugh softly with satisfaction)
'Chuckle' implies a laughing to oneself, with quiet amusement or modest satis-

faction. 'Chortle' is Lewis Carroll's famous 'chuckle' and 'snort' combined, from *Through the Looking-Glass*. In the poem *Jabberwocky*, Carroll says of the warrior whose 'beamish boy' had killed the Jabberwock that 'He chortled in his joy'.

cicerone see **chaperone**

cimbalom see **clavichord**

Cinemascope see **Cinerama**

Cinerama/Cinemascope (system of projecting a cinema film onto a wide screen)
Both terms are really proprietary names. 'Cinerama' – from 'cinema' and 'panorama' – was all the rage when it first appeared in 1951. The film was projected on to a wide, curved screen by three projectors simultaneously with stereo sound. Two years later came 'Cinemascope' (or 'Cinema-Scope') – from 'cinema' with the suffix '-scope'. This was an improvement in that although the basic system was the same, the film was projected by one projector. The first film shown in 'CinemaScope' was the American *The Robe* (1953). Subsequent single-lens 'Cinerama' was virtually indistinguishable from 'Cinemascope'.

cinnabar see **cinnamon**

cinnamon/cinnabar (red-coloured substance)
'Cinnamon' is the aromatic bark of a type of laurel tree in the East Indies. When the bark is dried the resultant substance can be used as a spice or in medicine. It is yellowish or reddish brown in colour. 'Cinnabar' is mercuric sulphide, a mineral used as a red pigment. Its name ultimately goes back to the Persian *zinjarf* (red lead).

Cinzano/Chianti/Campari (type of Italian wine or aperitif)
'Cinzano' is Italian vermouth, obtainable as red or white, sweet or dry. 'Chianti' is a dry red – less often white – wine, sold in distinctive straw-covered bottles. The name is also used indiscriminately of certain rather inferior Italian wines. 'Campari' is an aperitif consisting of bitters and usually drunk with soda. 'Cinzano' and

'Campari' are named after their manufacturers; 'Chianti' is properly from the Chianti Mountains in Tuscany.

Cistercian see **Capuchin**

cite see **quote**

citizen/denizen (inhabitant, resident)
A 'citizen' is the (usually native) inhabitant of a city or country. The word 'denizen' derives from Old French *deinz* (within) by assimilation in the fifteenth century with 'citizen', and refers to the inhabitant or resident of any place but normally one who was originally an alien and has been adopted. The word can apply also to animals and plants that have migrated, as well as to words borrowed from a foreign language.

citron see **citrus**

citrus/citron (sour yellow fruit)
The 'citrus' is a tree or shrub of the genus Citrus whose fruit includes the lemon, lime, orange, grapefruit and 'citron' itself. The 'citron' resembles a lemon but is larger and has a thicker rind.

cittern see **zither**

civic see **civil**

civil/civic/civilian (pertaining to a civilian or a citizen)
'Civil' is a general word that normally implies 'citizen', either as the native inhabitant of a state, as in such terms as 'civil' law or 'civil' affairs, or as a member of a military, ecclesiastical or political society. One thus has, respectively, a 'civil' award (not a military one), a 'civil' marriage (not a religious one) and the 'Civil' Service (as distinct from the military services). 'Civil' may also apply to the citizen as an individual, and define his 'civil' duty or 'civil' rights. 'Civic' has the basic sense 'pertaining to a city', as a 'civic' centre or a 'civic' function, although here it can extend to refer to a citizen seen as the inhabitant of a city, for example in 'civic' pride or 'civics', the school subject which is training in citizenship. 'Civilian' usually means

simply 'non-military', as in the 'civilian' population. Of an airline, however, one has, in this sense, 'civil' rather than 'civilian', so there are 'civil' passenger aircraft, and the body organising the National Air Traffic Services in Britain is entitled the 'Civil' Aviation Authority.

civilian see **civil**

clang/clank/clink/clonk/clunk (sharp sound made by one hard object striking another)
These onomatopoeic words can be usefully distinguished to apply to different objects. An iron gate slamming and a heavy bell struck 'clang'. Heavy chains rattling 'clank' – so does a suit of armour. Spoons placed on saucers and one wine glass brought into contact with another 'clink'. A plate or dish falling upside down on the floor 'clonks' – a slangish word but a valid one. A milk bottle set down on a doorstep and a car door slammed to, as Jimmy Savile OBE has shown, 'clunk'.

clank see **clang**

classic/classical (relating to class or the classics)
'Classic' is the attribute of something that is of the highest 'class' and serves as a standard or establishes one, as a 'classic' case or a 'classic' example. A 'classic' novel is one that has come to be regarded as one of the best, and so is now famous. 'Classical' applies to the 'classics', usually Roman or Greek, or to 'classicism'. There is thus a difference between a 'classic' play, which is one that serves as a standard (as the 'classic' novel just mentioned), and a 'classical' play, which is, say, a Greek or French one. Both words can overlap to mean 'refined', so that one can talk of 'classic' or 'classical' purity. 'Classical' music, however, is regarded as being opposed to romantic or light or popular, i.e. it is respectively pre-1800 (roughly), serious or traditional.

classical see **classic**

clavicembalo see **clavichord**

clavichord/clavicembalo/cembalo/ cimbalom (old keyboard instrument)
A 'clavichord', from the two Latin words for 'key' and 'string', resembles a square piano and has strings that are struck gently by metal blades projecting from the keys. The 'clavicembalo' is a misnomer. The name literally means 'keyed dulcimer', but its keys are plucked, not struck. 'Cembalo' is an abbreviation of this. It is a dulcimer having wires that are struck by hammers. A 'cimbalom' is a Hungarian dulcimer, with 'dulcimer' in all senses here an instrument, in the form of a flat box, that has wires stretched across bridges over a sounding-board. For an instrument something like a 'cimbalom' see **zither**.

cleanliness see **cleanness**

cleanness/cleanliness (state of being clean)
'Cleanness' refers to a temporary or permanent state of being clean. 'Cleanliness' implies being kept in a clean state and is often used figuratively, as 'cleanliness' of thought or heart.

clench/clinch (make fast, secure)
'Clench', an earlier word than 'clinch', means, 'grasp or close firmly', as one's fist, teeth or jaw. 'Clinch' has a wider use. Literally it means to drive a nail in or grasp one's opponent tightly in boxing or wrestling. Figuratively it means to settle decisively, as an argument or deal.

clinch see **clench**

clink see **clang**

clocks back see **clocks on**

clocks on/clocks back (adjustment of clocks by one hour to mark start or end of summer time)
When does which happen? You put 'clocks on' or forward by one hour in the spring, with the immediate result that you lose an hour's sleep and the more lasting consequence of having lighter evenings and, for a while, darker mornings. You put 'clocks back' by one hour in the autumn, thus gaining an extra hour in bed for once,

temporarily lighter early mornings, and a dreary succession of dark evenings. If in doubt when to do which, try the American mnemonic: 'Spring forward, fall back' ('fall', of course, being autumn).

clonk see **clang**

close call/close haul (narrow escape)
A 'close call' is the same as a 'close shave' or a 'close thing' – a near accident or narrow escape. 'That was a close call!' The phrase 'close haul' as such does not exist, although a boat can sail 'close-hauled'. This means that the boat is tacking on a course into the wind by means of sailing as close to the wind as the vessel will sail, keeping the sails trimmed as flat as possible. Such a course is not really dangerous – although obviously it will be more difficult with a constantly changing wind and rough water – and possibly the narrowest escape would be that of avoiding being blown back **leeward**. This can happen to novices, who may not be able to sail closer than around 55 degrees to the wind without suffering from excessive drift. A 'close call', however, can happen to beginners and experts alike in any kind of activity.

close haul see **close call**

clue/cue (sign, indication)
A 'clue' guides one in the direction of the solving of a problem or a mystery – but does not necessarily lead to the final solution. One might thus see a 'clue' to a friend's strange behaviour in his recent row with his boss. A 'cue' gives a hint or a suggestion. As such, it is not so positive as a 'clue'. So, put another way, your friend's encounter with the management might be a 'cue' to his strange behaviour.

clunk see **clang**

coarse/crude/rude (rough, vulgar, offensive)
Basically, 'coarse' has the implication of lack of refinement, inferiority, as of 'coarse' language or manners. 'Crude' – literally 'unrefined' as in 'crude' oil or sugar – suggests that there is a distinct absence of

polish or tact, so that a 'crude' joke is, to some, not only unfunny but offensive. 'Rude', apart from its meaning of 'robust' or 'sturdy', as in 'rude' health, implies a definite offensiveness or lack of politeness, partly because of roughness, partly through want of courtesy. A 'rude' reply is one that is consciously offensive; a 'crude' one may be unintentionally so, simply because the person knows no better.

cockatiel see **cockatoo**

cockatoo/cockatiel/marabou/caribou/ kinkajou/carcajou/sapajou (exotic bird or animal)
The 'cockatoo' is a crested parrot, a native of the East Indies and Australia. The 'cockatiel' is also an Australian parrot, and crested, but is smaller. It is common as a cagebird. The 'marabou' is a large stork, a native of Africa. Its soft downy feathers under its wing and tail have found favour with some women as an adornment for their hat. The 'caribou' is a species of North American reindeer. The 'kinkajou' is a small, brown, furry animal related to the racoon that lives in trees in Central and South America. The 'carcajou' is the American glutton, and the 'sapajou' is the capuchin monkey, a native of South America.

cocotte see **coquette**

coddle/cosset (pamper)
One usually 'coddles' invalids or children by pandering to their whims and generally overindulging them. To 'cosset' someone is to treat him as a pet, lavish attention on him. 'Cosset' is a dialect word for a pet lamb.

codger/curmudgeon (eccentric or crusty old person)
A 'codger' – possibly the word is related to 'cadger' – is usually an old, rather odd person. The term can be quite an affectionate one. 'He's a nice old codger' (cp. the gentlemen who deal with the *Daily Mirror*'s equivalent of 'Letters to the Editor'). A 'curmudgeon' is definitely not an affectionate term. It implies meanness or stinginess. Its actual origin is unknown,

although Dr Johnson in his *Dictionary* ascribed it to the French *coeur méchant* (spiteful heart).

cogent see **coherent**

coherent/cohesive/cogent (binding, meaningful)
'Coherent' literally means 'sticking together' and thus 'consistent' or 'logical', as in a 'coherent' report or policy. 'Cohesive', with the same basic meaning, emphasises the binding or uniting force. The word is chiefly used of physical objects, such as a 'cohesive' mass of some material, but one can talk of the 'cohesive' force of, say, a party or league of some kind. 'Cogent' means 'convincing', as when a speaker makes a number of 'cogent' points.

cohesive see **coherent**

coif see **quiff**

cole see **coleslaw**

coleslaw/slaw/kale/cole/kohlrabi (kind of cabbage)
'Coleslaw', from two Dutch words, means literally 'cabbage salad' and is a salad of sliced white cabbage. 'Slaw' is sliced or chopped cabbage eaten usually cold, i.e. uncooked, or less often, hot i.e. cooked. 'Kale' is a kind of cabbage with wrinkled leaves, although the name is also used for borecole or broccoli. 'Cole' is a general name for different kinds of cabbage, in particular rape. 'Kohlrabi', a word that is a blend of German *Kohl* (cabbage) and Italian *cauli rape* (cabbage turnips), is a variety of 'kale' with a stem swelling into a bulblike formation.

coliseum/Colosseum (large theatre)
A 'coliseum', now more familiar as the name of a number of theatres, cinemas, dance halls and the like, is properly any place for meetings or public entertainment. It is the generic variant of the 'Colosseum', the great amphitheatre in Rome built by Vespasian. Both words are, unsurprisingly, related to 'colossal'.

collaborate see **co-operate**

collate see **collect**

collect/collate/collocate (bring together, set in order)
To 'collect' is basically to 'bring or gather together', as a crowd, stamps, or water in a ditch. The actual order of gathering is often unimportant. To 'collate' is to compare things – usually texts, articles, written or printed entries and the like – in order to see if they agree or disagree. One might thus 'collate' one's entries for a competition, or one's notes for a lecture. There is a suggestion of 'collecting' as well. To 'collocate' is to arrange in proper order. A linguistic expert might thus 'collocate' the languages of West Africa. The term often suggests a place, as when a commanding officer 'collocates' his battle forces for action at a particular point.

collocate see **collect**

collude/connive/conspire (act or plot together)
'Colluding' implies a secret understanding, especially when something illegal or dishonest is involved. Agreeably, the word originates from the Latin verb meaning 'play with'. A similar sort of game is 'conniving', which suggests supporting something wrong, which one secretly approves, by deliberately avoiding showing any disapproval – by being, in other words, a secret accessory, or by turning a blind eye. This last sense is closest to the Latin original, meaning 'shut the eyes with'. 'Conspiring' – this time literally 'breathing together' – simply suggests agreeing to do something unlawful or illegal, especially secretly. This is the strongest, most active word, with 'connive' the weakest, least active.

Colosseum see **coliseum**

Comecon see **Comintern**

comfy/cosy (snug and homely)
'Comfy' is a pet abbreviation for 'comfortable', talking of some familiar or homely object, as a 'comfy' chair or a pair of 'comfy' slippers. 'Cosy' – spelled 'cozy' in

the USA – really means 'snugly comfortable', as a 'cosy' chair or a 'cosy' corner. Figuratively it means 'intimate', as when one has a 'cosy' little chat, although it can acquire a disparaging sense in such a phrase as a 'cosy' job, which is a cushy one, or a 'cosy' profit, which is an easy and large one.

comic/comical (causing amusement)
The essential difference is that 'comic' describes something that is supposed to be funny, and 'comical' – usually – something that is not. So one has on the one hand a 'comic' play, actor, novel or song, but a 'comical' sight, manner, face or gait. As a noun, 'comic' can mean a low-grade comedian.

comical see **comic**

Cominform see **Comintern**

Comintern/Cominform/Comecon
(Communist organisation)
The 'Comintern' was the Third Communist International, founded in 1919 and dissolved in 1943. It united various Communist countries and advocated violent or revolutionary measures. The 'Cominform' was an organisation existing from 1947 to 1956 established by the Communist parties of nine European countries including the USSR, France and Italy, for mutual advice and coordinated activity. 'Comecon', the acronym of 'Council for Mutual Economic Aid', is a confederation of nine Communist countries, including the USSR, Mongolia and Cuba, to coordinate their economic development. Founded in 1949, it is a kind of Eastern bloc Common Market.

commandant see **commander**

commander/commodore/commandant (high military rank)
A 'commander' is, in general, the chief commissioned officer, irrespective of rank, of a military unit, otherwise the 'C.O.'. When it comes to the three services, officers of equivalent rank, in descending order, are:

Navy commodore, commander, lieutenant commander

Army lieutenant general, lieutenant colonel, major
Air Force air commodore, wing commander, squadron leader

The WRNS equivalent of 'commodore' is 'commandant'. Moreover, apart from the naval rank, a 'commodore' is the senior captain of a line of merchant vessels and also the title of the president or head of a yacht club. Generally speaking a 'commandant' is the commanding officer of a particular place or body of troops, as of the Royal Army Medical College or an army barracks.

commissar see **commissioner**

commissary see **commissioner**

commissionaire see **commissioner**

commissioner/commissionaire/ commissary/commissar (public official)
A 'commissioner' is in principle someone appointed by a commission to carry out specified work. From this come such official titles as Parliamentary 'Commissioner', Health Service 'Commissioner', 'Commissioner' of Police, and so on. A 'commissionaire' is either, more familiarly, the uniformed doorkeeper at a hotel or club, or a member of the Corps of 'Commissionaires', which employs ex-servicemen, policemen, firemen, and merchant navy seamen. A 'commissary' is the (military) officer of a commissariat, which supplies provisions, transport and the like. It is also the title of someone given special power by a superior, or otherwise a deputy, such as the representative of a bishop in his absence. A 'commissar' was the title of the head of a government department, a 'commissariat', in the USSR before there were ministries and ministers, i.e. 1917–46. (His full title was 'People's Commissar'.)

commodore see **commander**

commute/compound (mitigate a punishment or sentence)
To 'commute' a punishment is to change it for one less severe, as when an offender has his sentence 'commuted' to five years'

imprisonment. To 'compound' a crime – which on the face of it would seem to make it worse – is to agree, for a financial consideration, not to prosecute or punish. For this word in another role see **compound**.

compact see **contract**

compile see **compose**

complacent/complaisant/compliant (pleasant or agreeable)
If one is self-satisfied, pleased with oneself, one may be said to be 'complacent', especially if secretly delighting in one's advantages. To be 'complaisant' is to be obliging with the aim of pleasing, but to be 'compliant' is to yield to another's wishes, whether to please or not.

complaisant see **complacent**

complement see **supplement**

complex see **complicated**

compliant see **complacent**

complicated/complex (difficult)
'Complicated' means 'difficult' because of several factors or points that must be taken into account, as a 'complicated' argument or a 'complicated' task. 'Complex' means 'difficult' because of an involved combination of factors, as a 'complex' problem or a 'complex' way of life.

compose (be made up of – or make up) see **consist of**

compose/compile/concoct (arrange, constitute)
To 'compose' something is to put it or arrange it in order to make a single finished product, often something written. One thus 'composes' a poem, a piece of music or a letter. To 'compile' something is to put (usually written or literary) materials in order so as to form a complete book or unit of some kind. In this way one can 'compile' an index, a register or a dictionary. Whether one 'composes' or 'compiles' a crossword is a matter of precision: to 'com-

pose' it implies imaginative or intellectual originality; to 'compile' it suggests setting the individual components – clues and words – in order. To 'concoct' a thing is to 'compose' it hastily, in fact to 'cook it up', as the origin of the word in Latin *concoctus* (cooked together) suggests.

compound (mitigate a punishment or sentence) see **commute**

compound/confound/confuse (complicate)
To 'compound' is to 'combine', as when a leader 'compounds' his followers – builds up a band of them. To 'confound' is to mingle in such a way that the individual components cannot readily be distinguished, or to throw in disorder or confusion. To 'confuse' is to combine without order or to fail to distinguish. In fact one often 'confuses' two things but 'confounds' more than two. Incidentally, it won't do to 'confuse' 'compound' with 'confound'. For 'compound' in another sense, see **commute**.

comprise (of) see **consist of**

compulsive/impulsive/impetuous (instinctive, spontaneous)
How does a 'compulsive' gesture differ from an 'impulsive' one? 'Compulsive', a word borrowed from psychology, is normally used in the sense 'strongly irrational'; thus someone who has a 'compulsive' desire for food cannot refrain from eating. By contrast, 'impulsive' suggests spontaneity, something done without thought for the consequences, as an 'impulsive' movement or an 'impulsive' act of generosity. 'Impetuous' implies an eagerness that borders on the rash, so that an 'impetuous' act of generosity might well make a large hole in one's pocket.

conciliate see **reconcile**

concoct see **compose**

concrete/cement (hard stonelike material)
Surprisingly often one hears people talking about a 'cement' path when they mean a

'concrete' one. 'Concrete' is made by mixing 'cement' – which is its binding agent – sand, broken pieces of stone and the like with water. This amalgam then hardens and you have an artificial stonelike surface. 'Cement' itself is made by burning a mixture of clay and limestone and is used in powder form.

condemn/contemn (disapprove of)
To 'condemn' something is to declare it to be bad or undesirable. To 'contemn' – a much rarer word, mainly only in legal use – means to treat with contempt, to scorn or despise. Since the noun and adjective 'contempt' and 'contemptible' are in reasonably common use, it's perhaps surprising that the verb is so rarely found.

conduit/culvert (water duct or course)
The basic difference between the two is that a 'conduit' carries water over a reasonable distance ('conducts' it), whereas a 'culvert' takes water across under something such as a road or railway. Both are normally underground, with a 'conduit' usually being a longish pipe or tube and a 'culvert' a fairly wide drain or sewer leading a shortish distance. The origin of 'culvert' is uncertain: there may perhaps be a link with the French *couvert* (covered).

confine/contain (limit, restrict)
To 'confine' something is to keep it within its recognised or acceptable limits, as when an invalid is 'confined' to his room or one 'confines' oneself to a few words. To 'contain' something is to check it to prevent it from breaking its normal bounds, such as 'containing' one's temper, the enemy, or an outbreak of disease. The implication is that something 'contained' would, if not checked, rapidly spread or increase.

confound see **compound**

confuse see **compound**

conga see **tango**

congregation/convention/convocation (meeting, assembly)
All three can be used, in rather special senses, of the assembly of an ecclesiastical,

academic or political body. As titles, one has 'Congregation' for the senate of Cambridge University, and the body of resident MAs at Oxford University, as well as for the permanent committee of the Roman (Catholic) College of Cardinals; 'Convention' for the period of English history when Parliament assembled without a summons from the sovereign, such as the one that restored Charles II to the throne in 1660; 'Convocation' for the ecclesiastical assemblies of the provinces of Canterbury and York in the Church of England that meet two or three times a year to discuss church laws, and also for the legislative assembly of Oxford University.

conjugal/connubial (pertaining to marriage)
There is a sizeable overlap in the use of the terms but on the whole it's a matter of rights and rites. 'Conjugal' means 'pertaining to the state of marriage', that is, to a married couple, as in 'conjugal' rights or 'conjugal' bliss. 'Connubial' relates to the marriage ceremony, so that one has 'connubial' vows and 'connubial' rites. The words, Latin in origin, mean respectively 'joined together' and 'married together'.

conjure see **adjure**

connive see **collude**

connote see **denote**

connubial see **conjugal**

consent see **assent**

consequent/subsequent (following)
'Consequent' means 'following as a result or effect', so that one might have a 'consequent' meeting to discuss proposals made at an earlier one. 'Subsequent' means 'following' in any way, so that a 'subsequent' meeting is simply one that happens to take place after an earlier one, or in fact after anything at all that had occurred earlier.

conserve/preserve (keep carefully)
To 'conserve' something is to keep it safe and sound, guard it against loss or damage – hence the 'conservation' of rural areas, old buildings and the like. To 'preserve' something is to keep it for a long time in a good condition, or keep it as it is now, so that one 'preserves' fruit, the peace and one's health. Illogically, if one 'preserves' fruit one can end up either with a 'preserve' or a 'conserve'; the latter suggests that sugar and other additives assist in the retention of the product's natural properties.

consistently/persistently (constantly)
To do something 'consistently' is to do it repeatedly but always in the same manner, as when someone works 'consistently'. If something is done 'persistently' it implies that the repetition is deliberate or calculated, as a correspondent who 'persistently' ignores your requests for a reply to your letter, or a child who is 'persistently' late for school.

consist in see **consist of**

consist of/consist in/comprise (of)/constitute/compose (be made up of – or make up)
A rather tricky collection. 'Consist of' is used of one thing being made up of one or more parts, components, materials, etc. Thus concrete 'consists' of cement, sand and stones mixed with water. 'Consist in' is usually followed by a verb, and means, more or less, 'be defined as': cheerfulness 'consists in' not letting things get you down. 'Comprise' can mean both 'consist of' – a house may 'comprise' three bedrooms, sitting room, dining room, kitchen and bathroom – and also 'make up', as the pages that 'comprise' this book. In other words 'comprise' can relate from single to plural or plural to singular, if the one comprehends the other. 'Comprise of' is also found, possibly because of the common use of 'of' with the past participle, as a course 'comprised of' ten lectures (which is the same as 'consisting of'). To 'constitute' is to make up: health and wealth can 'constitute' happiness. 'Compose' means much the same as 'constitute' but implies a degree of unity, often of dissimilar elements, as the varied ingredients that 'compose' a Christmas pudding.

conspire see **collude**

constantly see **continually**

constitute see **consist of**

contagious see **infectious**

contain see **confine**

contemn see **condemn**

contemptibly/contemptuously (with contempt)
If a person has behaved or acted 'contemptibly' he is usually held in contempt. A person who has behaved 'contemptuously' however, has himself expressed contempt for someone or something else. The same distinction goes for 'contemptible' and 'contemptuous'.

contemptuously see **contemptibly**

continually/continuously/constantly (repeatedly)
All three suggest a succession of occurrences. 'Continually' suggests that the recurrences are very close together, with small breaks or even none at all. Someone who is 'continually' cleaning his car thus does it very frequently, seemingly always. 'Continuously' suggests a succession that really is unbroken. If it rained 'continuously' last night it never stopped raining. 'Constantly' suggests that the action was repeated in the same manner, probably producing the same results each time. A person's proneness to colds, for example, might make him 'constantly' absent from work.

continuously see **continually**

contract/compact (agreement)
A 'contract' is a formal agreement, usually written and signed, as in marriage, or an engagement to perform, make regular payments and the like. A 'compact' is any mutual agreement, not necessarily a formal one. It is close to 'covenant', as a 'compact' made between two colleagues to help each other out or engage in mutually beneficial activities, legal or illegal. Formally, it

almost has the sense of 'treaty', as in a peace – or aggression – 'compact'.

contrary/converse (opposite)
A 'contrary' opinion is one that is either opposed to another or different from it. A 'converse' opinion, on the other hand, is always opposed to another.

contumacy/contumely (offensive behaviour)
Both words are accented on the first syllable; both express an objectionable attitude. 'Contumacy' is rebelliousness or wilful disobedience; 'contumely' is blatant contempt expressed in words or actions. The first word derives from Latin *contumax* (stubborn); the second from Latin *contumelia* (swelling together), with the former possibly derived from the latter.

contumely see **contumacy**

convention see **congregation**

converse see **contrary**

convocation see **congregation**

co-operate/collaborate (work together)
To 'co-operate' is to unite in work, to act jointly. The verb is often used of someone reluctant to be helpful, as when prisoners do not 'co-operate' with the authorities. To 'collaborate' is similar in meaning, but implies that the working together is for a specific purpose. Here the joint effort is much more likely to be for a sinister end, as of traitors who 'collaborate' with the enemy. There is an overlap, however, and some speakers and writers use the words indifferently.

coquette/cocotte (flirt)
A 'coquette' is a woman who seeks to gain the attention or admiration of a man out of vanity or for show. A 'cocotte' does likewise, but as a means to a different end – she is a prostitute, originally a Parisian one. Both words are related in some way to French *coq* (cockerel), of which they are a feminine form. Both *cocotte* and *poule* in modern French are words for 'hen' – and 'tart'.

cord/chord (string – or string-like object)
Both spellings are used for 'vocal cords/chords', yet 'cord' is the basic word for 'type of thick string'. The confusion is largely caused by a musical 'chord', in the sense 'notes played together' or 'string of an instrument'. This latter meaning is now found only in such set phrases as 'touch the right chord' or 'strike a chord' (recall), or in poetry – although Adelaide Ann Procter's 'Lost Chord' ('Seated one day at the organ, . . .') was 'one chord of music, like the sound of a great Amen', i.e. not a single string. The geometrical type – a straight line joining any two points on a curve – is 'chord'.

corporal punishment/capital punishment (penalty inflicted physically)
The two are emotive subjects, and in the heat of the moment may be confused. 'Corporal punishment' is that of the human body, traditionally by flogging, beating, slapping or smacking. Any child who has been subjected to it will know that there are mental undertones and overtones to the process as well as physical. 'Capital punishment' is execution – by any means, although the implication is by beheading, from Latin *caput, capitis* (head). 'Corporal', too, has its origin in the Latin – *corpus, corporis* (body).

corrode see **erode**

corundum see **carborundum**

corvette/vedette (fast naval vessel)
Originally, a 'corvette' was a three-masted sailing ship, ultimately derived from Latin *corbita* (ship of burden). In the modern sense it is a lightly armed fast vessel used for escorting convoys and midway in size between a destroyer and a gunboat. A 'vedette', from Italian *vedere* (to see), is a small naval launch, unarmed, used for reconnaissance work.

cosmonaut see **astronaut**

cosset see **coddle**

costumier/couturier (designer, maker or seller of clothes)

A 'costumier' makes or sells costumes, and also hires them to actors. A 'couturier' – from French *couture* (sewing) – designs and makes women's clothes. His – and also hers – is the art of the 'haute couture', the world of fashion.

cosy see **comfy**

councillor/counsellor (professional adviser)
A 'councillor' is essentially the member of a council, as a 'town councillor'. A 'counsellor' – one who counsels – is the common term in the USA to mean, among other things, a lawyer, especially one attending a trial, or a student's tutor. The word exists in some titles in Britain, however, notably as 'Counsellor of State' and, at a local and more homely level, 'marriage guidance counsellor'.

counsellor see **councillor**

courser see **charger**

couturier see **costumier**

crafty see **arty**

crass see **gross**

crawfish see **crayfish**

crayfish/crawfish (edible crustacean)
The 'crayfish' closely resembles the lobster, but is much smaller. The 'crawfish' actually is a lobster. The name denotes, especially, the spiny or rock lobster or *langouste*. 'Crawfish' is also, confusingly, the preferred American spelling of 'crayfish'. Both words have become firmly confused with 'fish' – which they are not. The origin lies in Old French *crevis* or *crevice*; the name of the creature in modern French is *écrevisse*.

credible/creditable/credulous (believable)
'Credible' means both 'believable', as a 'credible' story, and 'trustworthy', as a 'credible' backer or supporter. 'Creditable' means 'deserving credit', as a 'creditable' performance, or a 'creditable' result in an

examination. 'Credulous' refers to some-one who is over-ready to believe or gullible, or to a person's attitude or appearance, as a 'credulous' child, who will believe anything he is told.

creditable see **credible**

credulous see **credible**

crevasse see **crevice**

crevice/crevasse/abyss/chasm (rent or split, usually deep)
The only one that is not deep is 'crevice', which is a small crack that forms an opening, usually in something solid, as hard ground, rock or ice. A 'crevasse' is a deep cleft, usually in ice. An 'abyss' is a bottom-less, or seemingly bottomless, gulf, from the Greek word meaning 'without bottom'. A 'chasm' can be literal, when it is a deep or wide cleft or gorge, or figurative, when it denotes an abstract rending force, as the 'chasm' of death.

Crimplene see **poplin**

crimson/carnation/carmine/incar-nadine/cardinal/carnelian (shade of red)
It is remarkable that so many similar words should denote more or less the same colour. 'Crimson', is a deep, purplish red, as one sees in a 'crimson' complexion. 'Carnation' is a light red, almost pink – the colour of the flower, in fact. Its origin is the Latin *carnatio* (fleshiness), the reference being to the colour of flesh in paintings. 'Carmine' is virtually the same as 'crimson'; basically it is the pigment obtained from cochineal. The rolling Shakespearean 'incarnadine' has a primary suggestion of flesh colour, but a secondary sense of blood colour – the latter due to association with the words of the horrified Macbeth. 'Cardinal' is deep, rich red, the colour of a cardinal's robes. 'Carnelian', yet another word influenced by the flesh (Latin *caro, carnis*), is strictly speaking a red or reddish variety of chalcedony. A variant form of the word is 'cornelian': neither spelling should be confused with 'c(a)erulian' which is sky-blue.

cromlech/dolmen/menhir (type of large ancient standing stone)
A 'cromlech', from the Welsh *crom* (bent) and *llech* (stone) is a circle of single, standing stones, such as the one at Avebury. Unhelpfully, the word is also sometimes used to mean 'dolmen'. This is an ancient tomb or burial chamber looking rather like a rough and ready table with three or more upright stones and a horizontal flat stone on top. 'Dolmens' exist especially in Wales, Cornwall and Ireland as well as in Brittany. The name seems to be an invented one, from Breton *tol* (table) and *men* (stone), although some authorities derive it from Cornish *doll* (hole) and *men* (stone). There is no doubt that 'menhir' is simply Breton *men hir* (long stone). This is a single stone whether on its own or, as at Avebury, Stonehenge and the famous *alignements* at Carnac in Brittany, with others.

crotch/crutch (fork of the human body)
'Crotch' is used of the fork itself as a location, of the vital organs situated at the fork, or of this area of a pair of trousers, pants and the like. 'Crutch' is a popular anatomical term for the same area, with the usage not extended to other meanings. A particularly unpleasant below-the-belt blow is a kick in the 'crotch'.

crude see **coarse**

crumple/rumple (crush or press into irregular form or folds)
'Crumple' is used of the crushing of any kind of cloth or clothes, such as shirts, sheets, coats and curtains. 'Rumple' implies that the crushing or pressing is into smaller folds – a 'rumpled' sheet is thus merely a disarranged one – and is extended to mean 'ruffle' or 'tousle' applied to hair or an animal's coat.

crush/pash (infatuation, or the object of it)
A 'crush' is usually regarded as a feminine affair, the infatuation of a schoolgirl for her teacher (male or female) or, less often, of a woman for a man. 'Pash' can apply to both sexes – of both, for both – but its main application is among schoolchildren with

the target object either a teacher or a fellow pupil of the opposite or the same sex. In origin 'crush' suggests a passionate compulsion, and 'pash' a compulsive passion.

crutch see **crotch**

cudgel/bludgeon (short heavy stick used as a weapon)
A 'cudgel' is any stick used as a weapon; a 'bludgeon' – suggesting 'blunt', although the origin of the word is unknown – is more of a club, with one end heavier than the other. Both instruments provide the verbs that mean 'hit' (with the respective weapon). In addition one can 'cudgel' one's brains – rack them, and take up the 'cudgels' – join the defence on behalf of someone or something.

cue see **clue**

culvert see **conduit**

curmudgeon see **codger**

cyclotron/synchrotron/synchrocyclotron (nuclear accelerator)
The 'cyclotron' is the basic device. It imparts very high speeds to electrified particles by means of successive electric impulses. A 'synchrotron' is a 'cyclotron' in which the strength of the magnetic field is increased as the particles gain energy. By contrast a 'synchrocyclotron' is a 'cyclotron' in which the frequency of the electric field is *de*creased as the particles gain energy. The '-tron' suffix derives from 'electron'.

cynical/sceptical (distrustful)
'Cynical' means 'disbelieving' with a suggestion of disapproval. One can thus have a 'cynical' outlook or make a 'cynical' remark. 'Sceptical' is not so strong as 'cynical'; it implies a doubt, and usually a mild one, as might be expressed in a 'sceptical' look or by a 'sceptical' smile. Both Cynics and Sceptics were members of schools of Greek philosophy. The Cynics strove to develop the ethical teachings of Socrates (especially that virtue is only good); the Sceptics held that real knowledge of things is impossible.

cynosure see **sinecure**

czarevitch/cesarevitch/czarina/czarevna (member of the Russian imperial family)
Spellings of the titles vary, with 'ts-' often preferred to 'cz-' and '-wich' an alternative ending to '-vitch'. All, of course, are related to the czar (or tsar). The 'czarevitch' was originally the son of a czar; later the title became that of the czar's eldest son. The 'cesarevitch' was the title of the eldest son as heir to the throne. From it derives the 'Cesarewitch', the Newmarket race which in 1839 was instituted by the 21-year-old eldest son of Nicholas I, who was to become Alexander II. The 'czarina' – in Russian actually *tsaritsa* – was the wife of the czar, i.e. the Empress of Russia. The 'czarevna' was the daughter of the tsar. All words, as 'czar' itself, are related to 'Caesar' and 'Kaiser'.

czarevna see **czarevitch**

czarina see **czarevitch**

Dacron see **nylon**

dally see **delay**

damask/dimity (fabric with distinctive design)
'Damask', originally produced in Damascus, is a reversible fabric of linen, silk, cotton or wool with woven patterns, most usually seen in the dining room as a tablecloth. 'Dimity' – from the Greek *dimitos* (of double thread) – is a thin cotton fabric, white, dyed or printed, and woven with a

stripe or check of some kind of heavier yarn. It appears mainly in bedrooms as a bedspread, although it's also used for hangings and occasionally for clothes. Its stripes are sometimes raised and may be complemented by fancy figures.

dappled/piebald/skewbald (mottled, of a horse or pony)
A 'dappled' horse is a spotted one, such as a 'dappled' grey which is mainly grey with darker grey mottling or a 'dappled' bay which is bay (reddish brown) with darker mottling. A 'piebald' horse is white with black patches: the term derives from 'pie' (magpie) with 'bald' in the sense of 'marked with white'. 'Skewbald' horses are a mixture of white and some other colour, usually brown. The word seems to be modelled on 'piebald' but the 'skew' is hard to explain. Perhaps it has its origin in the Old French *escu* (shield) in reference to the 'quartered' appearance.

daring/derring-do (courage)
'Daring' is 'adventurous courage', 'boldness' as in a 'daring' escape or rescue. 'Derring-do' is something of a phony hybrid. It came about through a misunderstanding on the part of Spenser, who took the phrase 'derryng do' in a fifteenth century poem to be a noun – it in fact is 'daring to do'. It still serves as a pseudoarchaic epithet of 'daring' with the sense 'romantically heroic'. For another Spenserian slip, see **Sabbath**.

dash see **rush**

dastard see **bastard**

dazed/dazzled (bewildered by brightness)
Both words have a sense extended to include anything that stuns or overwhelms. Basically, 'dazed' implies a bewilderment, as when one is 'dazed' on hearing dramatic news, whereas 'dazzled' suggests a brilliance of some kind, literal, as of a flashlight, or figurative, as of a woman's radiant beauty.

dazzled see **dazed**

deadly/deathly (like death, or causing it)
Both words have both meanings, although 'deathly' is almost always figurative. One can thus talk of 'deadly' poison or a 'deadly' enemy, but a 'deathly' pallor or a 'deathly' hush.

deathly see **deadly**

debate/deliberate (discuss, consider)
The meanings of the words overlap up to a point, although 'deliberate' has the overtone of 'weigh up', which in fact it literally means. Both actions can be carried out by one person on his own, in spite of the implication of a joint discussion or consideration.

decathlon see **marathon**

deceitful see **deceptive**

decent/decorous (seemly, proper)
'Decent' suggests that good taste or standards or appearance are involved, as a 'decent' family or a 'decent' respect for law and order. With 'decorous' the emphasis is more on outward appearance or behaviour, as can be seen in someone's 'decorous' manner or heard in his 'decorous' speech. The shades of propriety merge, however, so that the related 'decorum' can mean both 'decency' and 'decorousness'.

deceptive/deceitful (deceiving)
It's a matter of intention: something or someone 'deceptive' may not intentionally be so; a 'deceitful' person, however, is one who deliberately deceives.

decidedly/decisively (definitely, markedly)
Confusion can lead to 'decisively' being used instead of 'decidedly', as when a team is wrongly said to have won a 'decisively' easy victory. 'Decidedly' means 'undeniably', as when someone is 'decidedly' forthright or outspoken; 'decisively' means 'showing decision', so that a matter is dealt with 'decisively' – or conclusively.

decisively see **decidedly**

decorous see **decent**

deductive/inductive (relating to process of reasoning)
'Deductive' reasoning is that in which a general statement is applied to a particular one, such as saying 'All cows are animals; this is a cow; therefore it is an animal.' This is formally known as syllogism. 'Inductive' is the opposite: a general principle is made as a result of the study of individual cases. It may, though, not lead to a one hundred per cent truth, since all individual cases would have to be studied. An example of 'inductive' reasoning is 'All calendars I have seen show twelve months in the year: I can therefore expect all calendars I see in the future to show twelve months in the year.'

defective/deficient (faulty, having a shortcoming)
Something that is 'defective' may be just imperfect, as 'defective' eyesight or a book which turns out to be a 'defective' copy. Something 'deficient' is always faulty, however, since it lacks its full quota of attributes. Thus a 'deficient' supply is one that falls short, and a person who has a 'deficient' memory has one which is unable to recall properly.

deficient see **defective**

deflation see **inflation**

deism/theism (belief in God or a god)
'Deism' is belief in a God (or god) who has created the world but has since become indifferent to it. The term is distinguished from atheism, pantheism and 'theism', which last denotes belief in one God or god who created the universe and went on to rule it. Alternatively, it can be used to mean simply a belief in the existence of a God or gods, in which sense it is distinguished merely from atheism. For more about belief in God see **atheist**.

delay/dally/dilly-dally/dither/shilly-shally (be slow or indecisive)
The basic word is 'delay' – 'be slow or tardy'. 'Dally' implies a loitering or lack of determination, as when a profligate 'dallies'

away his youth. 'Dilly-dally' and 'shilly-shally' are similar – the latter deriving from the semi-jocular query 'Shill I? Shall I?', although 'dilly-dally' suggests that hesitation leads to time being wasted, while 'shilly-shally' implies that indecision itself causes a waste of time. 'Dither' puts the emphasis on the hesitation, which is often accompanied by some kind of confusion or agitation.

delegate/relegate (consign, refer, classify)
To 'delegate' a task to a person is simply to give it to him. To 'relegate' something is often to place it in a lower position, as a football team in the League divisions, or an unwanted circular in the waste paper basket. 'Relegate' can, however, simply mean 'refer', as of a matter to a committee for discussion, or 'classify', as of a newly discovered scientific species to a particular family.

deliberate see **debate**

delusion/illusion (mental deception)
There is a nice difference between these classic confusibles. A 'delusion' is deception caused by something actually being other than it seems, as when a person is under the 'delusion' his food is being poisoned. 'Delusions' thus often refer to something sinister or harmful. An 'illusion' is deception caused by something *appearing* to be other than it really is, so that what is visualised may not exist at all. Thus a mirage is an 'illusion', not a 'delusion'. 'Illusions' are not necessarily unpleasant; they can often be pleasant, or at least harmless. There are, however, certain instances when either word can be used equally meaningfully, as 'If you think you're clever you're under an illusion (a delusion).'

demonstrate/remonstrate (show, point out)
Both words have as their root the Latin *monstrare* (show). To 'demonstrate' something is to show it clearly, normally for some specific purpose, as when a suspect 'demonstrates' his innocence – proves it by

pointing to particular facts or circumstances. To 'remonstrate' is to protest against something by pleading as if 'demonstrating'. The same suspect might 'remonstrate' with his accusers by protesting his innocence; only if he can clearly 'demonstrate' it, however, will he not be regarded as guilty.

denizen see **citizen**

denominator see **numerator**

denote/connote (mean, signify)
'Denote' has the direct meaning 'indicate': a high temperature usually 'denotes' fever, therefore, and thick, black clouds often 'denote' an approaching storm. 'Connote' means 'denote secondarily' i.e. signify something additional to the primary meaning. Thus 'home' 'denotes' living accommodation but it 'connotes' comfort and security.

deplore/deprecate/depreciate (feel reproach or disapproval for)
To 'deplore' a thing is to regret it, usually deeply. To 'deprecate' something is to express strong disapproval of it. If I therefore 'deplore' your behaviour I am upset by it; if I 'deprecate' it I say that I disapprove of it and probably give my reasons. To 'depreciate' has the basic sense 'lower in value', but can also mean 'disparage'. If a speaker makes several good, valid points, why 'depreciate' them simply because you don't agree? See also, out of interest, **self-deprecation.**

depository/repository (place where things are left or kept)
A 'depository' is a place such as a storehouse or depot (the word is a French cousin) where furniture and the like are kept safely. A 'repository' is on the whole smaller, such as a room, cupboard or chest where things are put for safe keeping or stored – or a place where something is discovered, as a back garden that turns out to be a 'repository' of tin cans and buried bones. Its use is extended to mean 'warehouse' or any place where things are sold, and also to designate the special place where a dead body is deposited.

deprecate see **deplore**

depreciate see **deplore**

depredation see **deprivation**

depressed area/distressed area/ development area/deprived area (area of economic depression or unemployment)
All four terms are government jargon. A 'depressed area' is one in which there is economic depression and unemployment, and a 'distressed area' one in which unemployment is marked. The terms are pre-war ones and the current terms for such areas are, respectively, a 'development area' and a 'special development area'. (Both these are officially known as 'assisted areas' in which, according to the Distribution of Industry Act (1945) 'assistance is offered by the government to encourage industrial development and the movement of office and other service employment'.) A 'deprived area' is one that is educationally deprived, i.e. a so-called 'priority area' in which the government has allocated resources for the improvement of educational facilities by means of a number of schemes such as the Urban Programme launched in 1968, the Educational Priority Area Project sponsored jointly by the Department of Education and Science and the Social Science Research Council, and the Community Development Project sponsored by the Home Office.

deprivation/depredation (loss)
'Deprivation' is the act of being deprived of something, so that one loses it: war often entails many 'deprivations'. 'Depredations' – the word is normally used in the plural – means 'destruction and robbery', as the 'depredations' that can be caused by birds on fruit bushes or locusts on crops. The word is related to 'prey'. War can also, of course, bring its 'depredations' as well as its 'deprivations'.

deprived area see **depressed area**

derogate see **abdicate**

derring-do see **daring**

déshabillé see **dishabille**

designed/destined/predestined
(planned, ordained)
'Designed' means 'intended', even if the desired aim is not actually achieved, as a train 'designed' to travel at over 100 m.p.h. 'Destined' implies that the result is achieved, whether it was desired or not – almost 'foreordained', in fact. Yuri Gagarin was thus 'destined' – and also 'designed' – to be the first man in space. 'Predestined' emphasises the preceding stage of something that (frequently) fails to achieve the desired aim, as an attempt to climb Everest which was 'predestined' to failure: looking back, you can see that it was never likely to have succeeded.

destined see **designed**

development area see **depressed area**

deviate see **digress**

devoted/devout (dedicated)
'Devoted' implies a positive show of loyalty, as with a 'devoted' husband, friend or admirer. 'Devout' expresses more of an attitude, one of sincerity and earnestness, as is shown by the 'devout' supporter of a campaign. The word has a religious connotation, which gives it a suggestion of reverence or even fanaticism.

devout see **devoted**

dialogue/duologue (conversation between two or more persons)
A misleading and rather devious couple, whose exact sense is indicated by the prefixes. A 'dialogue' – the prefix does not mean 'two' but, literally, 'through', 'by means of' – is a conversation between two *or more* persons. A 'duologue', where the prefix does mean 'two', is between two persons only, as in a play. The word was formed by analogy with 'monologue'.

diffident see **indifferent**

digress/diverge/deviate (turn aside)
One 'digresses' mainly when speaking, by wandering from the main topic. Two roads will 'diverge' if they run off at an increasingly widening angle from a common point. To 'deviate' is to turn, literally or figuratively, from a particular path or course, often only slightly or temporarily.

dilly-dally see **delay**

dimity see **damask**

dipsomaniac see **hypochondriac**

discerning/discriminating (choosing and distinguishing carefully)
'Discerning' tastes are ones that take minor features into account as well as the major, obvious ones. The word thus implies depth or acuteness of judgment. 'Discriminating' implies a similar attention to detail, but has the additional connotation of a rejection as well as a selection.

discomfit see **discomfort**

discomfort/discomfit (make uneasy)
To 'discomfort' a person is to disturb his comfort or happiness in some way, as bad news can do. To 'discomfit' is to confuse or disconcert: an airport strike can 'discomfit' your holiday plans considerably. The word is bookish, though, and need not often 'discomfit' you.

discrepancy/disparity (difference)
A 'discrepancy' implies that the difference should not in fact exist, as when one finds a 'discrepancy' in one's bank statement: the figures are not as they should be and not as they usually are. A 'disparity' emphasises the inequality of the difference: one expects the two things to be more alike. People are always ready to point to the 'disparity' in years when a forty-year-old marries someone half this age.

discriminating see **discerning**

dishabille/déshabillé (state of undress)
Both words are from the French. 'Dishabille', usually pronounced 'disabeel', is the state of being undressed, partly dressed, or dressed carelessly or negligently. 'Déshabillé', also written without accents, is 'days-a-bee-ay' and is usually reserved for

a specifically coy state of undress. *Partridge*, ever correct, points out that one is *in* 'dishabille' but *en* 'déshabillé'. The second term, however, has lost much of its stylishness now that the phenomenon itself has become so commonplace.

disinflation see **inflation**

disinterested/uninterested (not interested)
The two are not synonyms, and can mark a useful distinction. 'Disinterested' means 'impartial', as a 'disinterested' report or account. 'Uninterested' implies boredom through lack of interest. Some AGMs cause members to lapse into an 'uninterested' state. The noun of 'disinterested' is 'disinterest' or, if marked, 'disinterestedness'. Of 'uninterested' the noun is usually 'uninterest', or less often 'uninterestedness'.

disparity see **discrepancy**

dispel see **disperse**

disperse/dispel/dissipate (scatter, drive away)
'Disperse', meaning 'cause to go in different directions', usually applied to an organised body that can be tangibly split up, as a crowd or clouds. Of something intangible, or barely tangible, such as fog or smoke, both 'disperse' and 'dispel' are virtually interchangeable. 'Dissipate' has the additional sense of 'reduce to smaller parts', as of money or resources. When it comes to the nouns, 'dispersal' refers to the act of dispersing, 'dispersion' to the state of having been dispersed.

dissembling/dissimulating/simulating (pretending)
A 'dissembling' nature is one whose real quality is concealed. 'Dissimulating' and 'simulating' are opposites: 'dissimulating' meaning 'pretending not to have what you really do have' (or not to be what you really are); 'simulating' means 'pretending to have (or be) what you do not have (or are not)'. The last two are most often used as active verbs, while 'dissembling' is frequently used as an adjective.

dissentient see **dissenting**

dissenting/dissident/dissentient (disagreeing)
'Dissenting' means 'feeling or thinking differently'; 'dissident' suggests a strong or active disagreement, as of a 'dissident' voice or vote; 'dissentient' lays the emphasis on one's own views by comparison with those of the majority – at the time of the Reformation in England the Protestants were both 'dissident' and 'dissentient'.

dissident see **dissenting**

dissimulating see **dissembling**

dissipate see **disperse**

dissipated see **dissolute**

dissolute/dissipated (self-indulgent, morally lax)
'Dissolute' describes more the state – one of almost permanent dissipation. One could thus lead a 'dissolute' life, with 'dissolute' friends. With 'dissipated' the emphasis is on the action itself: a person's 'dissipated' appearance has a positive cause. The word is often used as a stronger variant of 'dissolute'. It has also, of course, the emotively neutral meaning 'scattered' (see **disperse**).

distinct/distinctive (marked)
'Distinct' means 'clear', 'easily noticed', as of a 'distinct' improvement in the economy or a 'distinct' nip in the air. The word frequently implies a comparison. 'Distinctive' means 'serving to distinguish' or 'characteristic', so that someone who speaks with a 'distinctive' authority is expected to do so, since such authority is one of his characteristics.

distinctive see **distinct**

distracted see **distraught**

distrait see **distraught**

distraught/distressed/distracted/distrait (mentally or physically disturbed)
A person who is 'distraught' usually

behaves irrationally under the pressure of a deep emotion such as fear or grief. A 'distressed' person is one seen to suffer as the result of a strong emotion or some kind of pain. With 'distracted' the disturbance is nearly always a mental one, and there is not necessarily any implication of physical suffering. The word can, in fact, mean little more than 'diverted'. 'Distrait', from the French, means 'absent-minded' – not so much 'distracted' as 'abstracted'.

distressed see **distraught**

distressed area see **depressed area**

distrust/mistrust (not trust)
The weaker word is 'mistrust', as in similar pairs of words with these prefixes such as 'disbelief/misbelief'. It means 'not trust' to any degree, even a slight one: if you 'mistrust' my motives, you have doubts about them. 'Distrust', on the other hand, means 'regard (one hundred per cent) with suspicion': if you 'distrust' my judgment you have no faith in it. Put another way, 'mistrust' is a more negative word; 'distrust' a positive one.

disturb/perturb (unsettle, agitate)
'Disturb' tends to apply to a physical or mental unsettling – a sudden hammering on the door at night would probably 'disturb' you both physically and mentally. 'Perturb' applies mainly to a mental state: one can be 'perturbed' by bad news or a vivid account of something unpleasant.

dither see **delay**

diverge see **digress**

divers see **diverse**

diverse/divers (various)
'Diverse' has the meaning 'of different or various kinds', such as 'diverse' opinions, painting materials or habits. 'Divers' is simply a quaint or poetic word meaning 'several', as in 'divers' complaints. It used to mean 'diverse', however, hence the 'divers manners' referred to by St Paul at the beginning of his Epistle to the Hebrews.

divine/dowse (search for water or metal hidden underground)
'Divine' is a more general word, meaning basically 'make known'. To 'divine' water is to discover it by means of a 'divining' rod of some kind. To 'dowse' – in spite of its appearance no relation to 'douse' – is more to search for water in this way. Thus 'divining' implies a finding; 'dowsing' merely a searching.

doddering/doting (senile)
Literally, 'doddering' is descriptive of one who dodders or trembles, shakes, and otherwise shows the enfeebled physical powers of extreme old age. A 'doddering' old man is really no more than an aged one, therefore, although the word is often used with the overtone of 'senile'. 'Doting' really does mean 'senile', with the lack of emotional stability that the word implies. The reference is to a feeble old man's pathetic affection – he 'dotes' on the past or a world in which he is no longer young.

dolmen see **cromlech**

dominating/domineering (controlling, governing)
'Dominating' can apply to an authority that is reasonable or unreasonable: a 'dominating' position may be simply a commanding one; a 'dominating' manner is usually a bossy one. 'Domineering' suggests a tyrannising or overbearing position, so that a 'domineering' manner is an unpleasantly haughty one.

domineering see **dominating**

doting see **doddering**

doubtful/dubious (unwilling to believe, open to question)
'Doubtful' suggests that more evidence is needed for something to be believed, as when one is 'doubtful' about a person's ability, or a book is of 'doubtful' content. 'Dubious' implies greater uncertainty than 'doubtful', so that 'dubious' hopes of winning are very small and a book of 'dubious' content has little merit and is not regarded as worth the buying or reading. 'Dubious' company is company that is

morally suspect; 'doubtful' company *may* be morally suspect.

downstage see **upstage**

dowse see **divine**

doze/drowse (be half asleep)
To 'doze' is to sleep lightly or fitfully; to 'drowse' is not so much to sleep as to feel sleepy, or at the most be half way between sleeping and waking. 'Drowse' usually implies a pleasant sensation, while 'doze' is simply factual.

drab/dreary (dull, tedious, colourless)
'Drab' is a more negative word, suggesting lack of colour or cheerfulness. Oddly, it derives from the French *drap* (cloth), meaning material that is undyed and therefore cheerless. 'Dreary' is a positive word suggesting sadness, active tedium and – possibly by association with 'weary' – tiredness and fatigue. Thus a 'drab' voice is an expressionless one, while a 'dreary' voice is a boring, depressing one.

dragoman see **dragon**

dragon/dragoon/dragoman/gorgon
(fearsomely powerful person)
Applied figuratively, a 'dragon' is a fierce or violent or domineering person, often one in authority. A 'dragoon' is properly a cavalryman or a mounted infantryman with a musket (the word derives from French *dragon* – the term for the hammer of a firearm). The noun is not in common use, although the verb – 'to force by rigorous and oppressive measures' – is quite common. Some 'dragons' do indeed 'dragoon'. A 'dragoman' is really in the wrong box – he is a professional interpreter in the Middle East, more to be revered than feared. All three words, however, fall under the additional influence of 'Draconian' meaning 'harsh', 'very severe', as were the laws of the Athenian statesman Draco in the seventh century BC. A 'dragon' is usually female; a 'gorgon' always is. The Gorgons, from the Greek *gorgos* (terrible), were the three mythological sisters whose glance turned their beholder to stone. The word still comes in

handy to describe a repulsive-looking woman.

dragoon see **dragon**

dram see **gram**

draught horse/dray horse (strong horse used for pulling loads)
A 'draught horse' is – increasingly was – one that works on a farm drawing loads, pulling ploughs and the like. A 'dray horse' is a strong carthorse or other powerful horse that is used for pulling a 'dray' – a low cart without fixed sides as that used by breweries.

dray horse see **draught horse**

dreary see **drab**

drowse see **doze**

dryad/naiad (nymph)
'Dryads' were thought to live in trees: the word has no connection with 'dry' – as distinct, say, from a water nymph – but comes from Greek *drys* (tree). 'Naiads' were indeed water nymphs, said to live in streams and springs. Their name is related to the Greek verb *naein* (to flow). For more mythological maidens see **nymph** itself.

dubious see **doubtful**

dumbfounded see **astonished**

duologue see **dialogue**

eatable/edible (fit or able to be eaten)
'Eatable' applies to something that is palatable. More often than not, its opposite

is used, so that 'uneatable' is used of food that is unpleasant or difficult to eat for some reason, as an oversalted stew or an underdone potato – 'quite uneatable'. 'Edible' means 'suitable for eating', such as an 'edible' fungus or plant. If something is 'inedible' it cannot be eaten however well it is prepared.

eccentric/erratic (deviating from the normal)
An 'eccentric' person deviates markedly from the normal; what he does is noticeably unusual. An 'erratic' person behaves in an irregular, inconsistent or unpredictable manner; you are not sure what he is going to do next. To this degree, an 'erratic' person can be said to be 'eccentric', since most people are normally consistent and reasonably predictable.

éclat/élan (spirit)
Two French words meaning respectively 'flash' and 'dash'. 'Éclat' implies a brilliance of some kind, as of success, reputation, performance or display. An orator of great 'éclat' thus speaks skilfully and with polish – and is no doubt famous for his eloquence. 'Élan' indicates ardour or zeal rather than accomplishment: someone who plays the part of Henry V with 'élan' does so with spirit but would have to play it with 'éclat' to give a really professional performance.

eclectic see **esoteric**

economic/economical (relating to the economy)
The words overlap, with one frequently used as the other. But to differentiate: 'economic' pertains to the economy, as an 'economic' crisis, to economics, as in the science of 'economic' geography, or to economy in the sense 'thrift', as in an 'economic' rent. 'Economical' is confined to this last sense, and means 'thrifty', as an 'economical' detergent (you need use only a little).

economical see **economic**

edible see **eatable**

edification see **education**

education/edification (instruction, enlightenment)
'For your edification . . .' someone begins ominously. Is he aiming to teach us a home truth or two? In origin, 'edification' is not related to 'education' but to 'edify', from Latin *aedificare* (to build). 'Edification' is the 'building up', therefore, of one's morality, and has the aim of increasing one's knowledge of right and wrong as well as improving one's mind. 'Education' is in its strictest sense the imparting of knowledge pure and simple.

effect see **affect**

effective/effectual/efficacious/ efficient (producing results)
'Effective' means 'producing an effect', so that one can give an 'effective' speech or take 'effective' steps to solve something. 'Effectual' means 'producing a particular effect' – one that was possibly not intended, as when warm, week-end weather leads to an 'effectual' mass exodus of city dwellers to the country. 'Efficacious' means 'capable of producing an effect' – but usually a medical one, and with the implication that the result is conditional on the application of the means, as an 'efficacious' medicine (it will work only if you take it). 'Efficient', of things or people, means 'effortlessly effective', as of a plan or an organiser. 'Efficacious' has a choice of nouns: 'efficaciousness', 'efficacity' or 'efficacy' – but the last can also double as the noun for 'effective'.

effectual see **effective**

effeminate/effete (unmanly, feeble)
'Effeminate' means 'womanish' of a man, hence 'unmanly', as of an 'effeminate' gesture, walk or voice. 'Effete' means 'worn out', hence 'weak', 'useless'. Oddly, the word applies properly to women, since it derives from Latin *effetus* (exhausted by bearing children). The word is thus related to 'foetus'.

effete see **effeminate**

51

efficacious see **effective**

efficient see **effective**

e.g./i.e. (abbreviation indicating that more precise information follows)
Both abbreviations are of Latin phrases, namely *exempli gratia* (for sake of an example) and *id est* (that is). 'E.g.' indicates that one or more specific examples follow what has been mentioned in general terms. Thus many crustaceans, 'e.g.' crabs, lobsters and shrimps, are edible. ('E.g.' introduces examples of what a crustacean is.) 'I.e.', on the other hand, gives an explanation of what has been mentioned, so that many crustaceans, 'i.e.' those sea creatures that have legs and a hard shell, are edible. ('I.e.' introduces an explanation of what a crustacean is.) The two abbreviations are often confused, especially in official notices. One hospital appointments card, for example, asks patients to 'notify the appointments clerk of any change in their personal particulars (i.e. change of address)'.

egoist/egotist (self-centred person)
The difference, in essence, is that an 'egoist', although self-centred, is not necessarily deliberately so; an 'egotist' is.

egotist see **egoist**

élan see **éclat**

elated see **elevated**

elder/older (older or senior)
'Elder' means 'older' only in family relationships, as an 'elder' brother or sister. Of two specified people, it means 'senior', as the 'elder' of two partners. 'Older' means 'older' in all other senses.

elect/élite (chosen group)
The 'elect' comprise any persons chosen for something – not necessarily the best. The 'élite', from the French *élire* (to elect) are, by contrast, the best, the most choice – usually of some group or set that is already of high or recognised quality, such as the 'élite' of the aristocracy or of the entertainment world.

elemental see **elementary**

elementary/elemental (basic, fundamental)
Literally, 'elementary' means 'pertaining to elements', so in some cases has a meaning close to 'primary'. Commonly, however, it means 'basic', 'simple', as in an 'elementary' fact, or argument for or against something. 'Elemental' means 'pertaining to the elements' – either chemical elements or, often, the forces of nature or of some spirit, as in the 'elemental' beauty of the polar regions or the 'elemental' grandeur of a symphony or portrait.

elevated/elated/exalted (raised up, set high)
'Elevated' has both a literal and figurative usage, so that an 'elevated' position can be a high one or a senior one. 'Elated' means 'proudly jubilant' – 'feeling high', in a way. 'Exalted' means 'nobly elevated', as an 'exalted' rank or 'exalted' style of writing.

élite see **elect**

elope see **escape**

elude see **avoid**

emend see **amend**

emigrant see **immigrant**

émigré see **immigrant**

Emmy/Grammy/Tony (American performing arts award)
An 'Emmy' – said to be an alteration of 'Immy', a jargon term for an image orthicon tube – is a statuette awarded by the American Academy of Television Arts and Sciences to an outstanding television programme or performer, the Oscar of television, therefore. A 'Grammy', from 'gramophone', is a gold-plated record awarded by the National Academy of Recording Arts and Sciences for achievement in gramophone recording. A 'Tony', named after the American actress Antoinette Perry, is the Broadway equivalent of an Oscar, i.e. an award for the theatre.

emotional/emotive (pertaining to the emotions)
'Emotional' means 'affected by or appealing to the emotions', as an 'emotional' greeting or an 'emotional' girl. 'Emotive' means 'tending to affect the emotions', 'not impassive'. Abortion is thus an 'emotive' issue.

emotive see **emotional**

empathy see **sympathy**

encumbent see **incumbent**

encumber/lumber (burden)
The words are close in meaning, although 'encumber' has more the sense of 'hamper', and 'lumber' that of 'saddle'. A passage thus 'encumbered' with furniture is one that it is difficult to get through, an obstructed one; a passage 'lumbered' with furniture is one that has an undue quantity of bulky furniture in it. The origins of the words reflect this distinction: 'encumber' derives from French *encombrer* (to block up), while 'lumber' seems to be from the other 'lumber' – to move clumsily, as to 'lumber along' – with a strong association with 'lumber', the now obsolete word for a pawnbroker's shop. 'Cumbersome' probably derives from 'encumber'. (For two confusible colleagues, see **incumbent**). The element '-umb-' or '-ump-' suggests clumsiness or bulkiness in a number of words – besides these particular two there are: 'clump', 'lump', 'bump', 'bumble', 'rumble', 'fumble', 'dump', 'tumble', 'stump', 'plump', 'mumps', 'hump', 'olump', 'stumble', among others. The Clumber spaniel, however, is not a noticeably heavy or awkward dog, although it is the largest of the English sporting spaniels. It was developed at Clumber Park, Nottinghamshire, towards the end of the eighteenth century.

endive see **chive**

enquiry/inquiry (request or demand for information)
Pedants claim there is a distinction. For the record, then: 'enquiry' is simply 'asking', as an 'enquiry' about one's health or where to book a seat on the train. 'Inquiry' is more of an investigation, so that police carry out 'inquiries' into a case. Most dictionaries, however, make no distinction between the two.

ensure see **assure**

enthralled see **thrilled**

en-tout-cas see **passe-partout**

enviable see **envious**

envious/enviable (expressing envy, or worthy of it)
'Envious' expresses envy, as an 'envious' expression, desire or look. 'Enviable' is 'causing envy', as an 'enviable' position, salary or charm.

epic/epos (long 'heroic' poem)
An 'epic', in the strict literary sense, is a long narrative poem, on a grand scale, about the deeds of warriors and heroes. An 'epic' can be primary (oral) or secondary (literary). Examples of a primary 'epic' are Homer's *Iliad* and *Odyssey* and the anonymous *Beowulf*, while secondary 'epics' include such works as Virgil's *Aeneid* and Milton's *Paradise Lost*. (Primary 'epics' may, much later, appear in a written version; basically, however, they are composed orally and recited. Secondary 'epics' appear only in written form.) An 'epos' is an early 'epic' poem of the primary kind, as the Homeric works above mentioned. Both words originate in Greek *epos* (word, song). 'Epic' has since come to be applied on a wider scale to a heroic-type novel or film such as Tolstoy's *War and Peace* (novel and film) and the grandiose cinematic creations of Cecil B. de Mille who as the clerihew records:

Was feeling ill
Because he couldn't put Moses
In the Wars of the Roses.

epigram/epitaph/epigraph (short saying or inscription)
An 'epigram' is a witty or pointed saying or a short satirical poem. An 'epitaph', from the Greek for 'funeral oration', is a commemorative 'epigraph' such as those seen

on tombs. An 'epigraph' itself is either an inscription, as that on a statue or building, or a quotation at the start of a book, head of a chapter, etc. An example of a combined 'epigram' and 'epitaph' is Lord Rochester's lines on Charles II:

Here lies our sovereign lord, the King,
Whose promise none relies on;
He never said a foolish thing,
Nor ever did a wise one.

epigraph see **epigram**

epitaph see **epigram**

epoch see **era**

epos see **epic**

epsilon/upsilon (letter of the Greek alphabet)
'Epsilon', literally 'e simple', is the fifth letter of the Greek alphabet: Ε, ε. 'Upsilon', or 'u simple', is the twentieth letter: Υ, υ. The first corresponds to English short 'e', as in 'epic', the second to 'u' or 'y', as in 'lyric' – as Greek respectively ἐπικός and λυρικός.

equable/equitable (fair, even)
Both words mean 'fair', but in different senses. 'Equable' means 'pleasant', as an 'equable' climate or an 'equable' nature. 'Equitable' means 'just', 'showing fair-mindedness', as an 'equitable' decision or an 'equitable' judge.

equitable see **equable**

era/epoch/aeon (age)
An 'era' is an age when conditions change and a new order begins, as the Christian 'era' or the 'era' of discovery. Geology uses 'era' for a major division of time, as the Mesozoic 'era', which extended for 160 million years. An 'epoch' is properly the start of an 'era', such as an 'epoch' of hostility, although in practice it is frequently used as a simple alternative for 'age'. The original sense still exists in 'epoch-making', however. An 'aeon' or 'eon' is an indefinitely long period of time. In geology it is the largest division of time, comprising two or more 'eras'. ('Epoch' for geologists is one of the main divisions of a geological period, such as the Holocene and **Pleistocene** 'epochs' which make up the Quaternary period.)

erode/corrode (eat away, gnaw away)
'Erode' has the sense 'destroy by slowly eating away', as of rain or a river current on soil or a bank, or figuratively, as of imprisonment 'eroding' a person's will. 'Corrode' implies a more sinister action, and not just eating away at one point but all over. Thus acid 'corrodes' metal and envy can 'corrode', i.e. impair, one's whole outlook on life.

erotic see **exotic**

erratic see **eccentric**

eruption/irruption (violent rushing or spreading)
The two are in fact opposites, with the same 'out' and 'in' prefixes as 'emigrant' and **immigrant**. An 'eruption' is an outbreak of something, as lava from a volcano or a rash on one's skin. An 'irruption', literally a 'break-in', is an inrush or invasion of something, as of water through a broken dam or sales shoppers storming a store. Sometimes 'irruption' is wrongly used to mean 'skin-rash' in place of 'eruption', possibly by false association with 'irritation'.

escape/elope (run away)
To 'escape' is to get away in general from something, usually something dangerous or unpleasant, as prison or an accident. To 'elope' primarily suggests running away with a lover in order to marry without parental consent, but it can also mean 'abscond', i.e. 'escape secretly', so that a shop-assistant might be accused of 'eloping' with the day's takings – making off with them.

esoteric/eclectic (superior, 'choosy')
'Esoteric' literally means 'intended for the few or the initiated' and derives from the Greek *esoterikos* (inner). 'Esoteric' poetry is thus written for the chosen or privileged few who can understand or appreciate it. The opposite, an even more 'esoteric'

word, is 'exoteric' – 'intended or fit for the public at large'. 'Eclectic' basically means 'selective', the implication being that something has been selected from numerous sources, as an 'eclectic' mind or an 'eclectic' taste in music. Loosely – and inaccurately – 'eclectic' is used to mean 'excellent', with little suggestion that a choice has been made.

especially see **specially**

esplanade see **parade**

essay/assay (try, attempt)
'Essay' is a stylish or semi-technical equivalent of 'try', as when one 'essays' one's strength or climbers 'essay' an ascent up the south face of a mountain. 'Assay' is strictly 'put to the test', 'analyse', in particular with regard to the testing or 'assaying' of metals or coins to establish the quantity of gold or the like that they contain. Unfortunately – or fortunately – one can both 'assay' one's strength as well as 'essay' it. It's a matter of choice, really. 'Assay', in fact, is the older word.

euphemism/euphuism (genteel style or turn of phrase)
A 'euphemism', from the Greek verb 'to speak fair', is a 'toned down' statement, the expression of something regarded as immodest, outrageous or indecent in genteel terms, as 'pass over' instead of 'die' or 'powder room' in place of 'women's lavatory'. 'Euphuism' is a literary term for an affected style of speaking or writing – originally that of the sixteenth-century English writer John Lyly. Euphues was the chief character in Lyly's *Euphues, The Anatomy of Wit* (1579) and *Euphues and his England* (1580), the language of which abounds in alliteration, antitheses and a whole range of similar mannered devices. Today 'euphuism' is virtually obsolete as a style, and 'euphemisms' have been so debased that they are more quaint than genteel.

euphuism see **euphemism**

evade see **avoid**

exacerbate see **aggravate**

exalted see **elevated**

example/sample/specimen (single unit or part of something designed to show the nature of the whole)
An 'example' is an illustration of something, often to indicate its standard or quality, as an 'example' of someone's painting or of a person's kindness. A 'sample' is an 'example' used for reference, and is usually an extract from something, as a 'sample' of someone's handwriting, of cloth or of a manufacturer's goods. It does not thus primarily denote quality. A 'specimen' is a 'sample' that is usually a scientific or medical one, as a 'specimen' of rock or of blood.

exasperate see **aggravate**

exceed/excel (surpass)
These are occasionally confused. To 'exceed' is to go beyond, with reference to a particular time, extent or quantity, as when a driver 'exceeds' the speed limit. If someone 'exceeds' in speed, strength, or stamina, for example, he is superior to others – and no doubt it is this sense that leads to confusion with 'excel', which of course means 'outdo', 'be better than'. One can thus 'excel' oneself by doing better than ever before – and by 'exceeding' one's previous limit or record.

excel see **exceed**

except/exempt (release from)
To 'except' something is to leave it out, so that if a person is 'excepted' from an invitation, he doesn't get one. To 'exempt' a person, however, is to free him from the obligation of doing something. Conscientious objectors were thus 'exempted' from military service, with the implication that what they did instead counted as military service. Put another way, to 'except' a person is to count him out; to 'exempt' him is not to count him in.

exceptionable see **exceptional**

55

exceptional/exceptionable (singular)
'Exceptional' means 'forming an exception', with the implication that the described object is unusual or of high standard, such as an 'exceptional' performance of a play of 'exceptional' interest. 'Exceptionable', meaning 'liable to be excepted to' is virtually the opposite, since it is a term of disapproval. Someone's 'exceptionable' behaviour is such that exception is taken to it, it is regarded as objectionable.

excerpt see **extract** (quoted passage)

excite/incite (stimulate)
To 'excite' is to stir into action, as a dog, a nerve or envy. To 'incite' has more the idea of encouraging, provoking or stinging to action – although the action itself may not be realised. A person 'incited' to an act of treason, therefore, may be a traitor or may not: it depends if he actually does the deed.

excoriate see **excruciate**

excruciate/excoriate/execrate (cause suffering to)
'Excruciate' is most common in its adjectival form, 'excruciating'. An 'excruciating' pain is one that causes severe pain or suffering. To 'excoriate' – literally 'strip the skin from' – is to flay verbally, denounce. To 'execrate' is to curse or abhor, to express strong hatred of. The derived adjective 'execrable' meaning 'deserved to be hated' is common.

execrate see **excruciate**

exempt see **except**

exotic/erotic (romantically exciting)
The two words do get confused. 'Exotic' literally means 'foreign' with reference to something imported from abroad but not acclimatised, as an 'exotic' plant or dish. The sense may be extended to apply to something that may still be abroad, such as the 'exotic' birds of the African jungle or 'exotic' spices of the East. The general overtone of the word is 'exciting because rare and mysteriously stirring'. This appeal to the senses no doubt reinforces its false association with 'erotic' which means, specifically, 'sexually exciting', as an 'erotic' poem or painting. Eros, the Greek god of love, lies behind the word. Both 'exotica' and 'erotica' are terms sometimes used for certain genres of pornographic literature. See also the confusibles **eccentric** and **esoteric**.

extempore/impromptu (done unprepared)
If you give an 'extempore' speech, you give it unmemorised – possibly referring to notes, but more likely using no notes at all. An 'impromptu' speech, on the other hand, is one not only necessarily unprepared but given at a moment's notice. A musical piece played 'extempore' is an improvised one; a musical 'impromptu' is one composed in such a way that it suggests improvisation. The words derive respectively from Latin terms: *ex tempore* (out of the time) and *in promptu* (in readiness).

extract/excerpt (quoted passage)
An 'extract' is any passage quoted, as an 'extract' from a new novel or a chairman's report. An 'excerpt' implies that the passage has been specially chosen, such as an 'excerpt' from a recently released record or from some important speech. The Latin verbs from which the words derive mean literally 'draw out' and 'pick out'.

extract/extricate (get out)
Two verbs. To 'extract' (see above entry) is basically 'draw out' as a tooth, or payment from an unwilling debtor. To 'extricate' is to get someone or something out of a difficulty, 'set free', as a splinter out of one's finger or, generously, a friend from debt.

extricate see **extract** (get out)

facility see faculty

faction see fraction

factitious see fictional

faculty/facility (ability, readiness)
'Faculty' is the ability or capability to do something, as a 'faculty' for hard work. 'Facility' is 'provision', in the sense of making something easier, as when one is afforded every 'facility' in some task. It also, however, in its more basic sense, means 'ability to do something easily'. Thus one person may have a 'faculty' for hard work (be able to do it), but another a 'facility' for hard work (be able to do it easily). In this basic sense there is also often a suggestion of readiness.

failing see fault

fallacious see fallible

fallible/fallacious (false, or liable to be false)
As used of people, 'fallible' indicates a liability to be deceived or mistaken, as a 'fallible' judge or authority, who cannot be relied on. Of things the word means 'liable to be false', as a 'fallible' rule (one that has exceptions). 'Fallacious' is used of things only and means 'containing a fallacy', therefore 'deceptive', as a 'fallacious' argument or 'fallacious' evidence.

famished see ravishing

fanatic see frantic

fancy/whimsy/whim (capricious notion)
A 'fancy' is an attractive, often casual, but usually unreal idea, as a childish 'fancy' or a poetic one. (The word is a contraction of 'fantasy'.) A 'whimsy' is also a fanciful idea, but one that is quaint or odd or possibly amusing or playful. 'His latest whimsy is to

paint his car red, white and blue.' A 'whim' may be simply a passing idea or a minor 'whimsy', especially one that is irrational. 'What she has for breakfast depends on the whim of the moment.'

fandango see flamenco

farandole see flamenco

farouche/louche (shy or shifty)
Two French words used mostly as vague vogue words. 'Farouche' seems almost to have opposite meanings: 'hostile' and 'shy'. Perhaps the best definition is a compromise – 'sullen', in which sense it is fairly often used. In origin the word goes back to Latin foras (out of doors, i.e. foreign or alien). 'Louche' literally means 'squinting', but is most often used in the sense 'shady', 'not straightforward'. As with 'farouche' there is a suggestion of foreignness or 'being on the wrong side'. They are not words to use with any degree of certainty, but they can on occasions impress.

fatal/fateful (causing death or destruction)
The two words are not fully interchangeable. 'Fatal' has the main senses of 'causing death', as a 'fatal' accident, or 'causing destruction', as a 'fatal' mistake (which can result in any kind of downfall or disaster). With reference to time, the adjectives each relate to 'fate' in a different sense. The 'fatal' hour is the one chosen by fate (as an active, usually evil, power) for some kind of catastrophe or inescapable doom. A 'fateful' hour is an important or decisive one, since it determines one's fate (i.e. one's future). However, in popular usage, especially in such phrases as 'the fatal day' (or 'the fateful day'), both words mean the same – 'momentous'.

fateful see fatal

fault/failing/foible (moral shortcoming)
'Fault' is the commonest word, and the strongest: 'His main fault is his lack of patience.' 'Failing' indicates a relatively minor shortcoming, possibly even a temporary one: 'Impatience is one of his failings.' 'Foible' is the mildest word, suggesting a weak point that may even be

amusing: 'Giving girls the glad eye is one of his foibles.' (The word is obsolete French for 'feeble'.)

feckless see **reckless**

felonious see **nefarious**

Fenians see **Sinn Féin**

ferment see **foment**

fervently/fervidly (ardently)
Both words have the sense 'ardently', but 'fervidly' emphasises the degree of heat or vehemence. Whereas, too, 'fervently' is often used of a mental state or emotion – one can wish, admire or desire something 'fervently' – 'fervidly' usually qualifies a concrete action, such as speaking, writing or pleading 'fervidly'.

fervidly see **fervently**

festal see **festive**

festive/festal (pertaining to a feast or festivity)
'Festive' applies more to something that is fitting for a feast or festival, such as a 'festive' occasion, mood or season. 'Festal' relates directly to the feast or festival itself, so that a 'festal' crowd is one actually present at a feast or festival – at either of which 'festal' music might be played or 'festal' games organised.

Fianna Fáil see **Sinn Féin**

fibula see **tibia**

fiction/figment (baseless story)
The two words are sometimes confused in the phrase 'figment of the imagination' (not 'fiction'). Basically a 'fiction' is a story invented with the aim of entertaining or deceiving: 'His account of his visit to Paris was pure fiction.' A 'figment' is a story or statement thought up in order to explain something: is the concept of racial equality a mere 'figment' of the mind, or is it a reality?

fictional/fictitious/factitious (unreal)
'Fictional' means 'pertaining to fiction', so

that someone's 'fictional' friends are imaginary ones. 'Fictitious' means 'invented', 'not real', as a 'fictitious' passport with a 'fictitious' name. 'Factitious', a comparatively rare word, means 'artificial', 'not spontaneous', as a person's 'factitious' delicacy of speech – he doesn't normally talk in this way, he is 'putting it on'.

fictitious see **fictional**

figment see **fiction**

Fine Gael see **Sinn Féin**

finicky/pernickety (fussy)
One sometimes hears the false but attractive blend 'fernickety'. Both words are colloquial, with 'finicky' meaning 'over-fussy', as a 'finicky' old woman or a 'finicky' design, and 'pernickety' having more the sense of 'unnecessarily fussy', as a 'pernickety' old man and 'pernickety' rules. A 'finicky' difference, therefore, but a real one. 'Finicky' is ultimately derived from 'fine'; 'pernickety' may possibly be an alteration of 'particular'.

flagrant see **blatant**

flail see **flay**

flair/flare (dazzling display)
It's not simply a confusion of spelling, since both words have an overtone of some kind of brilliance. 'Flair' is discerning talent or aptitude, as a 'flair' for graphic design or improvising a tune on the piano. 'Flare' is literally, of course, a sudden blaze, usually of light or fire. Figuratively it is a burst of temper, zeal, or some other emotion.

flamenco/fandango/farandole (lively dance)
The 'flamenco' is a lively Spanish dance, or the music or singing for it, in the Andalusian gypsy style. It is accompanied by the familiar hand clapping, finger snapping and castanet clacking known technically as *ialeo*. The 'fandango' is a Spanish courting dance in triple time, or the music for it. The movements begin slowly, then gradually increase in ardour and tempo. The

'farandole' is a lively dance of Provençal origin: all the dancers join hands and execute a variety of figures, usually progressing in a chain through the streets to the accompaniment of pipes and tabors. The 'carmagnole', the dance of the French Revolution, was a variety of the 'farandole'. The origin of the name 'flamenco' is explained variously. The *SOED* derives it from the Spanish for 'flamingo', which in turn is from the Portuguese word for 'flaming' – the reference being to the bird's pink or scarlet plumage. Presumably the dance and dancers reflect such a colour, either literally or in fieriness. A more likely derivation, however, would seem to be the Spanish for 'Fleming' or 'Flemish' – not referring to Flanders (whose own name is thought to mean 'Floodland'), but to the Andalusian gypsies known as the 'Flamencos', who are buxom and ruddy. (*They* could link up with the red-feathered bird.) Yet a third explanation sees the origin of the word in the Arabic *felag mangu* (fugitive peasant). There is no doubt that the dance has its roots in both gypsy and Arabic folk song, as well as Andalusian. The 'fandango' may derive from the Portuguese folk song known as *fado* (fate), while the 'farandole' could be a corruption of Provençal *fa* (make) and *roundelo* (round dance). The whole thing is rather a farrago (Latin for 'mixed fodder'). . . .

flammable see **inflammable**

flare see **flair**

flaunt see **flout**

flavour/savour (characteristic taste or smell)
A 'flavour' may appeal to smell as well as taste, and is often of something added to food or drink, as a drink with a lime 'flavour' or a spread having a cheese 'flavour'. 'Savour', a less common word, almost always implies a smell as well as a taste, and usually not a sweet one, as the 'savour' of a stew, soup or sauce.

flay/flail (hit or whip severely)
'Flay' has three senses. The basic one is 'strip the skin from', as when a dead animal is 'flayed'. From this comes the figurative meaning 'reprove with scathing severity', 'criticise viciously', as when one critic 'flays' another. A slang sense is 'fleece', i.e. overcharge, extort money from. 'Flail' is basically 'strike with a flail' (an instrument for threshing grain by hand), but is more commonly used today of 'flailing' arms or fists – ones that strike out wildly but do not hit. The two words are not related.

fleeting see **flying**

flinch/wince (draw back hastily with pain or to avoid pain)
If you 'flinch', you do so either when something painful actually happens (someone treads on your favourite corn) or at the thought of pain (the prospect of the dentist's chair). You 'wince', however, only when actually experiencing the pain, mental horror or whatever. 'I have not winced nor cried aloud', wrote W. E. Henley, and so 'My head is bloody, but unbowed.'

flounder/founder (struggle but sink)
To 'flounder' is to struggle, usually in water, but fail to keep afloat or abreast. Figuratively it is to struggle helplessly or hopelessly in some situation, as when 'floundering on' in a speech or stage performance. To 'founder' basically means 'sink or collapse', especially of ships filling with water and going to the bottom, or buildings falling or being razed to the ground. The word is also used in a specific technical sense of a horse going lame. Figuratively it means 'fail utterly', as of a bankrupt. 'Flounder' seems to derive from a combination of 'flounce' and 'founder' – possibly with an additional association with 'blunder'.

flourish/brandish (wave or display vigorously)
One can 'flourish' anything – a sword, a stick, one's arm – by waving it about or, as a flower in the button-hole, by displaying it ostentatiously. 'Brandish', however, is applied exclusively to weapons: to 'brandish' a sword or a knife is to wave it about threateningly.

E

flout/flaunt/vaunt (treat brazenly)
In a sense, 'flout' and 'flaunt' are opposites. To 'flout' means 'mock', as authority, the rules, etc., by treating them with contempt, so drawing the attention of others to them. To 'flaunt' means 'parade ostentatiously', as one's views or wealth, with the aim of drawing the attention of others to oneself. To 'vaunt' something is to boast about it, make it known by displaying it. This need not have, as 'flaunt' does, a disparaging sense. The word is, though, related to 'vain'.

fluorescent/phosphorescent (luminescent)
In scientific terms, a 'fluorescent' lamp is one in which light is produced by fluorescence, especially that initiated by the radiation of mercury vapour which causes a coating of phosphor on the inside of the tube. 'Phosphorescent' applies to a substance that glows as the result of slow oxidation of phosphorus, or, in particular, to some marine plants and animals that generate light by the oxidation of luciferin (a pigment) in the presence of luciferase (an enzyme).

flush see **blush**

flying/fleeting (rapid)
'Flying' means 'hasty', as a 'flying' visit or a 'flying' trip somewhere; 'fleeting' means 'brief', as a 'fleeting' glimpse or a 'fleeting' farewell.

foible see **fault**

foment/ferment (heat up)
'Foment' has two basic senses: 'promote', 'stoke up', as a rebellion or hatred, and 'apply warm water to', as a boil or abscess, to lessen the pain. To 'ferment' has, apart from the sense 'undergo chemical change and give off a gas', the meaning 'cause trouble'. In this latter sense it is virtually synonymous with 'foment', although often applied specifically to political unrest.

forage/foray (search)
To 'forage' is to search for food, supplies and the like, or to make a raid in search of some kind of plunder. To 'foray' is to plunder only, or 'pillage'. The words are related, and derive from French *forayer* (marauder).

foray see **forage**

forceful/forcible (showing force)
'Forceful' is literally, of course, 'full of force', and is used of someone or something acting or behaving with power or vigour, as a 'forceful' speaker making a 'forceful' speech with 'forceful' gestures. 'Forcible' means 'effected by force', as a 'forcible' explosion. It can, however, also mean 'producing a powerful effect', as a 'forcible' argument. There is a difference, therefore, between a 'forceful' performance, which is one made powerfully (with vigour) and a 'forcible' performance, which produces a powerful effect (but itself could be refined or restrained).

forcible see **forceful**

fortuitous see **fortunate**

fortunate/fortuitous (chance)
'Fortunate' means 'lucky', 'bringing good fortune', as a 'fortunate' meeting or discovery. 'Fortuitous' simply means 'produced by chance', so that a 'fortuitous' discovery is not necessarily a good one – or a bad one.

founder see **flounder**

fraction/faction (militant political or other body)
The basic difference is that a 'fraction' is a deviant or schismatic political group, while a 'faction' is normally a self-interested grouping within the main body. The term 'fraction' – literally a 'break-off' or 'splinter' group – came to be associated in the 1920s with the British Communist Party, and was officially defined as 'a Party (i.e. Communist) organisation inside a representative or delegate body' and also as 'a grouping of all the Communists and their followers inside a trade union or similar organisation'. In this sense it is clearly an approved group, not a schismatic one. 'Faction', however, has almost always been regarded as a grouping aiming to

achieve its goal by unscrupulous methods, usually resulting in party strife. It literally means 'action' group.

fragile/frail (delicate)
'Fragile' implies a liability to break, as literally china or glass or, figuratively, a truce. 'Frail,' which is rarely used literally, means 'weak', especially of health or morals.

frail see **fragile**

frantic/frenetic/fanatic/phrenetic (wild, unreasoning)
'Frantic' implies a desperation as well as a wild striving of some kind, as felt in 'frantic' pain or heard in a 'frantic' scream. 'Frenetic' and 'phrenetic' are near-synonyms meaning 'frenzied', although 'phrenetic' suggests 'half-crazed', particularly of religious beliefs or manias. The implication behind 'fanatic' – which produced the 'fan' – is that the enthusiasm or zeal is of unreasonable proportions. The word itself derives from Latin *fanaticus* (pertaining to a temple), while the other three words go back ultimately to Greek *phren* (midriff – the supposed seat of passions).

frenetic see **frantic**

frown/scowl (as verb: contract the brow)
To 'frown' is to contract the eyebrows to indicate displeasure or deep thought or puzzlement; to 'scowl' is to do likewise – but always angrily or sullenly.

frowsty see **fuggy**

frowzy see **fuggy**

fruit/fruition (awaited or desired product)
Apart from its literal sense, 'fruit' can mean 'the product of an action', as the 'fruits' of one's labours or the 'fruits' of learning. 'Fruition' is the realisation of what is wished for, so that if your hopes are brought to 'fruition' you have an entirely satisfactory outcome. Like 'fruit', 'fruition' can be used both literally and figuratively – meaning 'the bearing of fruit' – although rather surprisingly the two words are not related. 'Fruition' has come to be firmly

but wrongly associated with 'fruit'. It in fact derives from Late Latin *fruitio* (enjoyment).

fruition see **fruit**

fuddled see **muddled**

fuggy/fusty/frowsty/frowzy (stuffy, ill-smelling)
'Fuggy' is used of air filled with something fairly dense, as tobacco smoke. 'Fusty' suggests a mouldy, musty smell, or at any rate a stale one. (Figuratively it can mean 'old-fashioned', much as 'stuffy' can.) 'Frowsty' suggests both ill-smelling and musty and, very often, warm, as of a stuffy, heated living-room. 'Frowzy' hints at dirt, as well as an unsweet smell.

fuse/fuze (device in electrical or detonating mechanism)
Until quite recently, 'fuze' has been regarded in British English as an American spelling of 'fuse'. Early in 1978, however, the British government announced that NATO would henceforth distinguish between the two: 'fuse' is to be the spelling for 'wire or strip of fusible metal inserted in an electric circuit to prevent current overload', and 'fuze' – 'device designed to initiate an explosion'. The distinction seems a useful one.

fusty see **fuggy**

fuze see **fuse**

gabble see **babble**

gad/gallivant (go restlessly in search of pleasure)
To 'gad' – more often 'gad about' – implies

an idle search for pleasure. 'He's always gadding about at the week-end.' To 'gallivant' is to 'gad' with marked merriment or frivolity, even flirtatiously, by gad.

Gaelic see **Celtic**

Gaiety girls/Gibson girls (winsome maidens popular in the Naughty Nineties) The 'Gaiety girls' were chorus girls at the Gaiety Theatre, London, admired especially in the 1890s. They were famed for their prettiness and knack of charming their way to a title by means of their associations with the nobility. 'Gibson girls' existed only in paper form. They were drawings of willowy, wasp-waisted girls by the American cartoonist Charles Dana Gibson, and were also much in vogue at the turn of the century.

gall see **bile**

gallant see **valiant**

gallivant see **gad**

gammon see **ham**

gargantuan see **gigantic**

garish see **gaudy**

gaudy/garish (bright and in bad taste) 'Gaudy' colours are flamboyant ones, regarded as ostentatious and 'flashy'. 'Garish' suggests 'glaring' and a crude vividness. In combination 'garish' colours 'clash', whereas 'gaudy' ones tend to be 'loud'.

gazebo see **pagoda**

genie see **jinn**

genius see **jinn**

gerbil/jerboa (mouselike animal) 'Sir, What *is* a gerbil?' once wrote a puzzled reader to the editor of *The Times* in the course of correspondence on the creature. The animals are related: the 'gerbil' (or 'jerbil'), otherwise 'sand rat', is a rodent belonging to the mouse family found as a native in Asia, Africa and South Russia. It became popular as a pet in the USA and Britain in the mid-1960s. The 'jerboa', found in Asia and North Africa, is distinguished by its very long hind legs which it uses for travelling. Both animals have long, hairy tails; both are up to six inches long.

Gestapo/SS (Nazi military organisation) The two can be distinguished. The 'Gestapo', so abbreviated from *Geheime Staats-Polizei* (secret state police), was set up by Gœring in Prussia in 1933 and extended to the whole of Germany the following year. In 1936 it merged with the 'SS' or *Schutzstaffel* (protection squad), which was Hitler's personal army, otherwise known as the Blackshirts. The 'SS' was originally a section of the *Sturmabteilung* (storm troops), or Brownshirts.

gesticulate see **gesture**

gesture/gesticulate (use part of one's body to express an emotion or idea) You can 'gesture' with your body, head, arms, hands or face to get your meaning over. If you do so excitedly, you 'gesticulate', usually with waving arms. Both words are sometimes mispronounced with a hard 'g' as in 'guest', instead of a soft one, as in 'gentle'.

Gibson girls see **Gaiety girls**

gigantic/gargantuan (enormous) Strictly speaking, 'gigantic' is 'giant-like' and 'gargantuan' 'like Gargantua', the voracious character in Rabelais's *Gargantua and Pantagruel*. 'Gigantic' is used of anything very large or outsize such as a building, a success or an appetite. Gargantua, whose name originated from the Spanish *garganta* (gorge), had a spectacular capacity for eating and drinking. 'Gargantuan' is therefore an ideal word to describe a large appetite, meal or booze-up, but perhaps not so suitable for other huge objects.

girdle see **grill**

glance/glimpse (brief view)
A 'glance' is a quick view or sight of something or someone, so that full recognition is possible but only for a brief moment. A 'glimpse' implies that the object is only barely caught sight of, or partly seen, and that it may not be fully recognisable. One thus may see a 'glimpse' of red or catch a 'glimpse' of the sea (not see it completely).

glimpse see **glance**

glowering/lowering/louring (threatening, angry-looking)
A 'glowering' look is an angry or sullen one. It often hints at a **frown** or scowl. A 'lowering' look – the two words rhyme with 'towering' – is similar but less forceful. A 'lowering' or 'louring' sky is a threatening one, promising bad weather. (The spellings are interchangeable, with 'lowering' unrelated to 'low'.)

gorgon see **dragon**

gourmand/gourmet (one fond of good food)
'Gourmand' smacks of 'glutton' and in fact implies an excessive fondness of good food and drink. A 'gourmet', however, is a connoisseur of food and drink, otherwise, more refinedly, an epicure. 'Gourmand' derives from some French word of uncertain meaning; 'gourmet', although influenced in its meaning by 'gourmand', derives from a French word meaning 'wine taster' and is related to English 'groom', which in turn originally meant 'boy'. For further gastronomes, see **bon vivant**.

gourmet see **gourmand**

grab/grabble/grapple/grope (grasp, or try to grasp)
To 'grab' is to seize eagerly, usually with the hand. To 'grabble' is to feel or search with the hand, as when one 'grabbles' for something in the bottom of a bag or case. To 'grapple' is to seize something in order to fold it or put it in order, as when 'grappling' with the pages of the newspaper. Figuratively it means 'struggle to grasp with the mind', as when one 'grapples' with a problem. To 'grope'

is to feel about with the hand, usually when searching for something. One thus 'gropes' one's way in the dark or, figuratively, 'gropes' for the answer – searches for it uncertainly. All four verbs belong to the semantically linked 'grasping' group, as do 'grip', 'gripe', 'grapes' (which are all hooked together) and 'grasp' itself.

grabble see **grab**

graceful/gracious (having or showing grace)
'Graceful' means 'showing grace' as a 'graceful' gesture or a 'graceful' leap in the air. 'Gracious' means showing 'graciousness', i.e. 'kind', 'benevolent', 'courteous', as a 'gracious' deed. The word can imply a patronising or condescending manner, especially in such phrases as 'honoured by his gracious presence'. A 'gracious' smile, by the same token, can be a kind one or a condescending one. Of royalty, as 'by gracious permission of Her Majesty the Queen', the word is simply a polite epithet.

gracious see **graceful**

grain see **gram**

gram/dram/grain (small unit of weight)
A 'gram' (or 'gramme') is a decimal measure, formerly defined as one cubic centimetre of water at $4°$ C, now one thousandth of the International Prototype Kilogram – a cylinder of platinum-iridium kept in Paris. In avoirdupois, one ounce equals 28·35 'grams'. A 'dram' is, other than a 'wee drappie', one sixteenth of an ounce, and was formerly, with apothecaries, one eighth of an ounce. The 'grain' is the smallest British weight – one seven-thousandth of a pound, regarded as the average weight of a plump grain of corn. British and American 'grain' are identical.

Grammy see **Emmy**

grampus see **walrus**

grapple see **grab**

graticule/reticle (network of fine lines)
Not only are the words similar, but

'graticule' is frequently used to mean 'reticle' in the sense 'network of fine lines in the sight of an optical instrument'. The device is found in telescopes, for example, to enable measurements and accurate observations to be made. 'Graticule', however, has a second sense: 'grid of fine lines on a map indicating latitude and longitude'. Moreover, 'reticule' can be used as an alternative spelling for 'reticle', although more familiarly the '-ule' version applies, in a historical sense, to the small netted bag or purse formerly carried or worn by women and serving, in effect, as a kind of portable pocket – a forerunner of the modern handbag. 'Graticule' derives from Latin *craticula* (gridiron), while Latin *reticulum* means 'little net'.

griddle see **grill**

gridiron see **grill**

griffin see **gryphon**

griffon see **gryphon**

grill/griddle/gridiron/girdle (utensil for grilling)
A 'grill' is now normally a device on a cooker for grilling or broiling by directing heat downwards onto the food. In its original sense it is the same as a 'gridiron' – a set of parallel metal bars over a flame used for grilling meat and the like. (The 'iron' is by false association with the bars: the word is really a variant of 'griddle'.) A 'griddle' is usually a flat heated surface on the top of a stove for cooking oatcakes, biscuits and the like, and especially, of course, griddle-cakes. 'Girdle' is a variant of this in turn – hence the alternative 'girdlecakes'. No doubt 'girdle' proved easier to say and had an obvious association with a circular object: the iron plate itself is normally round.

grisly see **gruesome**

grope see **grab**

gross/crass (coarse, thick)
'Gross' has four basic meanings: 'unpleasantly fat' (she looks quite 'gross'), 'coarse' ('gross' behaviour), 'flagrant' (a 'gross' mistake), and 'total' (the 'gross' amount). 'Crass' overlaps fully with the second of these senses ('coarse') and partly with the first, where it means 'unusually great'. In this last sense its favourite companion word is 'stupidity', possibly since the very sound of 'crass' is expressive of foolishness and one's contempt for it. It conjures up, for a start, 'cretin' and 'ass'.

grudge see **begrudge**

gruesome/grisly (horrible, revolting)
'Gruesome', deriving from the French *grue* (shudder), is used of anything that makes one recoil or react in horror or revulsion, as a 'gruesome' sight or sound. 'Grisly' coincides in meaning with this, but has the additional sense of 'grim', 'formidable', as seen in someone's 'grisly' expression. Both words are commonly used in a semi-humorous sense. 'Rather grisly, you know – we had to stand in the corridor all the way.'

gryphon/griffon/griffin/wyvern (mythological winged creature)
'Gryphon' and 'griffon' are alternative spellings for the mythical monster that has the head and wings of an eagle and the body of a lion. (The spelling 'gryphon' 'is supposed to be dignified', notes the *SOED*.) It is also a heraldic figure resembling this creature. As a real creature, a 'griffon' is also a breed of toy dog, in particular the Brussels 'griffon', and a species of vulture found in southern Europe. A 'wyvern' (or 'wivern') is purely a heraldic beast: a two-legged dragon whose rear quarters are those of a serpent with a barbed tail. The word is related to to 'viper' but the original sense is obscure. 'Gryphon' derives from Greek *grypos* (curved, hook-beaked).

H

hack/hackney (type of horse)

A 'hack' is not a breed of horse but a definite type – a refined riding-horse. The term can also mean, however, an old, worn-out horse (hence the literary 'hack' and the tired 'hack' phrase). The word is an abbreviation of 'hackney', which is a harness horse with characteristic high-stepping, long-striding or smart-trotting gait. Its ancestor is the Norfolk trotter. The sense 'worn-out' is shared with 'hack' in such metaphorical uses as a 'hackneyed' phrase, which is a common or trite one. A 'hackney' carriage was the term used for a vehicle plying for hire in the nineteenth century, the predecessor of the modern taxi, which is still technically known thus. The origin of the word is uncertain, although it could derive from Hackney, now a London borough: horses were raised on pasture there and taken through the town to Smithfield Market via (appropriately enough) Mare Street.

hackney see **hack**

haft see **shaft**

hallelujah/hosannah (exclamation of praise to God)

'Hallelujah' – in hymns usually 'alleluia' – goes back ultimately to the Hebrew *hallelu* (praise ye) and *Jah* (Jehovah). Its most famous biblical location is in the opening verses of Revelation, from where come the words of the Hallelujah Chorus that triumphantly closes Part II of Handel's *Messiah*. 'Hosannah' from Hebrew *hoshi'ah nna* (save, I pray) occurs in both the Old and New Testaments as well as a number of hymns and was originally an appeal to God for deliverance by the Jews.

Hallowe'en see **All Saints' Day**

ham/gammon (type or cut of pork)

'Ham' is thigh of pig prepared for food, either fresh, or cured (salted and smoked). It is also the name of the upper part of the leg from which the meat comes. 'Gammon' is always cured and prepared like bacon, although served in thicker cuts than the normally thin rashers of bacon.

Hamitic see **Semitic**

handiwork/handwork (work done by hand)

To start with the basics: 'handwork' is work done by hand as distinct from that done by machine, e.g. lace-making. 'Handiwork' is work done or something made by the hands or by the personal agency of someone. In its general sense it is often contrasted with nature or God, that is, 'manmade' as distinct from 'natural' or 'divinely made'. The word is also used in some junior schools as an alternative to 'handicraft'. However, 'handiwork' is often used in place of 'handwork' in any of these senses, possibly because of the influence of 'handicraft'.

handwork see **handiwork**

harakiri/kamikaze (Japanese form of suicide)

'Harakiri' – sometimes, wrongly, 'harikari' – is a form of suicide carried out by ripping open the abdomen with a dagger or knife. It was notably practised by the higher classes, the *samurai*, when in disgrace or sentenced to death. The Japanese term is self-descriptive (belly cut). 'Kamikaze' became notorious in the Second World War as a form of suicidal crash dive performed by a Japanese aircraft, fully loaded with explosives, onto an enemy target, usually a ship. The word literally means 'god wind', and refers to the supposed divine wind that blew on a night in August 1281 destroying the navy of the invading Mongols.

harbinger see **herald**

harum-scarum see **helter-skelter**

hassle see **bustle**

haversack see **rucksack**

hecatomb see **catacomb**

heel over/keel over (overturn, collapse)
To 'heel over' is to cant or tilt or lean to
one side, of a ship. To 'keel over', of a ship,
is to turn right over so that the keel is
uppermost. Both expressions, especially
the second, are applied to any object that
leans or overturns; of a person, 'keel
over' means 'collapse'. 'Heel over' is not
connected with 'heel' but is probably
derived from an Old English word *heeld*
meaning 'incline'.

**helter-skelter/harum-scarum/
higgledy-piggledy** (in disorder or confusion)
English loves rhyming jingles like these.
(Oddly, many of them begin with 'h', as
'hocus-pocus', 'hoity-toity', 'hurly-burly',
'Humpty-Dumpty'.) 'Helter-skelter' implies disorderly haste, as of an enemy
fleeing or crowds hurrying out of a
stadium after a soccer match. By comparison the spiral slide known as a 'helter-
skelter' is a relatively organised device.
'Harum-scarum' suggests recklessness or
wildness, as of a passionate or capricious
person or his behaviour. 'Higgledy-
piggledy' is descriptive of a number of
objects in jumbled confusion, as of objects
in a 'glory-hole'. Etymological connections
with hares and pigs are only tentative.

herald/harbinger (messenger, forerunner)
A 'harbinger' is not just a poetic word for
'herald'. The word literally meant 'one who
provides lodgings for an army' and now has
the general sense of 'sign of something to
come', as the cuckoo is the 'harbinger' of
summer. A 'herald', by comparison, is
simply 'one who announces', a messenger –
hence the word's popularity as a newspaper
title. The 'g' in 'harbinger' is soft, as in
'messenger'.

heritage see **inheritance**

higgledy-piggledy see **helter-skelter**

Hindi see **Hindu**

Hindu/Hindustani/Hindi/Urdu (native,
religion or language of India)
A 'Hindu' is a native of India who adheres
to the country's dominant religion,
Hinduism. 'Hindustani' is the standard
language of northern India based on a
dialect of western 'Hindi' spoken around
Delhi. 'Hindi' is the name given either to
one of the modern Indic languages of
northern India, usually divided into eastern
and western 'Hindi', or to the literary
language derived from 'Hindustani' used
by 'Hindus'. 'Urdu' is a dialect of 'Hindustani' used by Muslims: it uses Arabic
characters and much of its vocabulary is of
Persian and Arabic origin. It also is the
official language of Pakistan (together with
English). See also **hoard**.

Hindustani see **Hindu**

historic/historical (relating to history)
'Historic' means 'important in history' as a
'historic' battle or a 'historic' speech.
'Historical' means 'concerned with history', such as a 'historical' novel or a
'historical' costume. A 'historical' map will
show 'historic' sites.

historical see **historic**

histrionics see **hysterics**

hoard/horde (collection, multitude of
things or people)
Which does a miser have, a 'hoard' of coins
or 'hordes' of coins? Possibly both,
although 'hoard' is the word meaning
'accumulation', especially of something
saved up for the future and hidden away.
A 'horde' is a large number of something,
nearly always people or animals. The
Golden 'Horde' was a troop of Mongol
Tartars that overran eastern Europe in the
thirteenth and fourteenth centuries.
('Golden' because of the magnificent
apparel of their leader Batu Khan, the
grandson of Genghis Khan.) The word is
related to 'Urdu': both of them mean
literally 'camp'.

honorary see **honourable**

honourable/honorary (worthy of, or given for, honour)
An 'honourable' award is one worthy of honour; an 'honorary' award is one given to serve as a token of honour, especially when not actually earned or won directly. Both words are used (with a capital 'H') as titles, the official abbreviation of which is, confusingly, 'Hon.'. 'Honourable' has a number of applications as a courtesy title. Among them, it is used as a prefix:
1 to the Christian names of the younger sons of earls and all children of viscounts and barons;
2 to the names of all justices of the High Court who are not Lord Justices or Lords of Appeal;
3 to the word 'member' or 'gentleman' in the House of Commons, when one MP is addressing or referring to another ('The Honourable Member for Ealing').
As a title, 'Honorary' means 'holding a position without being paid for it', as an 'Honorary' president, treasurer or secretary.

hoodoo/voodoo (spirit bringing bad luck)
A 'hoodoo' is a person or thing that brings bad luck or bad luck itself, a 'jinx'. 'Voodoo' is the genuine article: the 'black magic' rites of Negroes of the West Indies and the American South, involving sorcery and witchcraft and probably of African origin. Hence, too, it is the term used for one who practises these rites or for an object of 'voodoo' worship. The words are possibly related.

horde see **hoard**

hosannah see **hallelujah**

hovercraft/hydrofoil (vehicle able to travel over the water at speed)
Both vehicles appeared more or less simultaneously, at the end of the 1950s. The 'hovercraft' is the one that has the 'cushion of air' enabling it to travel over any relatively smooth surface. The name was invented by the designer of the craft, Sir Christopher Cockerell, as a 'not altogether appropriate word'. A 'hydrofoil' is a vessel fitted with hydrofoils: surfaces designed to lift the hull out of the water at speed (after 'aerofoil'). Unlike the 'hovercraft', it can travel over water only.

hulk see **hull**

hull/hulk (body of a ship)
The 'hull' of a ship is its frame or body, i.e. not including any sails, masts or superstructure. A 'hulk' is the body of an old or dismantled ship or wreck. A 'hulk' is also a term sometimes applied to a big person. (It suggests 'bulk', but that is simply a coincidence.)

hustle see **bustle**

hydrofoil see **hovercraft**

hydrometer/hygrometer (instrument for measuring liquid)
A 'hydrometer' is an instrument in the form of a cylindrical glass tube containing a weighted glass bulb. This is immersed in a liquid to measure its density or specific gravity (found by reading a calibration on the neck of the bulb). A 'hygrometer' is a device for measuring the relative humidity of the atmosphere. A number of types exist as e.g. evaporative, mechanical, electrical and dew-point. The French prefer the term *aréomètre* to *hydromètre* since the latter means 'water-spider'.

hygrometer see **hydrometer**

hypermarket see **supermarket**

hyperthermia see **hypothermia**

hypochondriac/dipsomaniac (one suffering from a morbid complaint)
A 'hypochondriac' is a person suffering from acute depression or, more generally, imagined ill-health. The term derives from the Greek, literally 'under the gristle'; the reference is to that part of the abdomen that lies under the cartilage of the breastbone. This region was supposed to be the seat of melancholy or 'black bile'. (For related concepts, see **bile, frantic**.) A 'dipsomaniac' is someone who suffers from a craving for alcohol, literally a 'thirst maniac'.

hypothermia/hyperthermia (condition of having the body temperature unusually cold – or hot)
The prefixes are the cause of the trouble, 'hypo' being 'under' and 'hyper' being 'over'. 'Hypothermia' is the distressing and often fatal condition prevalent among elderly people in cold weather, when the body temperature drops significantly below normal. 'Hyperthermia' is the opposite. The latter condition can be brought on by natural causes, such as intense heat, or induced, for example for therapeutic purposes.

hysterics/histrionics (violent emotional display)
'Hysterics', popularly, is a display resembling hysteria, with the familiar crying and/or laughing, gesticulating, babbling and the like. 'Histrionics' is a similar display, but a theatrical one, with vehement speech and exaggerated gestures – 'theatricals', in fact. The word derives from the Latin *histrio* (actor), while 'hysterics' has its origin in the Greek *hystera* (womb). It was originally thought that women were more likely to suffer from the disorder than men; science, subsequently, has proved otherwise.

ideal/idyllic (perfect, the best imaginable)
'Ideal' is very much a general word to describe something that is the best one can think of, as an 'ideal' picnic spot or 'ideal' timing. 'Idyllic' has a similar meaning, but in an aesthetic sense and often with a poetic flavour, as an 'idyllic' spot (one that is rustic, romantic, picturesque or the like). The essence of the word is in the origin of 'idyll' – Greek *eidyllion* (little picture).

idle/indolent (inactive, lazy)
The difference lies in the emotiveness:

'indolent' is a derogatory word, 'idle' is not. 'Idle' means 'not working', whether legitimately or not; 'indolent' means 'not working because lazy'.

idyllic see **ideal**

i.e. see **e.g.**

illegal/illicit/illegitimate (unlawful, improper)
There are three well-defined shades of meaning here. 'Illegal' means 'not legal', i.e. refers to something that is against the law and known to be forbidden, as 'illegal' entry into a country. 'Illicit' applies to something that is known to be 'illegal' but which is nevertheless deliberately done, usually regularly and secretly, as the 'illicit' import of drugs. (The implication is that, given other circumstances, the act could be legal.) 'Illegitimate' implies that what is done has not been authorised by law, has not been made lawful, as the familiar 'illegitimate' child born outside a lawful marriage.

illegitimate see **illegal**

illicit see **illegal**

illusion see **delusion**

imbrue see **imbue**

imbue/imbrue (soak, impregnate)
The root of both words is Latin *bibere* (to drink). 'Imbue' is basically 'fill', especially with reference to feelings: 'My visit to Rome imbued me with a real sense of history.' Similarly a teacher can 'imbue' his pupils with, for example, a regard for safety or a concern for the needs of others. 'Imbrue' is a more forceful word, and a rarer one. Literally, it is usually associated with blood: 'hands imbrued with blood' is a near hack phrase with some thriller writers. 'Imbue' used literally is normally applied to colours and scents, as a handkerchief 'imbued' with perfume.

immeasurable see **immense**

immense/immeasurable (vast, boundless)
'Immense' is simply 'very great', as an 'immense' size or quantity. 'Immeasurable', logically enough, has the implication that the object described is too great to be measured and often is therefore, by extension, priceless, as a jewel of 'immeasurable' value.

immersed see **submerged**

immigrant/emigrant/émigré/migrant (person leaving one country or place to go to another)
The prefixes hold the key: an 'immigrant' is someone who has come *in* to a country; an 'emigrant' is a person who has gone out of (Latin *ex-*) a country. An 'émigré' is a special kind of 'emigrant'. The original 'émigrés' fled from France at the time of the French Revolution. The word is now most frequently applied to political and religious refugees, in particular Russians and Jews. A 'migrant' is used of anyone or anything that moves regularly from one place to another, as 'migrant' workers, 'migrant' birds and fishes and even 'migrant' plants whose seeds are carried abroad. One person can, of course, be both an 'immigrant' and an 'emigrant', but not at the same time.

immoral/amoral (not moral)
'Immoral' is the opposite of 'moral', i.e. means 'having bad or low morals', 'not conforming to a moral standard'. 'Amoral' means 'having no morals', that is, no moral standards by which one can be judged. 'Immoral' is thus a positive epithet; 'amoral' is negative. Put more basically, 'immoral' connotes 'bad'; 'amoral' is neither good nor bad.

immunity/impunity (freedom from liability or penalty)
To have 'immunity' from something – usually unpleasant or disagreeable – is to be free from it, as 'immunity' from disease, attack or interference. 'Impunity' implies freedom from punishment or undesirable consequences. It is most commonly used in the phrase 'with impunity': 'Go on, criticise him, you can do it with impunity!'

imperial/imperious (domineering)
The basic meaning of 'imperial' is 'pertaining to an empire or emperor', as the 'imperial' palace or an 'imperial' decree. It also means 'commanding', in the sense 'emperor-like'. 'Imperious' implies a dictatorial attitude, but basically means 'domineering', as an 'imperious' voice or an 'imperious' gesture.

imperious see **imperial**

impersonate/personate (represent in personal form)
To 'impersonate' someone is to pretend to be him in some way. We are all familiar with the 'impersonations' of stage and television comics. More widely, every actor is 'impersonating' once he sets foot on the stage. It also means 'represent in bodily form', 'personify': the aim of many revolutionaries is to 'impersonate' the will of the common people. 'Personate' has the same meaning as 'impersonate' when it comes to acting: go to a local theatre group's production and you could see your bank manager 'personating' an American ranch hand. This sense is extended to mean 'pass oneself off as', often for fraudulent purposes, as when a pickpocket 'personates' a reporter at some public gathering. In the arts, especially painting, 'personate' means 'stand for' in the sense of representing an abstract quality or personal property. The snake usually 'personates' evil.

impertinent see **insolent**

impetuous see **compulsive**

impinge *see* **infringe**

implement see **instrument**

imply/infer (deduce – or mean)
Two fairly hoary confusibles: the diarist of *The Times* once (15 March 1977) used 'inferred' for 'implied' and caused an excited flutter among his readers. (He subsequently, but not too convincingly, referred readers to the *OED* in his defence.) In fact the two are indeed often used interchangeably, but strictly speaking: 'imply' means 'express indirectly' –

almost 'mean' – and 'infer' means 'derive by reasoning', 'deduce'. For some reason 'infer' is frequently used where many would prefer 'imply', but 'imply' hardly ever used instead of 'infer'. So if I 'imply' that you are deceitful, I say so indirectly; if I 'infer' that you are deceitful, I gather that you are from what you say or do, or from what I hear about you.

impracticable see **impractical**

impractical/impracticable/unpractical/unpracticable (not practical or practicable)
'Impractical' means 'not able to be put into practice although theoretically possible', as an 'impractical' plan (not a good one). Of a person, 'impractical' means 'no good at doing practical things'. 'Impracticable' means 'not manageable', 'not workable', as an 'impracticable' road (it cannot be used) or plan (it will not work). An 'impracticable' person is one hard to deal with, as someone who is stubborn or stupid. 'Unpractical' is not a common word, but it means 'not practical', as an 'unpractical' person (who cannot do practical things). 'Unpracticable' is a rarish alternative for 'impracticable'.

impromptu see **extempore**

impudent see **insolent**

mpugn *see* **infringe**

impulsive see **compulsive**

impunity see **immunity**

inapt see **inept**

incarnadine see **crimson**

inchoate see **incoherent**

incidental/accidental (fortuitous)
'Incidental' means 'happening or likely to happen in conjunction with something else'; 'accidental' means 'happening by chance', i.e. not in connection with something else. A season ticket is not only cheaper than a number of individual ones, it has the 'incidental' advantage of needing to be purchased only periodically instead of every day, and perhaps the 'accidental' advantage of fitting your inside pocket.

incite see **excite**

incoherent/inchoate (imperfectly expressed or formed)
The two are not synonymous, in spite of the definition of 'inchoate' given by the *Sunday Times* (25 September 1977) – one of those 'words which give you those chilly doubts when you use them' – as 'just begun, incomplete, imperfectly formulated, incoherent'. 'Incoherent' usually relates to thoughts or words with the sense 'not fitting together', 'rambling', as in an 'incoherent' speech or argument. 'Inchoate', something of a vogue word of the 1970s, means 'just begun', 'unformed', as an 'inchoate' mass of gas or the 'inchoate' church of the early Christians. Confusion with 'incoherent' may be due to false association with its near anagram, 'chaotic.'

inconsequent/inconsequential (irrelevant)
An 'inconsequent' remark is one that is not relevant to what has been said before; an 'inconsequential' remark is one that is trivial and that is of no consequence.

inconsequential see **inconsequent**

incumbent/encumbent (holder of a particular post)
Kenneth Hudson, in his *Dictionary of Diseased English* (Macmillan, 1977), points out that 'encumbent' is a 'strange and quite unjustified spelling of "incumbent", now common in the business world, especially in Australia' and suggests, very fairly, that the word has a false association with **encumber**. The term applies chiefly to the holder of a post in industry or commerce, and is possibly too recent – or Australian – to have been recorded in most British and American dictionaries. Even the *OED Supplement* (1972) has not managed to capture it. 'Incumbent', however, is a well documented word. It has the same meaning (in the business sense) as

'encumbent' although its precise definition is 'holder of an ecclesiastical office'. As things stand, therefore, the 'in-' spelling is the 'in' one and preferred in British English. Possibly in time the Australian version may be the one to gain the wider acceptance.

indifferent/diffident (showing little or no enthusiasm)
'Indifferent' means 'not caring', 'impartial', even 'apathetic': 'He was quite indifferent to her pleas'. 'Diffident' means 'lacking confidence', even 'shy'; a 'diffident' suggestion is one made reservedly or without much confidence.

indolent see **idle**

inductive see **deductive**

in effect see **in fact**

inept/inapt/unapt (inappropriate, unsuitable)
There is an overlap between 'inept' and 'inapt', but although an 'inept' remark is usually an absurd or silly one, an 'inapt' remark is simply one that is out of place or inappropriate. The words can apply to people: an 'inept' pupil is one slow to learn; an 'inapt' mechanic is one who lacks skill. 'Unapt' is not a common word, but can be used as an effective emphatic equivalent of 'not apt' or 'unsuitable'.

in fact/in effect (in reality)
'In fact' means 'in actual truth' and is used when explaining the real facts behind something that is false or doubtful: 'He thought he was right, but in fact he wasn't.' 'In effect' is used to mean 'in reality' when clarifying something or explaining it more precisely, especially when such clarification is apparently illogical or unexpected: 'We come now to what is, in effect, the highlight of the performance (you are intrigued or surprised that it is); 'You will start work on the twelfth, but your pay will in effect be from the first of the month' (illogically). From this it can be seen that in effect 'in effect' is basically rather different in meaning to 'in fact'.

infectious/contagious (communicable, 'catching')
Speaking strictly medically: an 'infectious' disease is one spread by germs, as colds or 'flu or typhoid; a 'contagious' disease is spread by actual bodily contact, or by contact with something that itself has been in bodily contact with the diseased person. Used figuratively, 'infectious' suggests that the 'source' of infection is agreeably irresistible, as 'infectious' laughter; 'contagious' emphasises the rapidity of spreading, as 'contagious' enthusiasm.

infer see **imply**

inflammable/flammable (catching fire easily)
The words illustrate the importance of prefixes: the 'in-' does not mean, as it often does, 'not', but simply 'in', i.e. 'in flame'. The two words therefore mean exactly the same, with the older word 'flammable' now revived and commonly used to avoid ambiguity in what could be a matter of life and death. In 1959 the British Standards Institution announced: 'It is the Institution's policy to encourage the use of the terms "flammable" and "non-flammable" rather than "inflammable" and "non-inflammable".'

inflation/reflation/deflation/disinflation (rate of increase, or decrease, in the supply of money in a country's economy)
'The words relating to inflation need to be treated with the greatest care' wrote the Editor of *The Times* in a memorandum on the subject circulated on the paper's staff. Basically, 'inflation' is an increase in the supply of money beyond its proper limits with a consequent increase in prices. The reverse of this is 'deflation', i.e. a reduction in the supply of money, with consequent fall in prices. 'Reflation' (meaning 're-inflation') should logically be used to mean another period of 'inflation' after a period of 'deflation', although in fact is commonly defined as 'the supply of money being restored to a higher level after deflation has occurred' ('A memorandum on style', *The Times*, 7 September 1977) – that is, not 'inflation', but a

recovery from 'deflation' and a slump, with or without a later stage of 'inflation'. 'Disinflation' is a post-war word used to indicate a slow increase in the supply of money in order to check 'inflation' without producing the disadvantages of 'deflation'. All four words have been vigorously batted around since the mid-1970s.

inflicted/afflicted (having something unpleasant imposed)
To be 'inflicted' with something or someone, as a heavy load of work or a mother-in-law to stay, implies that what is imposed must be borne as a necessary evil. To be 'afflicted' with a thing, usually a disease, implies positive suffering with associated distress or pain. The two are quite often confused: *Collins English Learner's Dictionary* under 'afflict' ('cause pain, disease etc.') gives the example 'afflict somebody with extra work' instead of 'inflict'.

infringe/impinge/impugn (oppose, counter, encroach)
To 'infringe' something is to violate or act contrary to it, as when one 'infringes' someone's rights or 'infringes' a law. The derivation is not from 'fringe' – as if one was 'edging in' where one had no right to – but from a Latin verb meaning literally 'break in'. To 'impinge' is to make an impact, often so as to spoil or affect adversely. Thus to 'impinge' on a person's spare time is to appropriate it unreasonably, to make unfair demands on it. To 'impugn' a thing is to question the truth of it, so that one can 'impugn' a statement or someone's words, call them in question.

ingenious/ingenuous (artful – or artless)
The confusion, where it exists, is not so much over the meaning of 'ingenious' but over the relationship to it of 'ingenuous'. There is also a similarity of meaning in the qualities the words describe – both 'ingenuity' and 'ingenuousness' (the respective nouns) are personal characteristics to be admired. Moreover, an 'ingenuous' person, by being sincere and frank and open, may unwittingly be quite 'ingenious', or clever at inventing or discovering things. However, enough no

doubt said to establish the difference between the two.

ingenuous see **ingenious**

inheritance/heritage (that which has been inherited)
An 'inheritance' is the property or possessions that pass to an heir, whether actually bequeathed, as a sum of money, or passed down by natural means, as a gift for languages. In a wider, although still personal sense, the word can apply to any quality or attribute passed down by one group of people to another, as the Viking 'inheritance' of English northcountrymen. 'Heritage' is a grander word and applies to some specific quality or possession that is, or can be, inherited – usually something valuable or beneficial, as 'our heritage the sea', but also an undesirable thing, as when poverty is regarded as the 'heritage' of war.

innuendo see **insinuation**

innumerable see **numerous**

inquiry see **enquiry**

insert/inset (as noun: something inserted)
An 'insert' is something placed in a complete entity, as an advertisement in the newspaper, an illustration plate in a book, an enclosure in a letter and the like. An 'inset' usually implies the insertion of something smaller in a larger entity, as a photograph in the corner of a larger one, a short scene in another in a play (for purposes of shifting scenery) and so on. Both words are accented on the first letter.

inset see **insert**

insinuation/innuendo/insinuendo
(indirect suggestion)
An 'insinuation', literally something 'brought in by winding', is an artful suggestion or hint, often an unpleasant one, as an 'insinuation' that one is being dishonest. It also has the sense 'ingratiation', applied to someone who has 'wound his way in' to someone else's company, or into a group activity such as a discussion.

An 'innuendo', derived from a medieval Latin formula – literally 'by nodding', indicating a parenthetical explanation, a 'that is to say' – is a derogatory indirect statement about someone attacking his character or behaviour, as an 'innuendo' that someone is a thief. It is thus more positive and forceful than an 'insinuation' which is merely a hint. An 'insinuendo' – the word is a blend of the other two – is a combined derogatory hint and statement. It is condemned by the *OED Supplement* as 'a tasteless word'; it would, moreover, seem to be a superfluous one.

insinuendo see **insinuation**

insipid see **tepid**

insolent/impudent/impertinent/pert (rude, cheeky)
'Insolent' is the strongest word here, implying an attitude that is insulting or unpleasantly arrogant, as seen in 'insolent' behaviour or heard in an 'insolent' remark. 'Impudent' implies shamelessness, which need not necessarily be insulting, so that an 'impudent' remark is one that is either disrespectful or brazen. 'Impertinent' – literally 'not pertinent', i.e. 'out of place' – is a word that implies intrusion or presumption: an 'impertinent' remark is one that is not called for and one which usually shows lack of respect. 'Pert' almost has the sense of 'engagingly cheeky', with a 'pert' remark suggesting a saucy but at the same time rather clever comment. (The old sense of 'pert' was indeed 'clever'.)

insouciant see **nonchalant**

instinctively/intuitively (naturally, innately)
'Instinctively' means 'by instinct', 'by an innate response', as when one 'instinctively' shades or screws up one's eyes when looking towards the sun. 'Intuitively' means that what is done results from the ability of the doer to understand a situation instantly without any reasoning process: 'She intuitively chose the longer route' (she knew it was the right one without being able to explain why).

institute see **institution**

institution/institute (organisation for promoting or studying something)
The difference is not always clear-cut. On the whole, an 'institution' is an establishment of some sort or its building, usually one of a kind, as a school (an educational 'institution'), hospital (medical 'institution') or charity (philanthropic 'institution'). Its field of activity is thus on the whole a broad one. By contrast an 'institute' concerns itself with a more specific object, frequently one that is studied rather than actively practised, as a cultural or scientific 'institute'. As with 'institution', the word is also used for the building or premises of the body. One thus has, for example, a literary 'institute' but a benevolent 'institution'. The names of a number of specialised bodies contain the word 'institute', as the Scott Polar Research Institute in Cambridge or the British Film Institute in London. In the field of education, the word is used for an establishment that specialises in technical subjects at post-secondary school level, as an 'institute' of technology. Generally, then, an 'institute' is more advanced and specialised in its field of activity than an 'institution'.

instrument/implement (tool, device)
An 'instrument' tends to be more precise or complex than an 'implement', as a musical 'instrument' or an electrical device or mechanism such as a telephone. An 'implement' is basically a tool, utensil or article used for a specific purpose, and usually performs a function that is subordinate or preparatory to the realising of a final product or process. Thus agricultural 'implements' are used for work such as ploughing, sowing and harrowing which is subordinate to the end process of the consumption or marketing of the produce, and kitchen 'implements' are used for the preparing and cooking of food as a process ancillary to the actual eating of the food. 'Implements' are thus a means to an end; most 'instruments' perform a function that is complete in itself.

insure see **assure**

intense/intensive (strong, concentrated)
'Intense' means 'occurring in a high or extreme degree', as 'intense' heat or anxiety. 'Intensive' means 'growing more intense', as an 'intensive' course or 'intensive' treatment, which can be carried to the limit of endurance or safety.

intensive see **intense**

intrusive/obtrusive (thrusting, prominent)
It's the prefixes again: 'intrusive' is 'thrusting in'; 'obtrusive' is 'thrusting forward or onto'. Both suggest an action performed without permission or reason. An 'intrusive' manner thus forces itself into other people's company; an 'obtrusive' manner forces other people to pay attention to it.

intuitively see **instinctively**

invective/inveighing (violent verbal attack)
'Invective' is usually an abusive verbal attack; 'inveighing' implies a vehement verbal attack, a 'railing'. Both words, as well as 'vehement', ultimately derive from Latin *vehere* (to carry, bear). 'Inveighing' is most common in the verbal form 'inveigh': 'He inveighed heavily against the rising cost of petrol.'

inveighing see **invective**

ionosphere see **atmosphere**

irruption see **eruption**

iterate see **repeat**

its see **it's**

it's/its (relating to 'it')
Possibly two of the commonest confusibles in the language: 'it's' does not mean 'belonging to it' (i.e. the apostrophe 's' is not a possessive one) but 'it is' or 'it has', as 'It's a long way and it's started to rain'. 'Its', *without* the apostrophe, does mean 'belonging to it'. 'Look at that fledgling – it's lost its mother!'

Jacobean/Jacobin/Jacobite (pertaining to James)
All three words relate to a James or Jacques, the Latin for which is *Jacobus*. 'Jacobean' relates to James I of England (reigned 1603–25) or his times, in particular with regard to the style of architecture and furnishings. A fine example of a 'Jacobean' mansion is Knole House, Kent. As a noun, a 'Jacobin' was a member of the society of French revolutionaries set up in 1789 who met in the Dominican convent of Saint-Jacques in Paris. The term came to be applied to an extreme political radical. A 'Jacobite' was an adherent of James II of England after his overthrow in 1688, or of his descendants, and in particular his son the Young Pretender – 'Bonnie Prince Charlie'.

Jacobin see **Jacobean**

Jacobite see **Jacobean**

jazzy/snazzy/natty (colourful and smart – of dress)
'Jazzy' implies bright colours, as perhaps sported in a 'jazzy' tie or scarf. 'Snazzy' really means 'flashily stylish', often with a suggestion of bright or gay patterns or colours (much as 'jazzy'). The origin of the word is obscure – possibly a blend of 'snappy' and 'jazzy'? 'Natty', which may derive from 'neat', means 'smart and trim', usually impressively so, as a 'natty' suit or uniform.

jerboa see **gerbil**

jeroboam/rehoboam/jorum (large vessel for holding wine)
First the definitions: a 'jorum' is a rarish word for a large bowl or vessel for holding drink, or the contents of such a bowl. A 'jeroboam' is a large wine bottle holding

2½–3 gallons; a 'rehoboam' is a very large bottle, containing 5 or 6 gallons (i.e. two 'jeroboams'). The origins are quaintly biblical: a 'jorum' is said to be named after Joram, who brought vessels of silver, gold and brass to David (II Samuel 8:10). A 'jeroboam' is named after Jeroboam, 'a mighty man of valour' (I Kings 14:16). The same gentleman, some claim, gave his name to that more lowly vessel, the 'jerry'. The 'rehoboam', modelled on the 'jeroboam', is said to have borrowed the name of Rehoboam, the first King of Judah (II Chronicles 13:7). There are also rich and rare vessels with names on the same lines such as 'methuselah', 'salmanazar', 'balthazar' and 'nebuchadnezzar'.

jersey/jumper (woollen garment worn on upper half of body)
Strictly speaking, the two are not interchangeable. A 'jersey' is close-fitting and heavy, while a 'jumper' is loose-fitting and light-weight. 'Jerseys' are mainly worn by men; 'jumpers' by women and children. The 'jersey' originated in Jersey, Channel Islands, where knitting was once an established industry. The 'jumper' is related neither to 'jump' nor to the child's garment called 'jumpers' (the one-piece suit also known as 'rompers'), but, apparently, derives from an old French word meaning 'short coat' – compare modern French *jupon* (petticoat) and *jupe* (skirt).

jinn/jinnee/genie/genius (spirit)
Alternative spellings increase the confusion here: moreover 'jinn' ('djinn', 'ginn') is really a plural word, the singular of which is 'jinnee' ('djinnee', 'jinni', 'djinni', 'genie'). The first three words thus are one and the same: a spirit, or class of spirits, influencing men for good or evil in Islam and Arabian mythology. The plural of the variant 'genie' is sometimes wrongly given as 'genii', but this is the plural of 'genius', a Latin word used to denote the attendant spirit that keeps watch over a person – or sometimes simply a demon or spirit in general. (The word 'genus', meaning 'class', 'order', as used scientifically, has the plural 'genera'.)

jinnee see **jinn**

jocose see **jocular**

jocular/jocose/jocund/jovial (merry, convivial)
Distinguishing nicely: 'jocular' is 'always making jokes', 'jocose' is 'playful', 'jocund' is 'cheerful' or 'light-hearted', and 'jovial' is 'hearty and good-humoured'. One might thus have a 'jocular' manner, a 'jocose' air, a 'jocund' companion, and a 'jovial' uncle. The first three relate to 'joke'; but 'jovial' to Jove or Jupiter. Those born under the planet Jupiter are said to be merry and sociable.

jocund see **jocular**

jorum see **jeroboam**

jovial see **jocular**

judicial/judicious (pertaining to judgment)
'Judicial' means 'pertaining to a judge or court of law', as 'judicial' proceedings or a 'judicial' survey. In a wider sense, the word means 'fair', 'just': a 'judicial' statement is an impartial one. 'Judicious' means 'having sound judgment', 'prudent', 'discreet', as a 'judicious' pause or remark.

judicious see **judicial**

judo/ju-jitsu (type of Japanese wrestling)
'Judo', literally 'soft art', is in fact a refined form of 'ju-jitsu' introduced in 1882 by Dr Jigoro Kano and using particular principles of movement and balance as a sport or form of physical exercise. 'Ju-jitsu' is the basic form of this. Its name has the same meaning, with 'judo' the Japanese adaptation of Chinese *jou tao*.

ju-jitsu see **judo**

jujube see **cashew**

jumper see **jersey**

junction/juncture (point at which two or more things meet)
'Junction' implies a coming together, as a railway 'junction' where the lines meet or a 'junction' box where electric wires unite.

'Juncture' describes either the point where two things are joined, as the 'juncture' of the head and neck, or a particular point in time, as a critical 'juncture' in a football match. One sometimes hears, wrongly, 'At this particular junction . . .'

juncture see **junction**

kale see **coleslaw**

kamikaze see **harakiri**

keck see **reach**

keel over see **heel over**

kerseymere see **cashmere**

kinkajou see **cockatoo**

kinky/kooky/quirky (eccentric, bizarre)
'Kinky', of people, often implies some kind of sexual perversion or oddity, in particular a homosexual one; of things the word usually applies to dress that suggests this, notably the so styled 'kinky boots' that came into fashion in the second half of the 1960s. In a more general sense the word means simply 'weird', 'bizarre'. 'Kooky' also means 'eccentric', but the overtones here are of craziness or crankiness. The word is often used with application to females – thus a 'kooky' career girl could lead a 'kooky' life. An Australian magazine, the *Melbourne National Revue*, billed the British comedy *No Sex Please, We're British!* as the 'funniest, kookiest night of your life' (31 August 1973). 'Quirky' means 'eccentric' with a suggestion of trickery or duplicity, as found in a 'quirky' book (it tries to dupe its readers) or a 'quirky'

speech (a 'devious' one). 'Kinky' derives from 'kink', i.e. 'twist'; 'kooky' is probably a perversion of 'cuckoo'.

knapsack see **rucksack**

kohlrabi see **coleslaw**

kooky see **kinky**

koruna see **krone**

kraal/laager (type of South African settlement)
A 'kraal' is a native village usually with a stockade and a central area for cattle or other animals. The word can apply to a cattle enclosure in general – in Sri Lanka, to an elephant enclosure. The Afrikaans word ultimately derives from Portuguese *curral* (enclosure), related to 'corral'. A 'laager', from German *Lager* (camp), is essentially an encampment set up inside a circle of wagons. It is commonly used figuratively to apply to a defensive position, especially one that expresses an entrenched policy or viewpoint: White South African advocates of racial segregation are sometimes accused of withdrawing or being driven 'back into their laager'.

kris see **kukri**

krona see **krone**

krone/krona/koruna ('crown' as unit of currency)
The 'krone' (plural *kroner*) is the monetary unit of Denmark and Norway, divided into 100 øre. The 'krona' (plural *kronor*) is the unit of Sweden, and the 'króna' (*krónur*) that of Iceland. These are respectively divided into 100 øre and *aurar*. The 'koruna' (plural *koruny*) is the unit of currency of Czechoslovakia equal to 100 *haleru* or heller. The 'Krone' (plural *Kronen*) was also formerly a German gold coin worth ten Marks or an Austrian silver coin equalling 100 heller.

kukri/kris (sword with a wavy blade)
A 'kukri' is a Gurkha knife with a short, wavy blade broadening towards the point. A 'kris', earlier sometimes spelt 'creese', is

a Malay or Indonesian dagger with a wavy blade that often has two scalloped cutting edges. The 'kukri', however, has a curved blade; the 'kris' a straight one.

kulak see **muzhik**

laager see **kraal**

la-di-da/lardy-dardy (pretentious)
There is a difference: 'la-di-da' relates to speech, to 'talking posh' (the phrase is imitative of the long 'a' sound used by southern or supposedly affected speakers, as in 'grass', or a drawled 'hear!, hear!'), while 'lardy-dardy' denotes pretentiousness of manner, a languid dandyism. It is quite on the cards, however, that someone who has a 'lardy-dardy' manner will also talk with a 'la-di-da' accent. Such speech and manner have long been regarded as typical of the English upper classes, and are the stock devices resorted to by actors to portray a member, or alleged member, of this stratum of society.

lag/laggard/sluggard (idle or slow person)
A 'lag' – often an 'old lag' – is normally a convict, one who has been 'lagged' or sentenced to penal servitude. (The word is not related to 'lag' in the sense 'dawdle'.) A 'laggard' is someone who lags behind or lingers, and a 'sluggard' is a person who is generally slow or slothful – not necessarily with the implication that he is slower than someone else.

laggard see **lag**

laissez-aller see **laissez-faire**

laissez-faire/laissez-passer/laissez-aller (entitlement to free action)
All three terms are French, of course, meaning respectively 'let do', 'let pass', 'let go'. (The '-ez' in each is sometimes written '-er'.) 'Laissez-faire' encapsulates the theory of government stating that the state should intervene as little as possible in economic affairs, i.e. should pursue a policy of 'non-interference' in trade and industry. A 'laissez-passer' is a permit or pass, usually a diplomatic one, to enter a particular area. 'Laissez-aller' is a general term indicating absence of restraint or unlimited freedom. The phrase 'Laissez-faire, laissez-aller', implying no interference and freedom of movement, is attributed to the eighteenth century French economist and royal physician François Quesnay.

laissez-passer see **laissez-faire**

Landsturm see **Landwehr**

Landwehr/Landsturm (German military reserve)
The 'Landwehr', literally 'land defence', is West Germany's first military reserve force, consisting of men under thirty-nine years of age with seven years of active service. The 'Landsturm' or 'land storm' is a subsidiary reserve comprising all untrained young men, and all ex-servicemen aged between thirty-nine and forty-five, i.e. those who are not in the 'Landwehr' or regular forces. There were no 'Landwehr' units in the Second World War since all servicemen were regulars; the 'Landsturm', however, was a reserve category of all men aged forty-five to fifty-five who were assigned to local defence battalions and later used in occupation duties and even ultimately in front line duties.

languid see **limpid**

lardy-dardy see **la-di-da**

largo/lento (slow musical tempo)
'Largo', literally 'broad', implies a slow dignified tempo, as in the well-known *Largo* by Handel. 'Lento' means just 'slow', as found, for example, in the second movement of some classical symphonies and sonatas.

lariat see **lasso**

larynx/pharynx (part of the throat)
The 'larynx' is the part of the throat at the upper end of the windpipe. It contains the vocal cords, so that laryngitis, or inflammation of the 'larynx', usually involves loss of voice. The 'pharynx' is the cavity connecting the mouth, nose and 'larynx' with the gullet. The 'pharynx' is thus situated above the 'larynx'.

lascivious see **licentious**

laser/maser (instrument for producing a beam of light of high intensity)
The 'maser' came first, around 1955. Originally the 'maser' emitted microwaves, hence its acronym which stands for '*m*icro*w*ave *a*mplification by the *s*timulated *e*mission of *r*adiation'. Later, 'masers' emitted waves in other parts of the spectrum, so that in 1960 the term was modified to 'laser', with the first letter of the acronym standing for '*l*ight'.

lasso/lariat (long rope with running noose for catching animals)
Both implements are used for catching horses and cattle, but the 'lariat' is also used for picketing animals while grazing. 'Lassos' tend to be found mostly in Spanish America, with 'lariats' also in use in Mexico. Both words are Spanish in origin: 'lasso' from *lazo*, 'lariat' from *la reata* (the picketing rope), in turn from the verb *reatar* (to tie again).

Latvian/Lithuanian (native or language of one of Baltic republics)
Latvia is a north-western Baltic republic, officially the Latvian Soviet Socialist Republic, whose population speaks 'Latvian' or Lettish – a language that is similar to 'Lithuanian' but more 'innovating'. Lithuania is slightly larger than Latvia and lies to the south of it. It, too, is a republic of the USSR. The Latvian capital is Riga, the Lithuanian Vilnius.

laudable/laudatory (deserving or expressing praise)
'Laudable' means 'praiseworthy', so that one can have a 'laudable' deed or effort.

'Laudatory' means 'expressing praise' and applies to a person's work or effort such as a 'laudatory' speech (one given in glowing terms) or a 'laudatory' review (a favourable one).

laudatory see **laudable**

lawful see **legal**

lay see **lie**

leave see **let**

lecherous see **licentious**

leeward/windward (exposed to – or protected from – the wind)
Confusible opposites. 'Leeward' means 'in the lee of the wind', i.e. sheltered from it ('lee' meaning 'shelter'); 'windward' therefore means 'exposed to the wind'. There are several groups of Leeward and Windward Islands around the world, with their names indicating their location relative to the wind. The Windward Islands in the West Indies, for example, are in the path of the north-east trade winds, while the Leewards, north-east of them, are sheltered from these winds.

legal/lawful (allowed by law)
The two words are often used more or less interchangeably, but it is possible to distinguish: 'legal' means 'authorised by law' or 'pertaining to the law', as a 'legal' application or the 'legal' profession; 'lawful' means 'permitted or recognised by law', i.e. not contrary to the law, as a 'lawful' act or 'lawful' access. But 'legal' can also mean 'permitted by law', as a 'legal' act. Confusion, therefore, is not general but limited. See also the related **illegal**.

leitmotiv see **motive**

leniency/lenity (mildness)
'Leniency' (or 'lenience') is the more general word, the noun from 'lenient', so that one can show 'leniency' in administering a punishment or in criticising someone's faults (by making allowances for them). 'Lenity' means more specifically 'mercifulness': 'The lenity of the judge's sentence was unexpected.'

lenity see **leniency**

lento see **largo**

let/leave (allow)
Does one 'let a person alone' or 'leave a person alone'? *Partridge* distinguishes: to 'let' a person alone is to stop bothering him, but to 'leave' him alone is to leave him as he is, on his own. However 'let' has its basic sense of 'allow', and 'leave' means 'go away from', so that 'let him alone' can mean 'allow him to stay on his own', and 'leave him alone' can mean 'go away and let him stay on his own' – in other words, there is little if any difference! What has happened is that 'leave' has colloquially come to be used to mean 'allow' – compare the established sense of the noun 'leave' = 'permission' – with the result that the two words, especially with 'alone', can be used interchangeably without any cause for confusion.

libertarian see **libertine**

libertine/libertarian (one who preaches or practises a form of liberty)
Originally a 'libertine' was a 'freedman' or, more narrowly, a freethinker in religious matters. The word is now used to describe someone who is 'free' in matters of morals, notably one who leads a sexually immoral life. A 'libertarian' is someone who advocates freedom of thought or conduct, or who holds the doctrine of free will. The latter word has thus acquired a noble aura, the former an ignoble one. But then crimes have more than once been committed in the name of liberty.

licentious/lascivious/lecherous (lewd, lustful)
'Licentious' literally means 'characterised by licence', that is, 'morally unrestrained'. 'Lascivious', from the Latin *lascivia* (wantonness) means 'inclined to lust'. 'Lecherous' – the word is related to 'lick' (compare French *lécher*) with its implied reference to gluttony and debauchery – means 'pertaining to free indulgence of lust'. 'Licentious' thus indicates the attitude, 'lascivious' the potential, and 'lecherous' the nitty-gritty.

lie/lay (be – or put – in a horizontal position)
Basically 'lie' is not transitive, and 'lay' not intransitive, that is, one can't 'lie' something and one must always 'lay' something. 'Lay' is, however, increasingly frequently used to mean 'lie', and in particular 'lie down' – see, for example, the line 'Come and lay down by my side' from the popular song 'Help me make it through the night', as well as widely elsewhere in the media. Is this usage incorrect? One might argue that 'lay' has the general sense 'cause to lie', so why can it not mean 'lie' itself? That is, the object pronoun is understood – 'Come and lay (yourself) down. . . .' Not only is 'lay' easier to say than 'lie', but the influence of such terms as 'lay-by', 'layabout' and 'lay-off' is strong. (Of these nouns, only 'layabout' can be objected to on grammatical grounds, since 'lay-by' has the implied object 'vehicle' and 'lay-off' that of 'workers'. A 'layabout' just 'lies about' – or lazes about). However, if the distinction between 'lie' and 'lay', as intransitive and transitive verbs, is to be observed, the correct forms of the present and past tenses are:

lie		*lay*
	Present	
I lie		I lay
I am lying		I am laying
	Past	
I lay		I laid
I was lying		I was laying
I have lain		I have laid

Neither set of forms should be confused with that of 'lie' meaning 'tell an untruth'. The forms for this verb are: I lie, I am lying; I lied, I was lying, I have lied.

limpid/languid (still)
'Limpid' is sometimes falsely influenced by 'limp'. In fact it means 'clear', 'lucid', as 'limpid' water, 'limpid' eyes or a 'limpid' style of writing. 'Languid', which in turn may wrongly suggest 'liquid', actually means 'flagging', 'dull', as 'languid' spirits or a 'languid' manner. A 'languid' wave of the hand, however, could coincidentally be a limp one.

litany see **liturgy**

Lithuanian see **Latvian**

liturgy/litany (form of church service)
The 'liturgy' is the actual form of public worship followed in a particular church, properly that of the eucharistic service of the Orthodox church. The word – from the Greek *leitourgía* (public duty) – is also used to apply to the Anglican *Book of Common Prayer* (see the word used in the Preface to this). The 'litany' – from Greek *litaneia* (an entreating) – is a liturgical form of prayer consisting of a series of requests and responses successively repeated. In the Anglican 'litany', for example, which is often said or sung at the beginning of Lent (the words are not related), the supplication 'Good Lord, deliver us' is repeated eight times, and 'We beseech thee to hear us, good Lord' twenty-one times.

livid/lurid (angry, terrible)
The figurative use of the words is the most common, with 'livid' meaning 'angry' and 'lurid' – 'fiercely intense': a 'lurid' report of a crime could make you simply 'livid'. The basic meaning of both words denotes a colour, with 'livid' being bluish-grey, as the colour of a bruise or a black eye, and 'lurid', strangely, either red or fiery, as a 'lurid' sky, or pale and ghastly, as the 'lurid' glare of snow and ice in the polar regions.

loadstone/lodestar (natural object used for guiding the way)
A 'loadstone' (or 'lodestone') is a variety of iron ore used as a magnet, and originally a 'way stone' used by sailors to guide ships. Loosely it is anything that attracts or has a magnetic pull, as the 'loadstone' of an exhibition. A 'lodestar' (or 'loadstar') is a star that shows the way, especially the Pole Star, or generally something or someone who serves as a guiding star. According to his contemporary, John Lydgate, Chaucer was the 'lodesterre' of the English language. 'Lode' is here related to 'lead' rather than to 'load' in the sense of 'burden'.

lodestar see **loadstone**

logistics see **strategy** (science of warfare)

louche see **farouche**

louring see **glowering**

lowering see **glowering**

lumber see **encumber**

lure/allure (as verb: to attract, entice)
To 'lure' is to attract deliberately, especially to something dangerous or sinful, as a decoy 'lures' a prey to a bait or trap, or the attractions of life in a city 'lure' people to come and live there. To 'allure' is to attract, not necessarily deliberately, by offering something really or apparently good: one can thus be 'allured' to the delights of music or into mistakenly confiding in someone. Both words are common as nouns.

lurid see **livid**

lustful see **lusty**

lusty/lustful (full of lust or lustiness)
'Lusty' means 'vigorous', 'hearty', as of a 'lusty' bull or a 'lusty' appetite. 'Lustful' means 'full of sexual desire', as seen in a 'lustful' look (a lecherous one). In fact 'lusty' meant 'lustful' as late as the seventeenth century, although 'lustful' had already established itself in its present sense a hundred years earlier.

luxuriant see **luxurious**

luxurious/luxuriant (rich, abundant)
The second of these is sometimes wrongly used instead of the first. 'Luxurious' means 'characterised by luxury', as a 'luxurious' hotel (a comfortable, well-appointed one) or a 'luxurious' life (one full of luxury). 'Luxuriant' means 'growing or producing abundantly', as 'luxuriant' grass (thick and dense) or 'luxuriant' soil (rich and fertile). Both ultimately derive from Latin *luxus* (abundance). The noun of 'luxurious' is 'luxuriousness'; of 'luxuriant' it is 'luxuriance'. The association between 'luxuriant' and 'lush' is purely fortuitous.

lynx see **minx**

M

macaque see **macaw**

macaroon/meringue (light sweet cake made of sugar and eggwhites)
A 'macaroon' – from a French word surprisingly related to 'macaroni' – is more of a cake or biscuit, and is often almond-flavoured. A 'meringue' – some trace the name back to the German town of Mehringen, where the cake was said to have been first made – is white, light, crumbly and either hollow or containing cream. The interesting false blend 'maroon' is sometimes heard, possibly inspired by 'marron' or the colour of chocolate.

macaw/macaque (exotic animal)
A 'macaw' is a large, long-tailed, brightly feathered parrot, a native of tropical and sub-tropical America. A 'macaque' (occasionally 'macaco') is a smallish monkey with cheek pouches and a short tail, found chiefly in Africa.

machismo see **sadism**

Mach one see **Mark one**

mackerel sky/mare's tail sky (type of cloud formation)
A 'mackerel sky' is one almost covered with bands of high, small, white, fleecy clouds (altocumulus or cirrocumulus) resembling the markings on a mackerel's back. Such a sky usually indicates the end of an unsettled or stormy period of weather, so is a good sign. A 'mare's tail sky', one with 'mare's tails', has thin wisps of long, flowing, grey clouds (cirrus) whose streaky appearance, caused by strong winds, resembles a horse's tail. A sky like this usually means bad weather since it indicates an approaching depression.

madam/madame (title or form of address for a woman)
'Madam' is the polite term of address,

especially to a married lady or an elderly one. 'Madame', accented on the second vowel, is sometimes similarly used, especially to impress. More regularly, however, 'madame' is a conventional title of respect for any woman who is not English-speaking, either on its own or prefixed to her name, as Madame Giroud, the former French Minister of Culture. Both forms can be used to mean 'brothel-keeper' (as a noun). 'Madame' as a title is also used, or assumed, by certain women who claim to be non-English-speaking, for example, 'palmists, milliners and musicians', as *Chambers* classes them. A 'madam-shop' is a small one which sells ready-to-wear clothes to 'fashionable women of mature taste'. A 'madam', or 'proper little madam' is a derogatory term sometimes applied to a pert young woman or girl – otherwise a **minx**. Both words derive, of course, from the French *ma dame* (my lady).

madame see **madam**

Mafia see **Maquis**

magenta/magnolia (shade of red)
'Magenta' is a reddish purple colour – that of the aniline dye discovered shortly after the French defeated the Austrians at the battle of Magenta (1859) in northern Italy. 'Magnolia' is the colour of the large fragrant flowers on the shrub named after the French botanist Pierre Magnol – strictly speaking white, yellow, pink or purple. On paint charts, however, 'magnolia' is used for a nondescript shade of pale pink.

magnificent/munificent (lavish)
'Magnificent' means generally grand or fine, as a 'magnificent' sunset or a 'magnificent' gesture (which could be a generous one). No doubt the latter sense leads to an association with 'munificent', which really does mean 'generous' or 'liberal' – the basis is Latin *munus* (a present).

magnolia see **magenta**

maharajah see **rajah**

mahatma see **rajah**

mahdi see **mufti**

malachite/marcasite (mineral used for making ornaments)
'Malachite' is a green mineral – basic copper carbonate – used for making ornamental objects such as vases. 'Marcasite' is a common mineral, known sometimes as white iron pyrites, that forms pale yellow crystals. It was used in the eighteenth century for making ornaments, notably costume jewellery. The origin of the words is, respectively, Greek *malache* (mallow) and Arabic *marqashitha* (of Markhashi – a region thought to have been located in north-eastern Persia).

malevolent/malignant (malicious, harmful)
'Malevolent' is literally 'wishing ill', as a 'malevolent' look or tone of voice. 'Malignant', a more powerful word, means 'wishing to cause harm' as a 'malignant' delight in someone else's misfortunes. With reference to diseases it means 'causing death', as a 'malignant' growth – contrasted with a 'benign' one which is not normally fatal.

malignant see **malevolent**

mambo see **tango**

mandarin see **tangerine**

manège see **ménage**

manzanilla see **amontillado**

Maquis/Mafia (secret militant organisation)
The 'Maquis' was the collective term for the French Resistance forces who counterattacked the Germans in the Second World War. Their name derives from the Corsican Italian word *macchia* (thicket); the dense scrub of Corsica was used originally as a refuge by fugitives from German conscription in 1942. The 'Mafia' is a criminal secret society of Sicilians or Italians, active either at home or in other countries, particularly the USA (where they also have the title Cosa Nostra, Italian for 'our thing'). The name originates from the Italian dialect word *mafia* (boldness), which probably goes back to the Arabic *mahyah* (boasting).

marabou see **cockatoo**

maraca see **marimba**

marathon/pentathlon/biathlon/ decathlon (sporting event, especially an Olympic one)
The 'marathon' is the great long distance race of the Olympic Games, since 1924 standardised at 26 miles 385 yards (42·195 kilometres). Its name comes from the story of the Greek messenger, possibly one Pheidippides, who ran some twenty-five miles from Marathon to Athens to bring news of the Greek victory over the Persians in 490 BC. (On arrival, he is said to have gasped '*Chairete, nikomen*' – 'Rejoice, we win' – before dropping dead.) The race did not figure in the original ancient Olympic Games. The 'pentathlon' (Greek for 'five contests') did, however, and comprised the long jump, running, throwing the discus, throwing the spear, and wrestling. The modern 'pentathlon' consists of riding, fencing, pistol-shooting, swimming and cross-country running, while the women's 'pentathlon', introduced in 1964, includes the shot put, high jump, hurdles, sprint or dash and long jump. The 'decathlon' ('ten contests') is a two-day contest of ten track and field events: the sprint or dash, running long jump, shot put, high jump, 400-metre race, 110-metre hurdles, discus throw, pole vault, javelin throw and 1,500-metre race. The 'biathlon' ('two contests') figures in the Winter Olympics and is a combination of cross-country skiing and rifle marksmanship – the competitor stops every five kilometres to fire five rounds at a target 100–250 metres away. The term 'marathon' has come to be applied to any long-distance race or endurance contest, notably the dance 'marathon', and has engendered such hideous half-breeds as 'talkathon', 'walkathon' and 'moviethon' (monstrous talks, walks and movie shows).

marcasite see **malachite**

mare's tail sky see **mackerel sky**

marimba/maraca (South American percussion instrument)
The 'marimba' is a sort of xylophone consisting of strips of wood of various lengths struck by hammers or sticks. The 'maraca' is basically a gourd filled with pebbles, seeds or other rattling objects and shaken to mark the rhythm. Both instruments feature in Latin American folk bands.

Mark one/Mach one (designation used for military equipment)
A 'Mark one' aircraft (for example) is the first of a number of successive types or modifications. A 'Mach one' aircraft is one that flies at a speed of 'Mach number one', i.e. at the speed of sound (about 760 m.p.h. at sea level). The term gets its name from the Austrian physicist and philosopher Ernst Mach (1838–1916). 'Mark one', 'mark two' etc., is not restricted to military usage, but can designate the first or subsequent model of virtually any manufactured product or piece of equipment. The confusion, when it arises, is more perhaps aural than visual. The usual abbreviated forms for the terms are Mk–1, Mk–2 (or Mk–I, Mk–II), etc., and M 1, M 2·05, etc.

maroon see **mulatto**

marquetry see **parquetry**

marsala see **amontillado**

maser see **laser**

masochism see **sadism**

masterful see **masterly**

masterly/masterful (superior)
'Masterly' means 'done like a master', so 'clever', 'skilful', as a 'masterly' touch, stroke or performance. 'Masterful' means 'acting like a master' in the sense 'imperious', 'commanding', as a 'masterful'

tone of voice or manner. But 'masterly' is occasionally used as an exact equivalent of 'masterful'.

matador/toreador (bullfighter)
The 'matador' is the one who actually kills the bull, from Spanish *matar* (to kill). The 'toreador', famous from his song in Bizet's *Carmen,* is a more general term for a bullfighter, usually one that is mounted, from Spanish *torear* (to fight bulls).

maudlin/mawkish (distastefully sentimental)
'Maudlin' is 'tearfully emotional' or 'weakly sentimental', the reference being to Mary Magdalene, who is often represented in art as weeping. 'Mawkish' – from an Old Norse word meaning 'maggot' – means 'sickly', 'slightly nauseating'. A 'mawkish' film might thus arouse a 'maudlin' sympathy for the hero/heroine/animal star or whoever.

Mauritanian/Moorish/Moresque (pertaining to the Moors or their land)
'Mauritanian' pertains to Mauritania, the west African republic situated mainly in the Sahara desert, or to Mauretania, the ancient kingdom in north-western Africa that included the territory now held by Morocco and part of Algeria. 'Moorish' pertains to the Moors, Muslims living in north-western Africa in what was Mauretania, or formerly a group of these people who invaded and conquered Spain in the eighth century. 'Moresque' or 'Mauresque' is the term applied to the 'Moorish' style of ornamental design (of architecture, furniture, etc.) associated in the West with films starring Rudolph Valentino. 'Mauritanian' should not, in turn, be confused with 'Mauritian', which relates to Mauritius, the island state east of Madagascar in the Indian Ocean.

mausoleum see **mortuary**

mawkish see **maudlin**

maxim/axiom/aphorism (saying)
A 'maxim' is a saying expressing what is generally held to be a general truth, especially a neatly phrased one, often even

a proverb, such as 'He who laughs last, laughs best.' An 'axiom' is not really a saying but the expression of a clearly established principle, such as 'More haste, less speed'. An 'aphorism' is very similar to a 'maxim' and is essentially, too, a terse saying embodying a general truth, such as 'Time is money' or 'People need people'. 'Axiom' and 'aphorism' derive from the Greek words meaning respectively 'requisite' and 'definition'. 'Maxim' originates from the Latin phrase *maxima propositio* (greatest proposition).

meander see **wander**

meistersingers/minnesingers
(medieval German singers and poets)
The 'meistersingers' (master singers), immortalised by Wagner, were members of one of the guilds, chiefly of working men, established in the fourteenth, fifteenth and sixteenth centuries in Germany for the cultivation of poetry and music. The 'minnesingers' (love singers) were a class of German lyric poets and singers who wrote and sang of love in the twelfth, thirteenth and fourteenth centuries, i.e. the German counterpart of troubadours. Thanks again to Wagner, the 'minnesinger' lives on in the figure of Tannhäuser and his opponent Wolfram of Eschenbach, who represent the lower and higher types of 'minnesinger' character.

Melanesia see **Micronesia**

melodic see **melodious**

melodious/melodic   (pertaining to melody)
'Melodious' means 'tuneful', 'producing a pleasant melody', as a 'melodious' voice. 'Melodic' is sometimes used in this sense, but technically means 'pertaining to melody', i.e. to the musical succession of single notes distinguished from harmony and rhythm in musical composition. The word is used in such expressions as 'melodic sequence', meaning the more or less exact repetition of a melody at a higher or lower level, as the third and fourth bars of *Three Blind Mice*.

ménage/menagerie/manège (home for animals or people)
A 'ménage' is a household or domestic establishment, the French word deriving ultimately from Latin *mansio* (mansion). In Scotland the word is used to apply to a kind of benefit society or an arrangement for selling on an instalment plan. The notorious 'ménage à trois' (household of three) is a household consisting of a man, a woman, and the lover of one of them. A 'menagerie' is now a collection of wild animals, sometimes by implication strange ones. The term originally meant 'management of a household'. 'Manège' – related to 'manage' rather than 'ménage' – is primarily the art of training and riding horses, and by extension the actual premises of a riding-school. 'Menagerie' is a useful word to describe, in a transferred sense, a set of weird or unusual people: 'The doctor's waiting-room was a real menagerie.' Both 'ménage' and 'manège' are often written without the accents.

menagerie see **ménage**

menhir see **cromlech**

meringue see **macaroon**

metacarpus see **tarsus**

metatarsus see **tarsus**

meter see **metre**

metre/meter (measure or measurer)
The spelling of these two is frequently confused, doubtless because the American spelling of 'metre', and of all words that in the British spelling end in '-metre', is consistently 'meter'. As a basic word, 'metre' is the unit of length and the poetic measure; 'meter' is 'instrument that measures', as a gas, electricity, water or parking 'meter'. The ending '-metre' is used for all units of length based on the 'metre', as 'kilometre', 'millimetre', 'centimetre', so that all other words, mainly measuring devices such as 'speedometer', 'thermometer' and 'altimeter', but including such mathematical terms as 'parameter', 'perimeter' and 'diameter', will end

in '-meter'. The two words have the same basic derivation: Greek *metron* (measure), although 'meter' is more directly from the English verb 'mete', as 'mete out' (measure out).

Micronesia/Melanesia/Polynesia (Pacific island group)
'Micronesia' comprises a number of island groups to the east of the Philippines, the main ones being the Marianas, the Caroline Islands and the Marshall Islands. 'Melanesia', which includes Fiji, New Caledonia, New Hebrides and Solomon Islands, among others, is in the south Pacific, north-east of Australia. 'Polynesia', which includes Hawaii, Samoa and Tonga, lies east of 'Melanesia' and 'Polynesia', and extends southwards to New Zealand. The three island groups form the three principal divisions of Oceania. The names are composed of Greek elements: 'Polynesia' – the first to be named – meaning 'many islands', 'Micronesia' – 'small islands', and 'Melanesia' – 'black islands' (either because the islands have a dark outline when seen from sea level, or because the natives are black-skinned).

migrant see **immigrant**

mildew see **mould**

millenary/millennium (period of one thousand years)
A 'millenary' is any period of a thousand years. A 'millennium' is also this, but more often the term is used in one of two specific ways: either to denote the period of a thousand years when Christ will reign on earth after his second coming, as foretold in Revelation 20, or to apply to a general lengthy period of happiness, good government or – ironically, perhaps – to a future 'golden age'. For similar confusibles see **centenary**.

millennium see **millenary**

milliard see **million**

million/billion/milliard (high number – 1 followed by six, nine or twelve noughts)
A 'million' is a thousand thousands, i.e.

1,000,000. The word literally means 'big thousand', and is said to have been invented in the fourteenth century by Marco Polo to describe the vast wealth of the East. The much travelled traveller dictated the tale of his journeyings to a fellow-prisoner in Genoa, and the subsequent somewhat far-fetched account came to be known, when in book form, as *Il milione*. A 'billion' varies. In Britain and France it is a million millions, or 1,000,000,000,000. In the USA it is a thousand millions, or 1,000,000,000. A 'milliard' is the word used in France and a number of other European countries to mean a thousand millions, i.e. the same as the American 'billion'.

millipede see **centipede**

miminy-piminy see **namby-pamby**

minced meat see **mincemeat**

mincemeat/minced meat (finely chopped meat or fruit)
'Mincemeat' is normally thought of as a mixture of minced apples, candied peel, suet and the like used with currants and raisins for filling mince pies. 'Minced meat' is simply meat that has been minced. However, 'mincemeat' is also sometimes used to mean 'minced meat' – and even 'minced' pies have been spotted on sale (although this seems to suggest that the pies themselves have been minced).

Ming/Tang/Ch'ing (Chinese dynasty)
The 'Ming' dynasty ruled from 1368 to 1644 and is famed for the association with fine porcelain, especially vases, produced by the imperial factory. The 'Tang' dynasty was much earlier, from AD 618 to AD 907, and is associated with the considerable territorial expansion of China (in particular the contact with Central Asia), the first development of printing, the political as well as religious importance of Buddhism, and the peak of Chinese poetry. The 'Ch'ing' was China's last dynasty, from 1644 to 1911, the one founded by the Manchus. Under it, the Chinese empire increased to three times the size of the previous 'Ming' dynasty,

the population more than doubled to 450 million, and an integrated national economy was established.

minnesingers see **meistersingers**

Minotaur/centaur/bucentaur (mythical creature – half beast, half man)
The (one and only) 'Minotaur' was the monster with the head of a bull and body of a man who was confined in the Cretan labyrinth and fed with human flesh. The creature was the offspring of Pasiphaë, wife of Minos, the king of Crete, and a bull. According to the Greek classic tale the 'Minotaur' – the name means 'bull of Minos' – was killed by Theseus with the help of Minos's daughter Ariadne, who guided Theseus out of the labyrinth with a thread after the deadly deed had been done. A 'centaur' was one of a race of monsters in Greek mythology who had the head, trunk and arms of a man and the body and legs of a horse. Chiron is one of the best-known 'centaurs', whose name has not been satisfactorily explained. The 'bucentaur' was not really a beast. It was the title of the state barge of Venice from which the doge and other officials performed annually, on Ascension Day, the ceremonial marriage of the state with the sea by dropping a ring into the Adriatic. The name is said to derive from Greek *bous* (ox) and *kentauros* (centaur), with reference to the figure-head of the barge which represented a mythical creature that was half bull, half man. The word could, however, originate from the Italian *buzino d'oro* (barque of gold). The last 'bucentaur' was destroyed by the French in 1798.

minx/lynx (bright-eyed creature)
A 'minx' is not a quadruped but a pert or flirtatious girl, deriving from 'minikin', meaning 'diminutive person' (in turn not related to 'manikin' but formed on the basis of the Old Dutch *minne*, 'love'). A 'lynx' is the animal sometimes known as a wildcat, which has lent its name to the expression 'lynx-eyed' – 'sharp-sighted'. Possibly the association with 'mink' aids the confusion: the fur of the 'lynx' has come to be used commercially, though not to the same extent as that of the mink.

Miocene see **Pleistocene**

miracle play/morality play/mystery play (type of medieval religious drama)
A 'miracle play' is one that sets a religious subject in dramatic form, such as a Bible story or the life of a saint, and presents the material in a series or cycle, as performed by the medieval craft guilds. York, Chester, Coventry and Wakefield are cities where famous 'miracle plays' were, or are said to have been, performed. A 'morality play', as its name implies, is an allegorical drama – rather later than the 'miracle play' – in which the characters are personifications of virtues and vices. The most famous 'morality play' is *Everyman*, which dates from about 1500. A 'mystery play' is often used as an alternative name for a 'miracle play'. In his *English Dramatic Literature*, however, Sir A. W. Ward makes the distinction that 'mystery plays' deal only with Gospel stories, while 'miracle plays' deal with the lives of the saints. This distinction is rather too fine, though, and rarely observed in general use.

misanthropist/misogynist/misogamist (one who hates his fellow men – or women)
The three are haters, respectively, of mankind, women and marriage. The 'mis-' element denotes the hating, the other halves of the words are the same as those in 'anthropology', 'gynaecologist' and 'bigamy'.

misogamist see **misanthropist**

misogynist see **misanthropist**

mistrust see **distrust**

misuse see **abuse**

Moguls see **Mongols**

mohair/moire/moiré/moygashel (type of fabric)
'Mohair' is the fleece of the Angora goat, used in plain weave for draperies and pile weave for fabrics. The association with 'hair' is a false one – the word comes from Arabic *mukhayyar* (select, choice), as applied to a cloth made of goat's hair.

'Moire' is a watered fabric, originally watered 'mohair' but now commonly watered silk or wool, and 'moiré' is a fabric of silk, rayon or the like which has a wave-like pattern pressed on it. Both words are a French borrowing of English 'mohair'. 'Moygashel' is a type of Irish linen used mainly for suits and costumes, as originally woven in the village of Moygashel in County Tyrone, Northern Ireland.

Mohammedan see **Muslim**

Mohawks/Mohicans (North American Indian tribe)
The 'Mohawks', whose name relates not to hawks but comes from an Indian word meaning 'they eat animal things' (the tribe was formerly supposed to be man-eating), are the most easterly of the Iroquois Five Nations and once lived along the Mohawk river, in New York state. The 'Mohicans' – their name is Algonquian for 'wolf' – were formerly concentrated in the upper Hudson Valley and are now a confederacy of North American Indians whose native tongue is Algonquian. They are famous largely thanks to Fenimore Cooper's novel *The Last of the Mohicans*, in which the 'last of the Mohicans' is Uncas who, with his father Chingachgook and their friend Natty Bumppo, frustrates the attempts of Magua, the evil Indian Huron leader, to block the efforts of Alice and Cora Munro to join their father, who is the British commander of Fort William Henry, near Lake Champlain.

Mohicans see **Mohawks**

moire see **mohair**

moiré see **mohair**

molto/mosso (musical direction)
Both words, of course, are Italian. 'Molto means 'much', 'very', as in '*molto vivace*' – 'very lively'. 'Mosso' means 'fast' (literally 'moved') as in '*più mosso*' – 'faster', and '*meno mosso*' – 'slower' (literally 'more moved' and 'less moved').

Mongols/Moguls (Asian rulers and conquerors)

'Mongols' are properly natives of Mongolia, but historically – the more familiar usage – were members of the Mongol Empire that in the thirteenth century extended over the larger part of Asia, reaching the Dnieper river in the west. The 'Moguls' were the 'Mongol' conquerors of India ruling from 1526 to 1857 (nominally from 1803) when the last of the emperors was dethroned. The 'Great Mogul' or 'Grand Mogul' was the title, as used by Europeans, of the emperor of Delhi. In modern use a 'mogul' is a 'king', 'baron' or 'boss' of some kind of commercial empire, as a 'movie mogul'. The historical 'Moguls' were noted for their rich works of art and jewellery, which were produced in India during the 'Mogul' empire.

monsoon/simoom/sirocco (strong, hot wind)
The 'monsoon' is a seasonal wind of the Indian Ocean and southern Asia that blows from the south-west in summer and the north-east in winter. The summer 'monsoon' is the notorious one, with its heavy rains. The 'simoom' or 'simoon' is a hot, sand-laden, suffocating wind that blows over the deserts of North Africa and Syria in spring and summer. The 'sirocco' is a hot, dry, dust-laden wind, a 'simoom' in fact, blowing from North Africa and affecting parts of southern Europe, or a warm, sultry, south or south-east wind with rain in the same regions.

Montilla see **amontillado**

mooch see **moon**

moon/mooch/mope (move about aimlessly or listlessly)
If you 'moon' about, you wander around dreamily or idly, as if moonstruck. If you 'mooch' about you are acting rather furtively, whether hanging about or slouching along somewhere. If you 'mope' – the only verb of the three not colloquial – you may not be moving at all, but sunk in a listless apathy (the word comes from the obsolete verb 'mop', meaning 'pull a wry face').

Moorish see **Mauritanian**

moot see **move**

mope see **moon**

morality play see **miracle play**

Moresque see **Mauritanian**

morgue see **mortuary**

morpheme see **phoneme**

Morrison shelter see **Anderson shelter**

mortgagee/mortgagor (one who mortgages property – or to whom property is mortgaged)
The confusion lies perhaps more in the process of mortgaging than the suffixes, with '-ee' denoting the person to whom something is done, sold, given, sent, etc. (as 'addressee', 'employee', 'internee', 'examinee') and '-or' used for the person who does, sells, gives, etc. ('donor', 'dedicator', 'vendor', 'consignor'). In practice the 'mortgagee' is usually a building society (to whom the property is mortgaged), and the 'mortgagor' the house buyer (who is mortgaging the property). That is, the 'mortgagor' must repay the 'mortgagee' the loan he has been given.

mortgagor see **mortgagee**

mortuary/morgue/mausoleum (place for the dead to lie)
A 'mortuary' is a place where the dead are temporarily kept before being buried or cremated. A 'morgue', more common in American than British usage, is a place where the bodies of people found dead, whether or not in suspicious circumstances, are laid out for identification. A 'mausoleum' is a grand tomb of some kind – originally the one erected at Halicarnassus in Asia Minor around 350 BC for Mausolus, the ruler of Caria. (It was one of the wonders of the ancient world; fragments of the original frieze are in the British Museum.) The original 'Morgue' was a building in Paris used for the same purpose as a modern 'morgue', with the actual name itself of uncertain origin. Both 'morgue' and 'mausoleum' are used figuratively to

mean a large, dreary room: 'My hotel bedroom was a real morgue'; 'The waiting room at the station is a proper mausoleum of a place.'

Moslem see **Muslim**

mosso see **molto**

Mothering Sunday see **Mother's Day**

Mother's Day/Mothering Sunday (day when traditionally presents are given by children to their mothers)
The former, which is relatively recent, and American, has commercially ousted the latter, which is quite old, and of English origin. An Act of Congress of 1913 in the USA set aside the second Sunday in May for remembering mothers. In the Second World War, American troops introduced 'Mother's Day' to Britain, where it subsequently became confused with 'Mothering Sunday'. This in the church calendar is the fourth Sunday in Lent, otherwise Mid-Lent Sunday, Refreshment Sunday or Laetare Sunday (and any date from 1 March to 4 April) when traditionally the mother church (the principal or oldest one in the district) was visited and schoolchildren and apprentices were given a day's holiday to be at home with their parents. 'Father's Day', celebrated on the third Sunday in June, is a similar import from America.

motif see **motive**

motive/motif/leitmotiv (subject or theme of a work of art)
The basic meaning of 'motive', of course, is 'what induces a person to act', but the term is used in the arts as an alternative to 'motif', which is the distinctive feature or theme in an artistic, literary or musical composition. (In music the word applies specifically to a brief passage from which longer passages are developed – otherwise a 'figure'.) In design, a 'motive' or 'motif' is a particular repeated figure, as a lace ornament sewn on a dress or a pattern printed on wallpaper. A 'leitmotiv', from the German (leading motive), is a term used in musical drama for a theme associated

throughout the work with a particular person, situation or idea. Wagner made the 'leitmotiv' his speciality.

mould/mildew (growth of minute fungi associated with disease or decay)
The main distinction is that 'mould' grows on vegetable or animal matter, especially food, while 'mildew' forms on plants and fabrics, such as paper and leather, when exposed to moisture. The words are not related: 'mildew' is a form of Old English 'honeydew'.

mousse/soufflé (light sweet or savoury dish)
A 'mousse' – from the French for 'moss' or 'froth' – is a light, sweet pudding with cream, beaten eggs, gelatine, etc., served chilled. A 'soufflé' – French 'puffed' – is a light, savoury, baked dish made fluffy with beaten eggwhites and containing fish, cheese or other ingredients. There exist savoury 'mousses' and sweet 'soufflés', but with these it's usually a casual or careless extension of the name.

move/moot (raise or propose)
To 'move' a point or matter is to make a formal request or application. 'Mr Briggs then moved that the meeting be adjourned.' To 'moot' a point is to raise it for discussion. 'Mrs Jones mooted the question of the subscription' (she wanted it to be discussed). The second verb becomes an adjective in the fixed phrase 'moot point', meaning a debatable one and by implication a doubtful one. The phrase is sometimes spoken as if it was 'mute point', by false association with this more common word. (This would mean a point that was not spoken, and presumably one that might therefore be in doubt. The legal phrase 'to stand mute' means not to plead in court.) 'Moot' has its origin in the Old English *mot* or *gemot* (meeting, assembly).

moygashel see **mohair**

muddled/fuddled/addled (mixed, confused, bemused)
'Muddled' is the general word. 'Fuddled' has the specific sense 'muddled by drink', while 'addled' means 'mentally confused' –

the word usually occurs in such phrases as 'addle-brained' or 'addle-headed'. There is an association with 'addled' eggs – ones that are bad or spoiled.

mufti/mahdi (Muslim leader)
The 'mufti' is the Muslim legal adviser who is consulted on religious matters. Under the Ottoman empire the word was used as the title of the official head of the state religion, or of one of his deputies, with the 'Grand Mufti' being the head of the Muslim Arab community in Jerusalem. 'Mufti' in the sense 'plain clothes' derives from the fact that the official is a civilian. The 'mahdi', with Muslims, is the title of the expected spiritual and temporal ruler who, it is believed, will set up a reign of righteousness throughout the world. There have been a number of claimants to the title, notably Mohammed Ahmed (died 1885) who established in the Egyptian Sudan an independent government that lasted until 1898. The titles mean, respectively, 'one who delivers a judgment' and 'the guided one'.

mulatto/maroon (Negro or part Negro)
A 'mulatto' is the offspring of one white parent and one Negro, i.e. a half-breed. The word, which is Spanish, goes back ultimately to Latin *mulus* (mule), with reference to the person's hybrid origin. (A mule is a cross between an ass and a horse.) A 'maroon' was a Negro – originally a runaway slave – living in the wilder parts of the West Indies in the seventeenth and eighteenth centuries. The derivation is not from 'maroon' meaning the dark brownish red colour, but the verb meaning 'strand on an island'.

munificent see **magnificent**

munitions see **ammunition**

Muslim/Moslem/Mohammedan/Mussulman (follower of Islam or of Mohammed)
Mohammed was the founder of Islam, so that the four terms are closely related and in many ways overlap. The distinction is chiefly one of preference and usage. 'Muslim' is currently the preferred form,

with 'Moslem' being obsolescent, 'Moham-medan' relating more to Mohammed than the Islam religion as a whole, and 'Mussulman' (plural strictly speaking 'Mussulmans') decidedly archaic. 'Moslem' survives in such proper titles as the 'Moslem League' – the Muslim political organisation founded in India in 1906 whose demands in 1940 for an independent Muslim state led to the establishment of Pakistan. The name 'Muslim' comes from the Arabic *aslama* (he resigned himself, i.e. to God), to which 'salaam' is also related.

Mussulman see **Muslim**

muzhik/kulak (Russian peasant)
A 'muzhik', still often spelt 'moujik', is the basic word for the Russian peasant, seen as a rustic countryman as opposed to a more or less sophisticated town-dweller. The word now has a distinct pre-revolutionary flavour. A 'kulak', literally 'fist', was a special sort of 'muzhik' – a rich and often hard-fisted 'exploiting' peasant who employed hired labour or owned machinery. 'Kulaks' were also largely pre-revolutionary, although a number were still in existence after 1917, and many of these organised a grain strike in 1927–8 as a protest at the uncompetitive prices offered them by the state. By 1934, when three-quarters of all Soviet farms had been collectivised, most remaining 'kulaks' had either been resettled in remote parts of the USSR, or arrested and their property and lands confiscated.

mystery play see **miracle play**

nabob/nawab/nizam (official in India)
A 'nabob', properly the title of certain Muslim officials in the Mogul empire, was

the term that came to apply to an English-man who had grown rich in India, or, by extension, to any wealthy person. The word is a variant of 'nawab', which is closer to the Urdu (literally 'deputy governor'). The 'nizam' was the title of the ruler of Hyderabad, India, from about 1700 to 1950, and was also used to apply to a soldier in the regular Turkish army.

naiad see **dryad**

**namby-pamby/niminy-piminy/
miminy-piminy** (affected)
'Namby-pamby' usually means 'weakly sentimental'. It was originally the nick-name, Namby Pamby, invented by Henry Carey for the English poet Ambrose Philips (died 1749). Carey – who among other things wrote 'Sally in our Alley' – used the name as the title of a poem he composed in 1726 to ridicule Philips's verses. 'Niminy-piminy' means 'affectedly refined', with the phrase a meaningless imitation of mincing speech. 'Miminy-piminy', no doubt influenced by it, means 'absurdly affected', 'ridiculously finicky'.

natty see **jazzy**

naturalist/naturist (one who studies things in a natural state)
One term can sometimes be misread or misunderstood for the other. A 'naturalist' studies natural history, and is often a specialist such as a zoologist or botanist. A 'naturist' is an alternative term for a nudist. Many nudists prefer this word, regarding 'nudist' as emphasising the wrong aspect of what they think of as 'social nakedness'. But 'naturist' as a semantic cover-up is rather transparent.

naturist see **naturalist**

nawab see **nabob**

Nazarene/Nazarite (member of religious group)
A 'Nazarene' is basically a native or inhabitant of Nazareth, while 'The Nazarene' was one of the titles of Christ. The term is used to mean 'Christian' by some Jews and Muslims, and the 'Nazarenes' were also a

sect of early Jewish Christians who retained the Mosaic ritual. The name was also adopted by a group of early nineteenth century German artists. Among the ancient Hebrews, a 'Nazarite' was a religious devotee who had taken certain vows of abstinence (see Numbers 6 for what they were). Here the derivation of the name is not 'Nazareth' but Hebrew *nazar* (consecrate).

Nazarite see **Nazarene**

nefarious/felonious (wicked)
'Nefarious' means 'very wicked', 'iniquitous', as 'nefarious' deeds or practices. 'Felonious' means 'pertaining to a felony', i.e. a grave crime such as murder or burglary. (Felonies were, until 1967, officially distinguished from misdemeanours, which were lesser offences.)

neglectful/negligent (careless, disregardful)
'Neglectful', which means 'characterised by neglect', refers to the actual act of neglect, so that if one is 'neglectful' in one's duty one does not do something that should be done. 'Negligent' means virtually the same, but refers to the *habit* of neglect. Someone who is 'negligent' in his duties, therefore, fails to do, in general, what he ought to do. A 'neglectful' person shows 'neglect'; someone who is 'negligent' shows 'negligence'.

negligent see **neglectful**

neuralgia/neuritis/neurosis/ neurasthenia (nervous disorder)
Possibly the first two are confused the most. 'Neuralgia' is pain along the course of a nerve, especially in the areas round the nose and mouth (so-called trigeminal neuralgia, or tic douloureux) or the throat and ear (glossopharyngeal neuralgia). Authorities differ as to whether the '-itis' of 'neuritis' really does mean 'inflammation' (in this case, of a nerve) as it normally does. The *Encyclopaedia Britannica*, defining 'neuritis' as a 'degenerative, non-inflammatory disease of nerve tissue', recommends 'nerve disease' as a more accurate term. The disease can be experienced any-

where in the body, with pain and a pricking or burning numbness in the affected part. 'Neurosis' is an emotional disorder, with obsessions, compulsions, and often associated physical complaints that, however, show no objective evidence of disease. (The '-osis' denotes a verbal noun.) 'Neurasthenia' is nervous debility or exhaustion, as from overwork or prolonged mental strain, its symptoms being vague complaints of a physical nature. The 'asthenia' is Greek 'weakness'.

neurasthenia see **neuralgia**

neuritis see **neuralgia**

neurosis see **neuralgia**

niche see **nook**

niminy-piminy see **namby-pamby**

nitrate/nitrite/nitride (chemical compound of nitre or some related substance)
The suffixes tell all: a 'nitrate' is the salt of nitric acid (HNO_3), and also a fertiliser consisting of potassium nitrate or sodium nitrate; a 'nitrite' is the salt of nitrous acid (HNO_2); a 'nitride' is a binary compound of nitrogen. The suffixes thus denote, respectively, 'salt of an acid with name ending in -ic', 'salt of an acid with name ending in -ous', and 'binary compound'. (For the significance of chemical suffixes, see Appendix I, Table 2, page 149.)

nitride see **nitrate**

nitrite see **nitrate**

nizam see **nabob**

noisome see **obnoxious**

nonchalant/insouciant (casual, unconcerned)
'Nonchalant' means 'coolly unconcerned', 'indifferent', as a 'nonchalant' air or attitude. The word is the participial form of the archaic French verb *nonchaloir*, with *chaloir* in turn deriving from Latin *calere* (to be hot). 'Insouciant' means 'free from concern', 'carefree', being *'sans souci'*, as an 'insouciant' whistle.

nook/niche (recess)
Although similar, the two words do not seem to be related. A 'nook' is a corner or any small recess, especially one that is obscure, remote or cosy. An 'inglenook' is a chimney corner. The word is often used in the phrase 'every nook and cranny', where 'cranny' is a small narrow opening or chink or **crevice**. A 'niche', going back ultimately to Latin *nidus* (nest), is either an ornamental recess for a statue or something similarly decorative, or a place or a position that is just right for someone or something: 'At last he's found a niche for himself' (he's found a good job, a secure position, a role in life, or the like).

notable/noticeable (significant, appreciable)
A 'notable' difference is a big one, and 'notable' progress is great or considerable progress. A 'noticeable' difference may well be a small one, but one that can nevertheless be discerned or appreciated; 'noticeable' progress is progress that can clearly be seen. These two confusibles are surprisingly common.

noticeable see **notable**

nourish see **nurse**

noxious see **obnoxious**

numerator/denominator (mathematical term expressing the figure in a fraction)
The 'numerator' is the number written above the line in the fraction, showing how many parts of a unit are taken; the 'denominator' is the number below the line, showing the number of equal parts into which the unit is divided. The words are Latin ones meaning respectively 'counter' and 'namer'. Thus in $2\frac{3}{8}$, the 'numerator' is 3 and the 'denominator' is 8.

numerous/innumerable (very many)
'Numerous' simply means 'of great number'. 'We have been there on numerous occasions' thus means that we have been there very often. 'Innumerable' is literally 'countless'. It is a more forceful word than 'numerous' and means in effect 'of very great number'.

nurse/nurture/nourish/cherish (tend carefully)
To 'nurse' somebody or something implies a constant tending or fostering. One can literally 'nurse' a person back to health or 'nurse' a grievance (foster it by brooding over it). To 'nurture' a person suggests training him as well as supporting him in some way. It is often used of children or young people generally. The word is related to 'nourish', which has an implication of the provision of food or nutriment, especially to promote healthy development. To 'cherish' is to hold dear, used of a person or thing: if you 'cherish' a close friend you will presumably 'cherish' his friendship. There is a certain overlap of meaning of almost all the words, with 'nurse' the predominant idea behind them.

nurture see **nurse**

nylon/rayon/Dacron/Orlon/Bri-Nylon (name of a synthetic fibre)
'Rayon' came first, with its final '-on' spawning the endings of all the other names, as well as West German perlon, East German dederon, Japanese niplon and Russian kapron. The 'ray' may be arbitrary but, more likely, the word is simply the French *rayon* (ray), with reference to the fibre's thin strands or filaments. 'Rayon' is basically any textile made from cellulose, and is what used to be known as artificial silk. The term originated around 1924. It was followed by 'nylon' in 1938, which was the word used to describe, more specifically, a synthetic polyamide capable of extrusion when molten into fibres, sheets, etc. The name was based on both 'cotton' and 'rayon' with the 'ny-' an arbitrary element. The letters of 'nylon' do not stand, as is sometimes thought, for 'New York' and 'London', and still less are they the acronym of 'Now *you*, lousy old *N*ipponese!', an exclamation said to have been made by one of the material's inventors. (The name was in fact chosen out of 350 words as the result of a competition. It may be no coincidence that '-ny-' also occurs in 'vinyl', a basic ingredient of many artificial fabrics.) 'Dacron' is an American form of Terylene made by Du Pont. One of its chief attri-

butes is its combined resilience and crease-resistance. 'Orlon', also made by Du Pont, is mainly used as a wool substitute in knitwear. 'Bri-Nylon' is a type of 'nylon' manufactured by British Nylon Spinners.

nymph/sylph/sibyl (bewitching woman)
A 'nymph', in Greek mythology, is a minor goddess – a beautiful maiden inhabiting the sea, rivers, woods, trees, mountains, meadows and the like, and often attending a more important deity. Greek *nymphe* means 'bride'. A 'sylph' is one of a race of imaginary beings supposed to inhabit the air, that is, one of the four 'elements' (with salamanders inhabiting fire, undines water, and gnomes – the only males – the earth). The word was probably invented by the sixteenth century Swiss-German physician and alchemist Paracelsus, perhaps based on a blend of Latin *sylvestris* (of the woods) and 'nymph'. Both 'nymph' and 'sylph' are extended to describe a beautiful woman or girl in general, with 'sylph' perhaps being a more graceful or 'airy' female. A 'sibyl' was a woman in ancient Greece or Rome who was said to possess powers of prophecy or divination, with her name derived from Greek *Sibulla*, of uncertain meaning (perhaps *theosoulle*, 'divinely wise'). She is the old maid of the three. The word should not be confused with the female forename, of the same origin, that is now usually spelt Sybil.

obbligato/ostinato (special part in musical piece or score)
Strictly speaking, 'obbligato' applies to a part that must be played – it is obligatory (as opposed to 'ad lib.'). The term can also be used, however, for an extra part, such as

a violin 'obbligato', with the meaning 'violin ad lib.'. So what should mean 'obligatory' can on occasions mean 'optional'. 'Ostinato' – the Italian for 'obstinate' – refers to a constantly recurring melodic fragment, as often found in a 'basso ostinato' or ground bass – which is 'obbligato' in the literal sense of the word.

obdurate see **obstinate**

object/subject (thing or person to which attention is directed)
Why an 'object of interest' but a 'subject of conversation'? The difference lies in the concept: 'object' implies an end or goal, as an interesting 'object' or an 'object' of study; 'subject' implies a means to an end, as a school 'subject' or the 'subject' of a portrait. Furthermore 'object' implies an aim that can be short or long term. There is thus a difference between the 'object' of one's research (the purpose of it), and the 'subject' of one's research (what one is actually studying).

obnoxious/noxious/noisome (offensive)
'Obnoxious' means 'objectionable', usually highly so, as 'obnoxious' behaviour or an 'obnoxious' remark. 'Noxious' means 'injurious', as a 'noxious' gas. Both words are related to Latin *noxa* (hurt). 'Noisome', which is related not to 'noise' but to 'annoy', means 'offensive', 'disgusting', usually of a smell. In a figurative sense, however, both it and 'noxious' can mean 'harmful', as a 'noisome' or 'noxious' task – one that is sickening.

obscure/abstruse (hard to understand, difficult)
'Obscure', from Latin *obscurus* (dark) means 'not clear' or 'not expressing meaning clearly' as an 'obscure' remark or an 'obscure' text. 'Abstruse' means 'difficult to understand', from Latin *abstrusus* (concealed), as an 'abstruse' statement or idea. The bogus blend 'obstruse' is sometimes heard, perhaps by false association with 'obtuse'.

observance see **observation**

observation/observance (act of observing)
'Observation' is the noun of 'observe' in the sense 'watch carefully' and 'remark', as 'He was kept under constant observation' and 'That's an interesting observation.' 'Observance' is the noun of 'observe' in the sense 'keep (a law)' or 'celebrate' (e.g. a festival), as in Shakespeare's 'custom more honour'd in the breach than the observance' and the Lord's Day Observance Society.

obstinate/obdurate (persistent, stubborn)
The words derive from the Latin for, respectively, 'determined' and 'hardened'. 'Obstinate' means 'not yielding', often perversely so, as an 'obstinate' child who refuses to obey, and 'obstinate' resistance which is difficult to overcome. 'Obdurate' means 'not easy to influence or change', with the suggestion of a hard line being taken – a hardened offender may well have an 'obdurate' conscience.

obtrusive see **intrusive**

occidental see **oriental**

occupied/preoccupied (engaged, busied)
'How will you preoccupy yourselves?' a television reporter asked a couple facing a two days' wait at an airport. To 'occupy' oneself is to busy oneself, be engaged in doing something. To be 'preoccupied' – one does not normally 'preoccupy' oneself as a conscious process – is to be engrossed in something, to be occupied to such an extent that one is oblivious to everything else.

ochre see **amber**

oculist see **optician**

odium/opprobrium (reproach)
The two Latin words mean 'hatred' and 'infamy'. Public 'odium' is general public dislike or hatred of someone or something. 'Opprobrium' is disgrace or reproach incurred by conduct that is regarded as shameful. The respective adjectives 'odious' and 'opprobrious' are also confused, with 'odious' sometimes falsely conjuring up

'odorous' – which can mean bad-smelling as well as fragrant – and the phrase 'be in bad odour' (be disliked).

official/officious (pertaining to an office)
'Official' is 'authoritative', as an 'official' announcement made by someone in his 'official' capacity. 'Officious' means 'fussily dutiful', especially ostentatiously so, as an 'officious' waiter. In diplomatic circles, however, an 'officious' statement is the opposite of an 'official' one – it is informal, or unofficial, in fact.

officious see **official**

older see **elder**

onyx/sardonyx/sardius/sardine (type of precious stone)
An 'onyx' is a kind of chalcedony (a type of quartz) with different colours in layers or bands. It is used for cameos in particular. A 'sardonyx' is a type of 'onyx' containing layers or bands of sard, which is the yellow or orange-red kind of chalcedony known as cornelian. 'Sardonyx' is used mainly in jewellery – it is the 'sardine stone' mentioned in Revelation. 'Sardius' is an alternative word for sard, but it was also the name of the precious stone in the breastplate of the Jewish high priest, in fact thought to have been a ruby.

op-art/pop-art (art form of the mid-twentieth century)
'Op-art' – or 'optical art' – is an international form of art that uses optical illusion as its basis, especially so as to produce emotional or visual stimulation and to create the illusion of movement. This is achieved by the careful arrangement and manipulation of colours and geometric forms, particularly repetitive ones. 'Pop-art', which is mainly of British and American inspiration – names such as David Hockney, Roy Lichtenstein and Andy Warhol have become internationally famous through their association with it – essentially reflects the mass media oriented society of the West, with representations of everyday objects such as typewriters and canned goods. The 'pop' is 'popular', but also suggests the explosive effect, or 'pop',

produced on the viewer by many of the form's works. One definition of 'pop-art' by Richard Hamilton, an English exponent of it, is 'Popular/Transient/Expendable/ Low-Cost /Mass-Produced /Young /Witty/ Sexy / Gimmicky / Glamorous / Big Business. . . .' By the end of the 1970s both 'op-art' and 'pop-art' had lost much of their sense of immediacy and iconoclasm.

operative see **operator**

operator/operative (one operating a machine or piece of equipment)
In industrial terms, an 'operator' is some-one operating a specialised piece of equipment, whether sophisticated, as a computer, or reasonably complex, as a copy lathe. An 'operative' is a factory worker, quite often a skilled one, who operates fairly standard machinery, as a loom 'operative'. The greater the skill, however, the more likely the 'operative' will become an 'operator'.

ophthalmologist see **optician**

opossum see **possum**

opprobrium see **odium**

optician/oculist/ophthalmologist/ optometrist (one specialising in eyes)
To the myopic man in the street, an 'optician' is a man who makes or sells spectacles. In fact 'opticians' also sell, reasonably enough, optical instruments, and are divided into 'ophthalmic', who can test sight if registered by the General Optical Council, and 'dispensing', who can make up prescriptions. The term 'oculist' is now rather dated. It used to apply to a doctor of medicine who was skilled in examining and treating the eye. An 'ophthalmologist' is a professional title of either an eye specialist or eye surgeon or, at a less exalted level, an 'ophthalmic optician'. The term derives from the Greek *ophthalmos* (eye), with Latin *oculus* (eye) giving 'oculist'. An 'optometrist' is a specialist in optometry, the examination of the eye for defects and faults of refraction and the prescription of correctional lenses and exercises. Unlike an 'ophthalmologist'

he does not use drugs or surgery.

optometrist see **optician**

oration/orison (special address)
An 'oration' is a formal speech, especially on an occasion such as a funeral or the presentation of academic awards. It is a grand word that suggests stylishness and a considerable display of rhetoric. An 'orison' is a prayer, public or private. The word, which is related in origin to 'oration', is rather archaic and usually used in the plural. 'Nymph, in thy orisons Be all my sins remembered', Hamlet entreats Ophelia in his 'To be or not to be' speech.

ordinal/cardinal (class of numbers)
'Ordinal' numbers state the order (first, second, third, etc.); 'cardinal' numbers are the basic ones (one, two, three, etc.). Latin *cardinalis* means 'pertaining to a hinge'.

ordinal/ordinary (order of church service)
An 'ordinal' is a directory of church services in general, or a book containing the forms for the 'ordination' of priests. An 'ordinary' is a book containing the order for divine service, especially the mass or, specifically, the service of the mass exclusive of the canon (that part of the service between the Sanctus and the communion). While in ecclesiastical circles, it might be useful to note that an 'ordinary' is also a bishop or archbishop or his deputy regarded as a legal authority. Such a dignitary should not, of course, be confused with a 'cardinal', one of the officials who elects the Pope. All the terms are more widely used in the Roman Catholic church than the Anglican, although the 'ordinary' is an official long established in both Anglican and Common law.

ordinary see **ordinal** (order of church service)

organdie/organza/organzine (type of fine fabric)
'Organdie' is a thin, translucent, usually stiffened muslin with a lasting crisp finish and in colour white, dyed or printed. It is used chiefly for dresses and curtains and

any suitable 'display' of fabric. 'Organza' is made from a mixture of silk or nylon with cotton – it's similar to 'organzie' but not as fine. 'Organzine' is a silk yarn used in weaving silk fabrics. 'Organza' may be an alteration of the trade name 'Lorganza' but the origin of 'organdie' and 'organzine is a mystery. (*Webster* traces 'organzine' back to the town of Urgench in the Soviet Union, where it was said to have been first manufactured.)

organza see **organdie**

organzine see **organdie**

orgastic see **orgiastic**

orgiastic/orgastic (wild, passionate)
'Orgiastic' pertains to 'orgy'; 'orgastic' to 'orgasm'. The latter word is not limited to the physiological sense, since the basic meaning of 'orgasm' is 'immoderate excitement'. In this sense, therefore an 'orgy' could be said to be 'orgastic' as it, too, connotes great indulgence. The alternative (and more common) adjective for 'orgasm' – 'orgasmic' – has come to be used in the 1970s as a 'hip' term of approval: 'How did it go last night?' 'Orgasmic!'

oriental/occidental (Eastern – or Western)
'Oriental' is 'Eastern', and 'occidental' is 'Western'. The 'Orient' is a rather vague geographical term applied to either the countries of Asia generally – and especially Japan – or the countries to the east of the Mediterranean, such as Iran. The 'Occident', a less common word, is the countries of Europe and the USA – by contrast with those of the 'Orient'. The *SOED* notes that 'Orient', in modern American usage, can occasionally be used to mean Europe. This may increase the confusion over the words. Americans, too, can reach the Far Eastern 'Orient' more rapidly by travelling west!

orison see **oration**

Orlon see **nylon**

orotund see **rotund**

orthopaedic/paediatric (pertaining to children's diseases)
'Orthopaedic' relates to the correction of diseases and deformities of the skeletal system, notably the spine, bones, joints and muscles, especially, although not exclusively, in children. The two Greek elements making up the word are 'right' and 'child'. 'Paediatric' relates, simply, to the study and treatment of children's diseases in general.

ostensibly see **ostentatiously**

ostensively see **ostentatiously**

ostentatiously/ostensibly/ostensively
(characterised by showing or demonstrating)
'Ostentatiously' means 'in the manner of a pretentious display', 'so as to deliberately draw attention': 'He ostentatiously straightened the picture on the wall.' 'Ostensibly' means 'outwardly appearing as such', 'professedly': 'He borrowed some money, ostensibly to pay the rent' (but really to back a horse that he hoped would be a winner). 'Ostensively', a rarer word, can be used as an alternative to 'ostensibly', but is primarily a term confined to logic meaning 'in a manner that is immediately demonstrative', 'proving directly'.

ostinato see **obbligato**

outrageous/outré (shocking)
'Outrageous' means either 'very bad' or 'very offensive', as an 'outrageous' crime (which could be either, or both). The word is not, unfortunately, related to 'rage', but derives from an Old French verb, *outrer* (to exceed). It is the past participle of this verb that gives *outré*, meaning 'exceeding the bounds of what is regarded as usual and proper', or simply 'eccentric', 'bizarre' as 'outré' clothes or an 'outré' remark. The word is usually pronounced 'ootray'.

outré see **outrageous**

overtone see **undertone**

Oxford Group/Oxford Movement
(religious movement)
The 'Oxford Group' was an early nickname

for Moral Rearmament, or Buchmanism. (Buchman won support for his ideas at Oxford University in 1921, but the movement has no special association with the city.) The 'Oxford Movement' was the one started in the Church of England by J. H. Newman (later Cardinal Newman), John Keble and others at Oxford University in 1833 with the aim of guiding Anglicanism towards High Church principles or Anglo-Catholicism.

Oxford Movement see **Oxford Group**

P

pace see **vice**

paediatric see **orthopaedic**

pagoda/pergola/portico/gazebo (exotic structure)
The 'pagoda' is well known as the many-storeyed temple or sacred building in India, China, Burma, etc., constructed over the relics of the Buddha or a saint. A 'pergola' is an arbour, or a construction resembling one, formed out of horizontal trellis-work on columns or posts over which vines or other plants are trained. A 'portico' is a kind of porch over the entrance to a temple, church or other building, consisting of a roof supported by columns or piers. A 'gazebo' is a belvedere – a construction such as a turret, pavilion or summerhouse that commands an impressive view. One tentative etymology of the word – a blend of 'gaze' and Latin *videbo* (I shall see) – is as whimsical as the structure itself.

palate/palette (potential artistic vehicle)
Confusion is not normally found in the true sense of the words, respectively 'roof of the mouth' and 'board on which artist

mixes his colours', but in the transferred or metaphorical sense, especially as used by wine writers and music critics. Thus a wine with a 'well-rounded palate' is one which has a full-bodied (or whatever) taste. But what did the music critic of *The Times* mean when he wrote of Prokofiev seeming to represent 'a clean palette and a breath of fresh air' (4 March 1976)? In other words, was his metaphor from painting or wine-drinking? Both a 'clean palette' and a 'clear palate' would represent a latent vehicle for some kind of artistic experience. The use of 'palate' to mean 'sense of taste' is, of course, incorrect, since the taste buds are on the tongue, not on the roof of the mouth.

palette see **palate**

palimpsest see **papyrus**

palmy see **barmy**

palsied see **paralysed**

pampas see **prairie**

panacea/placebo (type of medicine)
A 'panacea' is a remedy for all diseases, a cure for all ills, both physical and figurative. (The word comes from the Greek meaning 'all healing'.) A 'placebo' is a medicine given more to please or placate than to benefit, since the drug that the patient supposes it contains has been replaced by an inactive substance such as sugar. Its application is thus entirely psychological. 'Placebo' is Latin for 'I shall please', this being the opening word of the Latin rite of Vespers for the Dead.

panoply see **canopy**

papyrus/palimpsest (ancient document)
A 'papyrus' is an ancient document or manuscript written on sheets made from the 'papyrus' or paper reed, formerly abundant in Egypt. (The word is actually related to 'paper'.) A 'palimpsest' is a parchment on which the writing has been partially or completely rubbed out to make room for another text. The term is also used of a monumental brass that has been turned and engraved on the reverse side

with a new text. The origin of the word is the Greek *palin* (again) and *psestos* (rubbed smooth).

parade/promenade/esplanade (public place or road designed for walking or driving)
A 'parade' can be a 'promenade' or a place for walking for pleasure or display, although as the name of a street a 'Parade' is usually short, with a row or block of shops. A 'promenade' is usually associated with a seafront at a resort, where it is a road for strolling or driving that runs beside the sea. An 'esplanade' is either a level space between a fortress and a town such as the one at Edinburgh Castle, where the Tattoo is held, or a term used in much the same sense as 'promenade' to apply to a road running along a seafront. The word comes from Latin, via Spanish, with the basic meaning 'levelled'.

parakeet/paroquet/popinjay (kind of parrot)
A 'parakeet' is a kind of small, slender parrot, usually with a long, pointed tail, such as the Australian, or grass 'parakeet'. The word is the anglicised variant of 'paroquet', which is the Old French form. 'Popinjay' means 'parrot' only in an archaic sense. It was also used to apply to the figure of a parrot used as a target for shooting practice. In modern use a 'popinjay' is either a fop or dandy or, in some regions, an alternative name for the green woodpecker. All words are probably related to 'parrot', which in turn may derive from the proper name 'Pierrot' – although one theory traces 'parakeet' and 'paroquet' back to the Italian *parchito* (little parson).

paralysed/petrified/palsied (unable to move)
To be 'paralysed' is to have no power to contract one's muscles; to be 'petrified' is literally to be turned into stone. To be 'paralysed' or 'petrified' with fear, say, means to be unable to move as a result of being terrified. If there is any difference in the shades of meaning it is that a 'paralysed' person cannot make the necessary movements to escape, but a 'petrified' one is rooted to the spot by his rigidity. 'Palsied'

means 'affected with palsy' – a paralysis accompanied by tremulous movements – and hence 'paralysed', although in a secondary sense 'palsied' means 'trembling' or 'tottering'.

parameter see **perimeter**

parochial see **provincial**

paroquet see **parakeet**

parquetry/marquetry (mosaic work in wood)
'Parquetry' is essentially mosaic woodwork in floors or wainscoting. 'Marquetry' is inlaid work of variously coloured woods or other materials mainly in furniture. French *marqueter* means 'to chequer', 'to inlay'.

partially see **partly**

particular/peculiar (special)
The 'particular' advantages of something are the specific or exceptional ones; the 'peculiar' advantages are the distinctive or exclusive ones – possibly even rather unusual or unexpected ones. 'A particular advantage of this job is that I can be home by 4.30.' 'A peculiar advantage of this job is that I can work on Sunday and have Monday off.' A similar distinction exists between the words when used with such nouns as 'interest', 'difficulty', 'problem', 'liking', 'influence'.

partly/partially (not wholly)
'Partly' is the opposite of 'wholly', meaning thus 'in part', 'to some degree'; 'partially' is the opposite of 'completely' and means 'not fully'. A 'partially' blind person crossing the road might thus be 'partly' responsible for a car having to brake suddenly: he cannot be fully blamed as his sight is not perfect.

pash see **crush**

passe-partout/en-tout-cas (type of frame or border)
'Passe-partout' – French for 'passes everywhere' – is the term used for the strips of adhesive paper fastening the two pieces of glass that contain a photograph. (The word

can also apply to the whole frame made with such strips.) 'En-tout-cas' – French for 'in any case' – is the term, properly a trade name, used for a type of all-weather hard tennis court. The phrase is also sometimes used to mean a combined umbrella and parasol.

pastry/pasty/patty/pâté (kind of pie or cake)
'Pastry' is the baked crust of pies or tarts, made of paste or dough; a 'pastry' is a small individual cake, such as a fancy cake. A 'pasty' is a pie filled with anything savoury, or sweet, such as a meat 'pasty', fish 'pasty' or apple 'pasty'. Such a pie has a crust of 'pastry', and is normally not large in size. A 'patty' is a small pie or 'pasty', or a small flat cake of minced beef or some other food – there are even peppermint 'patties'. 'Pâté' is a paste or spread of finely ground liver, meat or fish, usually served as a starter or hors d'oeuvre. 'Pâté de foie gras' – literally 'pastry of fat liver' – is goose liver paste filling, regarded by some gourmets as a worthy rival to caviare. All the words are basically related to 'paste'.

pasty see **pastry**

pâté see **pastry**

pathos/bathos (sad or sentimental sensation)
'Pathos' is that quality of speech or music that evokes a feeling of pity or sympathetic sadness: 'The tale was told with a pathos that drew tears from all those present.' 'Bathos' is at best insincere 'pathos'; at worst it is a descent in speech or music 'from the sublime to the ridiculous'. Pope illustrates 'bathos' with the lines:
Ye Gods! annihilate but Space and Time
And make two lovers happy.
Both words are Greek, meaning respectively 'suffering' and 'depth'.

patty see **pastry**

peculiar see **particular**

Peke see **Pom**

pellagra/podagra (disease)
'Pellagra' – possibly from Italian *pelle agre*

(rough skin) – is a non-contagious disease caused by a deficient diet and marked by skin changes, nervous dysfunction, and diarrhoea. 'Podagra', from the Greek meaning 'foot seizure', is gout – properly in the feet.

pendant/pennant/pennon (type of flag)
A 'pendant' is anything hanging, as an ornament, chandelier, length of rope or ... 'pennant', which is properly a long triangular flag used for signalling, with its widest end next to the mast. In practice a 'pennant' can be any flag used as an emblem. In the USA it is a flag awarded for success in athletics. The sense also coincides to a large degree with 'pennon', which is a distinctive flag having various forms, such as tapering, triangular or swallow-tailed. Originally it was the flag on the lance of a knight. There is thus little difference between the latter words, although a 'pennon' is usually longer and narrower than a 'pennant'.

pennant see **pendant**

pennon see **pendant**

pentathlon see **marathon**

perceptive/percipient/perspicacious/ perspicuous (intelligent, clear, lucid)
'Perceptive' means 'understanding readily or quickly', as a 'perceptive' remark. 'Percipient' means simply 'showing understanding', as, again, in a 'percipient' remark. 'Perspicacious' means 'having the ability to see and distinguish', 'discerning', as a 'perspicacious' mind or wit. 'Perspicuous' means 'clear', 'easily understood', as a 'perspicuous' reason, or 'expressing clearly': 'He is quite clear and perspicuous.' Both 'perceptive' and 'percipient' are commonly used of people: 'He is very perceptive' means 'He understands things well'; 'He is a percipient arguer' means 'He argues with understanding.' The nouns of these adjectives are: of 'perceptive' – 'perceptivity', of 'percipient' – 'percipience', of 'perspicacious' – 'perspicacity' (or less commonly 'perspicaciousness').

percipient see **perceptive**

percolate see **pervade**

peremptory see **perfunctory**

perennial see **annual**

perfunctory/peremptory (brief)
'Perfunctory' means 'performed merely as a routine or an uninteresting duty', 'casual', as a 'perfunctory' inspection (a brief, superficial one) or a 'perfunctory' piece of work (done half-heartedly or carelessly). 'Peremptory' means 'dictatorial', and implies a command that is absolute. Such commands or orders are given in a 'peremptory' tone, i.e. an abrupt one.

pergola see **pagoda**

perigee see **apogee**

perimeter/parameter/periphery
(mathematical term defining length or quantity)
A 'perimeter' is the outer border of a two-dimensional figure or the length of such a border. 'Parameter' has a number of precise and vague senses. Of these, two precise meanings belong to mathematics and statistics. One mathematical definition is 'the line or quantity serving to determine a point, line, figure or quantity in a class of things'. From this evolved the statistical usage: 'a quantity which determines the distribution of a random variable, and which can be estimated from sample data.' (An example of this might be 'fertility and mortality parameters', meaning approximately 'the extent to which people give birth and die'.) This sense has itself given birth to a vogue word of vaguest meaning, as in: 'By the parameters of her upbringing, she's a very well educated person.' In this loose usage 'parameter' simply means 'standard', 'limit', 'condition', 'criterion'. A 'periphery' is much more precise; it is the external boundary of any surface or area, especially a rounded one.

periphery see **perimeter**

permeate see **pervade**

pernickety see **finicky**

perquisite see **requirement**

perseverance see **persistence**

persistence/perseverance/pertinacity/ tenacity (resoluteness, stubbornness)
'Persistence' can be a favourable or unfavourable word, implying either dogged resolve or prolonged annoyance. 'Perseverance' implies an activity maintained in spite of difficulties. 'Pertinacity' suggests an essentially unfavourable doggedness, although the word can also be used in a favourable sense ('They fought with considerable courage and pertinacity'). 'Tenacity' means 'the quality of holding fast', as the 'tenacity' of the attack of an enemy or, more literally, of a firmly binding glue.

persistently see **consistently**

personate see **impersonate**

perspicacious see **perceptive**

perspicuous see **perceptive**

pert see **insolent**

pertinacity see **persistence**

perturb see **disturb**

pervade/permeate/percolate (spread, extend, penetrate)
To 'pervade' is to extend an activity, influence, presence or the like, as the wit that 'pervades' a new novel, or the scent of spring flowers that 'pervades' a room. To 'permeate' is to penetrate or pass through, literally or figuratively, as water that 'permeates' the soil or the new teaching methods that have 'permeated' the schools. To 'percolate' is to 'permeate', but slowly, especially of liquids, as water that 'percolates' through the sand or the new ideas that are beginning to 'percolate' into people's minds. The word is from the Latin with literal meaning 'strain through'.

peseta/peso (unit of currency of Spanish-speaking countries)
The 'peseta' is the basic unit of currency of Spain, equal to 100 *céntimos*. The 'peso' is the unit of Mexico, Cuba, the Philippines and Spanish American countries (equal usually to 100 *centavos*). The 'peso' was also a former Spanish gold coin with a value of eight *reales*.

peso see **peseta**

petrified see **paralysed**

Pharisee see **Philistine**

pharynx see **larynx**

phase see **phrase**

phial/philtre (small bottle – or the drug it contains)
Two rather archaic confusibles. A 'phial' is a small glass vessel for liquids, usually medicine or some kind of potion. A 'philtre' is the potion or drug itself, especially one supposed to arouse amorous feelings, or any magic potion. The 'phil-' element means 'love', as in 'philanthropic' or 'Francophile'.

philanderer see **philanthropist**

philanthropist/philanderer (one who loves his fellow men – or women)
A 'philanthropist' loves all mankind. The word is usually used to apply to a benefactor of some kind. A 'philanderer', from the Greek meaning literally 'man lover', is not one who loves men, but a man who loves women, otherwise a male flirt. Philander was, in an old ballad, the lover of Phillis, and in Beaumont and Fletcher's *Laws of Candy* the lover of Erota. Hence a 'philander-er', or 'Philander-like' person.

Philistine/Pharisee (nickname for a despised person)
The original 'Philistines' were the warlike people who occupied the southern coast of Palestine and harassed the Israelites. The term is now applied to anyone looked down on as lacking in culture or aesthetic refinement, or any 'boor' in general. The 'Phari-

sees', from a Hebrew word meaning 'separated', were the Jewish sect who observed the religious law strictly and claimed a consequent superior sanctity. The word is now used of any self-righteous or hypocritical person.

philtre see **phial**

phoneme/morpheme (linguistic unit)
A 'phoneme' is the basic sound unit in a language. In English it is often, but by no means always, represented by a single letter. In 'phoneme', for example, there are six 'phonemes': one for 'ph', two for 'o' (which is really, in standard speech, something like 'er' followed by 'oo'), one for 'n', one for 'e' and one for 'm'. 'Phonemes' in English are usually represented not by conventional letters but by special symbols, such as those of the International Phonetic Alphabet, in which 'phoneme' appears as *fəuni:m*. (The colon indicates a long vowel sound.) A 'morpheme' is a minimal linguistic unit, often a prefix, root, suffix or ending in a word. In 'confusible', for example, there are three 'morphemes': the prefix 'con-', the root '-fus-' and the suffix '-ible'. The terms derive respectively from the Greek words for 'sound speech' and 'form', with 'morpheme' based on the word 'phoneme'. Both words are quite recent: 'phoneme' was first used in 1923, and 'morpheme' followed two years later.

phosphorescent see **fluorescent**

phrase/phase (unit of a whole)
The two words are surprisingly often confused, with 'phrase' often used for 'phase'. A 'phrase' – from Greek *phrasis* (speech) – is a group of words in speech, notes in music, or motions in dancing that acts as a unit and, with other such units, makes a complete work. In this sense the meaning is thus close to 'stage', which is the basic meaning of 'phase'. A 'phase', however, is not necessarily a repeated or like unit but normally a unit of change or development, such as a 'phase' of the moon (e.g. first quarter or full moon). Doubtless the temptation to say 'phrase' instead of 'phase' has been increased by the association of the Government's 'Pay Code' or

'Phase Four', introduced in 1978 to control inflation, with a 'wage freeze', i.e. a jumble of 'pay', 'stage', 'wage', 'freeze' and 'phrase'.

phrenetic see **frantic**

piazza see **plaza**

piccalilli see **pickles**

pickles/piccalilli/chilli (seasoned relish)
'Pickles' are vegetables such as cucumbers, onions and cauliflowers that have been preserved in vinegar, brine and the like. 'Piccalilli' – which word is probably a blend of 'pickle' and 'chilli' – is a highly seasoned 'pickle' of East Indian origin made of chopped vegetables and hot spices, the whole usually yellowish in colour. 'Chilli', originally an Aztec word, is the pod of a species of capsicum used in 'pickles' and sauces and, in dried form, as the chief ingredient of Cayenne pepper. 'Chilli con carne' – Spanish for 'chilli with meat' – is a Mexican dish made from meat and finely chopped red pepper, usually served with beans, and 'chilli' sauce is made of tomatoes cooked with 'chilli', spices and other seasonings. The preferred American spelling of the word is 'chili'.

piebald see **dappled**

pigeon/wigeon (kind of game bird)
Both birds may end up in a game pie, but they are not related. The 'wigeon' – more usually spelt 'widgeon' – is a kind of wild duck of a size between a mallard and a teal and does not belong to the family called Columbidae that includes the 'pigeon' and dove. Possibly the false association is caused either by 'wigeon' suggesting 'wood pigeon' or by the jingle effect of both words together, itself an unconscious harkback to those nursery tale characters Chicken-Licken, Hen-Len, Turkey-Lurkey and Goose-Loose.

pilaster see **pillar**

pile/pyre (heap of wood on which a dead body is burnt)
The confusion is mainly due to 'funeral

pile' (or 'funeral pyre'). A 'funeral pile' is a heap of wood on which a dead *or* living person or a sacrifice of any kind is burnt. A 'funeral pyre' is a 'pile' of wood for burning a dead body. The first word is basic 'pile'; the second derives from Greek *pyr* (fire).

pillar/pilaster (upright column)
A 'pillar' can be any shape in section – usually round or square – and can be used as a support or stand on its own. A 'pilaster' is a square or triangular 'pillar' with a capital and a base, that forms part of a wall, from which it projects. It may either bear some of the weight or be purely for decoration. Its association with walls, and resemblance to 'plaster', may obscure the word's real meaning.

pimento/pimiento (strong-tasting fruit)
A 'pimento' is the dried fruit of the *Pimenta officinalis*, otherwise known as allspice, or the name of the tree itself. A 'pimiento' is a red Spanish pepper with a sweet, pungent flavour. The 'pimento' berry is used in baking and is often an ingredient of mincemeat. 'Pimento' is often used for 'pimiento', but not the other way round. The confusion is the fault of early Spanish explorers, who seeing the 'pimento' thought it was a type of pepper and called it *pimienta* (pepper).

pimiento see **pimento**

pimp see **poof**

pincers see **pliers**

piquant see **pungent**

piteous see **pitiful**

pitiable see **pitiful**

pitiful/pitiable/piteous (causing pity)
'Pitiful' implies that the person or thing excites pity or is contemptible, as respectively a 'pitiful' sight or a 'pitiful' display of knowledge. 'Pitiable' means 'lamentable', 'wretched', as a 'pitiable' old man living in a 'pitiable' shack in a 'pitiable' condition. 'Piteous' implies an exhibition of suffering and misery, as heard in a

'piteous' groan or seen in a 'piteous' sight. (A 'pitiful' sight itself need not necessarily imply a condition of suffering: a field of flattened corn after heavy rain might be a 'pitiful' sight since one would pity the farmer rather than the corn.)

pizzazz see **razzmatazz**

placebo see **panacea**

plain see **plane**

plane/plain (flat or level surface)
The confusion is not between 'plane' = 'smoothing tool', 'aeroplane' and 'plain' = 'flat stretch of land' but between 'plain' and 'plane' in the sense 'flat or level surface', either as a mathematical term or in extended use (e.g. a moral 'plane'). It's a matter of spotting the spelling: 'plain' means only the flat stretch of land. All the other senses are 'plane'. (There is of course the noun 'plain' in knitting, as the opposite of 'purl', but this comes direct from the adjective 'plain' meaning 'ordinary', 'simple'.) The two words are in fact of identical origin – Latin *planus* (plain), with the spelling 'plane' differentiated only in the seventeenth century.

plangent see **pungent**

plaza/piazza (square on the continent)
The words are respectively Spanish and Italian, and related to 'place'. Both are used for a public square or open space in a town or city, although a 'piazza' can also be an arcade or covered walk, for example round a square or running along the front of a building.

Pleistocene/Pliocene/Miocene
(geological epoch)
In chronological order, the epochs are 'Miocene', 'Pliocene', 'Pleistocene', their Greek names meaning 'less recent', 'more recent', and 'most recent'. The 'Pleistocene' epoch includes the Ice Age, which was roughly a million years ago, immediately preceding historic times. The 'Pliocene' epoch was around fifteen million years ago, and the 'Miocene' thirty-five million.

pliers/pincers (tool with pivoted limbs forming a pair of jaws)
'Pliers' are small 'pincers' used for bending (plying) wire, holding small objects, and the like. 'Pincers' are used for gripping (pinching) things. Unlike 'pliers' the jaws are rounded, with a sizeable circular area between them. The jaws of 'pliers' are straight, or slightly tapering.

Pliocene see **Pleistocene**

podagra see **pellagra**

poignant see **pungent**

polyester see **polythene**

Polynesia see **Micronesia**

polystyrene see **polythene**

polythene/polystyrene/polyurethane/ polyester (plastic or similar artificial product)
All terms refer to a type of polymer, which is a chemical compound of high molecular weight derived either by a combination of many smaller molecules – Greek *polymeres* means 'of many parts' – or by the condensation of many smaller molecules so as to eliminate water, alcohol, etc. 'Polythene' is a plastic polymer of ethylene, used for containers, electric insulation, packaging and the like. 'Polystyrene' is a clear plastic polymer of styrene having good mechanical properties and, among other things, the ability to resist moisture and chemicals, so that it is used for the housings of such large domestic appliances as refrigerators and air conditioners. 'Polyurethane' is a polymer of urethane best known as a flexible foam for upholstery material, mattresses and the like. 'Polyester' is a term used for a number of polymerised esters (compounds formed by the condensation of an alcohol and an acid with the elimination of water) familiar in a wide range of clothing and home furnishings.

polyurethane see **polythene**

Pom/Peke/pug (breed of toy dog)
The 'Pom' or Pomeranian is said to have

been bred down to its present five pounds or less from a thirty-pound sheepdog in Pomerania, a region now mostly in Poland along the Baltic coast. A toy dog with erect ears, it has a thick coat standing out around its neck and shoulders. The breed was a favourite with Queen Victoria. The 'Peke' or Pekinese came to Britain from China in 1860 after the sacking of the Summer Palace in Peking when three Allied officers brought back five of the Imperial pets. Most of today's 'Pekes', however, are descendants of those smuggled out of China at the end of the last century. Their distinctive feature is their wide, flat head and short, wrinkled muzzle. The 'pug' also originated in China and became especially popular in the Netherlands in the sixteenth century (the name of the breed is of Dutch origin). This is the dog, rather bigger than a 'Peke', with a wrinkled face, upturned nose and tight, curled tail. The breed is neither noticeably 'pugnacious' nor unduly 'pygmy', in spite of the suggested association with these words.

pomade/pomander (scented medicinal substance)
'Pomade' is a scented ointment for the scalp and hair – originally for the skin and perhaps made with apples (French *pommes*). 'Pomander' is, or was, a blend of aromatic substances, often in the form of a ball, carried on the person as a perfume or guard against infection. Apples come in here, too, as the name derives from Old French *pome d'ambre* (apple of amber). The present form of the word is a corruption of earlier 'pomeamber'.

pomander see **pomade**

ponce see **poof**

poof/ponce/pimp (sexually or morally suspect person)
A 'poof' is a slang term – either from 'puff' meaning 'braggart' or the disdainful interjection 'poof!' – for a male homosexual or effeminate man. Confusion with 'ponce' is largely due to the verb 'ponce' meaning 'move or walk about effeminately'. Properly a 'ponce' – the origin may be in

'pounce' – is someone who lives off a prostitute's earnings. This sense links the word with 'pimp', who is a man that solicits for a prostitute or a brothel, in other words a procurer. The term is also used of any contemptible person, especially a tale-bearer. The suggestion that 'pimps' originated in the Dorset village of Pimperne, near Blandford, seems a little unrealistic.

pop-art see **op-art**

popinjay see **parakeet**

poplin/Crimplene/Terylene (strong fabric used for clothing)
'Poplin' is a finely-ribbed mercerised cotton material used chiefly for dresses, blouses, children's wear and the like. It is said to have been originally made either in the Belgian textile town of Poperinge or in the papal city of Avignon, in the south of France. If the latter, it is possible the word came to English from Italian *papalina* (papal) via French *popeline*. 'Crimplene' is a crimped form of 'Terylene', which itself is a synthetic polyester fibre made from *ter*ephthalic acid and eth*ylene* glycol.

portico see **pagoda**

pose/propose/propound (suggest, put forward)
To 'pose' is to put or set a problem or question, often a difficult or embarrassing one. The word was originally 'appose', a variant of 'oppose'. To 'propose' something is simply to offer it for consideration or acceptance, and this is the basic meaning of 'propound', which is, though, a considerably more bookish word.

possum/opossum (kind of animal with a pouch and distinctive toes)
'Possum' can be simply a colloquial term for 'opossum', although the phrase 'to play possum', meaning to pretend to be unconscious, as the animal itself does to escape danger, is a fixed one. If a distinction is made, however, the 'opossum' is the North American animal, properly *Didelphis virginiana*, that lives in trees or close to water, is about the size of a large cat, and has a pouch and a thumbed hind-foot. Its name

derives from a Virginian Indian word meaning 'white beast'. The variant 'possum', on the other hand, is often reserved for one of a number of Australian animals – all phalangers, i.e. having webbed toes – that resemble the true American 'opossum'.

postulate see **stipulate**

potash/potassium (chemical element or its compound)
'Potash' – originally 'pot ashes', a translation of the early Dutch *potasschen* – is 'potassium' carbonate (K_2CO_3), a crude impure form of which was got from wood *ash* evaporating in *pots*. Caustic 'potash' is 'potassium' hydroxide (KOH). 'Potash' is thus always a compound of 'potassium', which itself is a silvery white metallic element with chemical symbol K (from Latin *kalium*, related to 'alkali'). Compounds of 'potassium' are used as fertilisers and for manufacturing specially hard glasses.

potassium see **potash**

prairie/pampas (extensive grassy plain in America)
'Prairies', from French *pré* (field, meadow), are tracts of treeless grassland with fertile soil as found, typically, in the upper Mississippi valley (in the USA) and in Canada. The 'pampas' are in South America. They are vast grassy plains in the rain shadow of the Andes, in Argentina, with the word originating in the Quechua *pampa* (plain). Similar plains north of the Amazon are known as 'llanos' – Spanish for 'plains'.

precede see **proceed**

precipitately/precipitously (hurriedly)
The basic distinction is between 'precipitate' meaning 'rash' and 'precipitous' meaning 'steep'. To leave a room 'precipitately' is thus to hurry out of it without regard for the consequences of your action; to leave it 'precipitously' is to rush headlong out of it for some reason.

precipitously see **precipitately**

précis see **résumé**

predestined see **designed**

predicate see **predict**

predict/predicate (state)
To 'predict' a thing is to foretell or prophesy it: 'An easy win for the home team this afternoon is predicted.' To 'predicate' something is to state that it is real or true: 'I think we may predicate that his motives are sincere' – that is, we may confidently say that they are. In American usage, 'predicate' can mean 'base': 'We are predicating our plans on those assumptions.' In general English usage, too, 'predicate' can mean 'imply', 'connote': 'Grass predicates greenness.' The words literally mean 'say before' and 'state before'.

predominate/preponderate (prevail)
To 'predominate' is to dominate over all others, to be more widely prevalent or noticeable, as a forest in which pine trees 'predominate'. To 'preponderate' is literally 'to exceed in weight', hence to 'predominate' in power, force or influence. 'These reasons preponderate over all others.' In practice, however, the terms are often used to mean exactly the same: 'to prevail' or 'to exceed'. Even so, 'preponderate' has a definite connotation of weight or authority.

preface/prelude/prologue (preliminary part of something)
A 'preface' is a preliminary statement by the author or editor of a book explaining its aim and range. Unlike an introduction, it is by convention not regarded as forming a part of the work as a whole. In a general sense it is anything preliminary or preceding. A 'prelude' is literally something 'played beforehand', and is a preliminary event, act or performance of some kind that hints of something greater to come. In musical terms a 'prelude' is either a piece preceding an important movement, such as the 'preludes' that precede the fugues in Bach's Forty-Eight, or an independent piece, as Chopin's twenty-four piano Preludes which are complete in

themselves. Both 'preface' and 'prologue' have the same original sense in, respectively, Latin and Greek – 'spoken beforehand'. A 'prologue' is usually found in a play, where it is an introductory speech drawing the attention of the audience to the theme of the play. More loosely it is the 'preface' or introduction to any poem or novel. One of the most famous 'prologues' in English is the one to Chaucer's *Canterbury Tales*.

prefatory see **preparatory**

preliminary see **preparatory**

prelude see **preface**

premonition see **presentiment**

preoccupied see **occupied**

preparatory/prefatory/preliminary (introductory)
A 'preparatory' remark at the beginning of a speech is one that 'prepares' those present for the speech as a whole – virtually an introduction, in fact. A 'prefatory' remark is one that explains the theme or aim of the speech – one that acts as a preface. A 'preliminary' remark might well not relate directly to the speech at all, but simply be one that precedes it. 'Preliminary' notices or examinations, however, are ones that precede more important notices or exams – the ones before the real thing. The word literally means 'before the threshold'.

preponderate see **predominate**

prerequisite see **requirement**

prescience see **presentiment**

presentiment/prescience/premonition (a feeling beforehand)
A 'presentiment' (not, incidentally, a 'presentment', which is an act of presenting or a legal statement) is a feeling that something evil or unpleasant is going to happen – a foreboding. 'Prescience' is knowing or seeing something beforehand, literally or figuratively – in other words foreknowledge or foresight. A 'premoni-

tion' is similar to a 'presentiment', but has the implication that the feeling is more of a warning, and therefore that possibly the unpleasantness or evil to come can perhaps be avoided or at least mitigated.

preserve see **conserve** (keep carefully) or **reservation** (tract of land set apart for special purpose)

presume/assume (suppose, take for granted)
'You'll come, I presume?': the implication is that I'm taking it for granted that you will, and I would be surprised if you didn't. 'You'll come, I assume?': the implication is that I am expecting you to because I have so decided or because it is your duty or obligation to. 'Assume' thus almost hints at an already completed action or a precondition, while 'presume' relates to a simultaneous action or one in the future. To use 'assume' for 'presume' can seem presumptious, as well as being incorrect.

pretension/pretentiousness (claim)
Both words can mean 'state of pretending to be more important or clever than one really is', but in addition 'pretension' has the basic meaning 'claim', as in 'I have no pretensions to being an expert on this'.

pretentiousness see **pretension**

preternatural see **supernatural**

prim/prissy/sissy (fussy, 'old-maidish')
'Prim' means 'formal and correct', 'demure', although applied to a woman it implies prudishness: 'a prim little miss'. 'Prissy' is used more of men in much the same sense: 'prudishly prim', with a hint even of effeminacy. 'Sissy' or 'cissy' is a favourite children's word for 'coward' although it, too, can be used of a man or boy to mean 'effeminate or girlish person'. The origin of 'prim' is not clear – there may be a connection with 'prime', i.e. 'excellent'. 'Prissy' seems to be a combination of 'prim' and 'sissy', with 'sissy' itself probably derived from 'sister'.

primary see **prime**

prime/primary (first)
'Prime' has the implication of 'first in importance or quality', as the 'Prime' Minister or 'prime' beef. 'Primary' relates mainly to being either first in time or great (but not first) in importance, as a 'primary' cause or a 'primary' consideration.

primeval/primordial (primitive, elementary)
'Primeval' means 'belonging to the first or earliest times', 'very old', as a 'primeval' forest. 'Primordial' relates to the very earliest times, the real beginning, as 'primordial' life or matter. The origin of the word is in Latin *primus* (first) and *ordiri* (to begin).

primordial see **primeval**

primp see **prink**

prink/primp (dress carefully)
To 'prink' oneself up is to smarten oneself up, especially fussily or showily. To 'primp' – sometimes used as an equivalent for 'prink' – properly means to dress or deck with nicety or affectation. The senses are thus very close. Possibly the difference can be effectively expressed by the associated words 'prank' and 'prim', to which the verbs are apparently respectively related.

prissy see **prim**

procedure/proceedings (course of action)
'At this point in the procedure' one sometimes hears, instead of 'proceedings'. A 'procedure' is the way of doing something, as a special 'procedure' for booking seats. The word has a legal or parliamentary ring to it. The 'proceedings' are the action itself with a specially defined sense in 'record of the transactions of a society' and 'legal action in court'.

proceed/precede (go ahead)
To 'proceed' is to go ahead, especially after stopping. To 'precede' is to *be* ahead, whether moving or not, in either time or importance. Barons 'precede' baronets in rank, and both could 'proceed' in a procession. The trouble is caused by the prefixes, since both 'pro-' and 'pre-' can mean 'before'.

proceedings see **procedure**

proclaim see **announce**

proclivity see **propensity**

procure see **secure**

prodigy see **progeny**

profligate see **prolific**

progeny/prodigy/protégé (special kind of child)
'Progeny' is a general word for offspring. It is a singular word with a collective meaning. A 'prodigy' is a child – or any person – who has special gifts or talents: Mozart, giving public recitals of his own works at six, was a musical 'prodigy'. (The word is related to 'prodigious' in the sense 'unusual', 'wonderful'.) A 'protégé' is a person, either a child or someone older, who is under the protection or patronage of another. The term, which is French for 'protected', was first used in English in 1778. No doubt the exclusive association of all three words with children is partly due to the biblical story of the Prodigal Son – but 'prodigal' here means simply 'wasteful', 'extravagant'.

prolific/prolix/profligate (abundant, excessive)
'Prolific' is the commonest word of the three, meaning 'producing abundantly', as a 'prolific' writer. 'Prolix' means 'excessively or tediously lengthy', especially of a person who reads or writes. Marcel Proust was perhaps a 'prolix' writer as well as a 'prolific' one. 'Profligate' means 'utterly immoral' or 'recklessly extravagant'. Some people regard Proust as having been both.

prolix see **prolific**

prologue see **preface**

promenade see **parade**

prone see **prostrate**

H

pronounce see **announce**

propensity/proclivity (tendency)
Both words mean 'natural or habitual inclination', but 'proclivity' has the implication of an innate predisposition, especially towards something undesirable or unwholesome. One might thus have a 'propensity' for exaggerating but a 'proclivity' for extravagance. This 'bad' connotation is reflected in the word's Latin origin: *clivus* is a slope. 'Propensity', on the other hand, is literally merely a 'hanging forward'.

propitious see **auspicious**

proposal/proposition (offer, suggestion)
A 'proposal' is any plan put forward for acception or rejection. A 'proposition' is specifically an advantageous offer, as a business 'proposition' or a paying 'proposition'. However, 'proposition' does not have this connotation in some specialised senses; in mathematics and music, for example, 'proposition' means simply 'statement'.

propose see **pose**

proposition see **proposal**

propound see **pose**

prostrate/prone/supine (lying flat)
Both 'prostrate' and 'prone' means 'lying face downwards', with 'prostrate' having the implication of doing so as a sign of humiliation or submission. 'Supine' means 'lying on one's back'. Where 'prostrate' means 'overcome by illness or grief', however, one may be lying in any position – or not lying at all.

protagonist see **antagonist**

protégé see **progeny**

provided see **providing**

providing/provided (if, on condition that)
'Providing' implies the fulfilment of a condition: 'Providing he's not late we can leave at seven', i.e. 'If he is not late, we shall

be able to leave at seven.' 'Provided' implies a stipulation: 'Provided he's not late, we can leave at seven', i.e. 'If he does as he should, and arrives on time, we can leave at seven.' But in practice the words are frequently used interchangeably. A distinction can be made, however, provided one is careful.

provincial/parochial (narrow-minded)
The references are to the inhabitants of, respectively, a province and a parish, both limited areas. When used to mean 'narrow-minded', 'provincial' has a connotation of the rustic or 'country-bumpkin', and 'parochial' the implication that the outlook or opinion is not only narrow but limited. These nuances are brought out in phrases such as 'provincial manners' and 'parochial interests'.

psychiatrist see **psychologist**

psychologist/psychiatrist (one who has made a scientific study of the mind)
'Psychologist' is the broader term, for one who is trained in psychology, the study of the mind, or of mental states and processes in general. A 'psychiatrist' actually treats mental diseases or disorders. The '-iatrist' ending is Greek *iatros* (physician), as in 'paediatrician' (doctor specialising in the treatment of children's diseases).

pug see **Pom**

puke see **reach**

pulsar see **quasar**

pungent/poignant/piquant/plangent (sharp, painful)
'Pungent' means 'sharp to the taste or smell', 'biting' or, figuratively, 'powerful', as 'pungent' criticism. 'Poignant' shares the literal sense of 'pungent' but is more commonly used figuratively to mean 'painful' or 'moving' as a 'poignant' remark (which could be either). 'Piquant' means 'agreeably pungent', as a 'piquant' sauce or 'piquant' wit. 'Plangent' means either 'resounding noisily' as 'plangent' waves, or 'resounding mournfully' as the 'plangent' sound of a violin. The word's association

with 'plaintive' is justified, since both senses derive from Latin *plangere* (to beat – in the latter case, the breast).

puny/pusillanimous (feeble)
'Puny' means 'of less than normal size and strength', hence 'weakly', 'petty', as a 'puny' fellow or a 'puny' excuse. It derives from 'puisne', which spelling, pronounced the same way, is still in legal use for a junior judge in the High Court. The word is French: *puis* (after) *né* (born). (The belief was that a child born later would be more frail than those born before him.) 'Pusillanimous' means literally 'petty-spirited', that is, 'cowardly', 'faint-hearted'.

pusillanimous see **puny**

pyre see **pile**

Quadragesima see **Quinquagesima**

quail see **quiver**

quake see **quiver**

qualmish see **queasy**

quantum see **quota**

quark see **quasar**

quasar/pulsar/quark (scientific phenomenon of unknown or uncertain origin)
The three are relative newcomers to the scientific scene. 'Quasars' were discovered in 1963. They are starlike objects with a high-energy electromagnetic radiation of unknown constitution or structure. The most common theory to explain a 'quasar'

is that of the 'black hole': a dense cloud of gas in the centre of a galaxy collapses under its own weight to form a 'black hole' which then becomes the nucleus of a 'quasar'. The word derives from '*quasi*-stell*ar* source'. A 'pulsar', or '*puls*ating st*ar*', is a source of pulsed radio signals detected within a galaxy but outside the solar system, now thought to be a rapidly rotating neutron star. The 'pulsar' made its debut in the astronomical field in 1968. A 'quark' is the term used for one of three hypothetical particles with three corresponding anti-particles (antiquarks) which have been postulated on the basis of all other particles in the universe. The 'quark' was first propounded in 1964 and owes its name to the 'three quarks for Muster Mark' in Joyce's *Finnegans Wake*.

quaver see **quiver**

queasy/qualmish/squeamish (sickened, nauseated)
To feel 'queasy' is to feel sick. A 'queasy' stomach is upset by 'queasy' food. The origin of the suggestive word is uncertain – possibly a blend of 'queer' and 'uneasy'. 'Qualmish', of course, relates to 'qualms', which are momentary feelings of nausea or sudden misgivings. 'Squeamish' means 'easily nauseated or sickened' or 'easily shocked'. 'There's no need to be squeamish; any man should be able to change a baby's nappies.'

quiff/coif (type of covering for the head)
A 'quiff' is a lock or curl of hair on the forehead, especially a single, oiled one. A 'coif', from which 'quiff' may derive, is a hood-shaped cap worn under a veil, as by nuns or, as a historical garment, an ecclesiastical or legal headdress worn by men from the twelfth to the sixteenth century. Later, it was a close-fitting white or coloured cap worn by women (from the sixteenth to the eighteenth century.)

Quinquagesima/Quadragesima
(Sunday in the church calendar)
'Quinquagesima' is the Sunday before Lent. Latin *quinquaginta* means 'fifty' and this Sunday is fifty days before Easter, reckoning inclusively. 'Quadragesima' is

the following Sunday, i.e. the first in Lent. Although *quadraginta* means 'forty', the Sunday is not forty days before Easter, however reckoned. Possibly the name was given on an analogy with 'Quinquagesima', or refers to the forty days of Lent. See also the even more illogical **Septuagesima**.

quirky see **kinky**

quiver/quaver/quake/quail   (tremble, show fear)
To 'quiver' is to shake with a slight but rapid motion, as with fear or excitement. To 'quaver' is to shake tremulously, as with apprehension or weakness. To 'quake' is to shake or shudder, as with cold, weakness, fear or anger. To 'quail' is not to shake at all, but to shrink or flinch with fear.

quorum see **quota**

quota/quorum/quantum (required amount)
A 'quota' is the fixed or due amount or number of something, or the proportional part of a word. The word comes from medieval Latin *quota pars* (how great a part). A 'quorum' is the term used for the required number of people needed for business to be transacted, as at a meeting. For Parliament to sit, for example, there must be a 'quorum' of forty MPs, i.e. a minimum number of forty. Latin *quorum* (of whom) was a word used in commissions in a sentence translating as: 'of whom we will that you . . . be one'. A 'quantum' – Latin 'how great' or 'how much' – is a required, desired or permitted amount. The term is used in physics to apply to a unit quantity of energy proportional to a frequency of radiation.

quote/cite (repeat the words of another)
To 'quote' is to repeat someone else's words by way of illustration or as an authority. To 'cite' is either to 'quote' or simply to name someone or something, but specifically as an authority. Unexpectedly, the two words are not related: 'quote' derives from Latin *quot* (how many) – the reference being to marking a text or passage with numbers, i.e. dividing it into chapters

and verses – and 'cite' comes from Latin *ciere* (to set moving).

rabbit see **babble**

rabble see **babble**

rabid see **avid**

raise see **rise**

raise the anchor see **weigh anchor**

rajah/maharajah/mahatma (title of Indian ruler or leader)
'Rajah', which is ultimately related to Latin *rex* (king), is the title of an Indian king or prince or a Malay chief. 'Maharajah', meaning 'great rajah' is the title of certain of the greater Indian princes. 'Mahatma', meaning 'great-souled', was the title given to a wise and holy Buddhist leader in India. The most famous of the 'Mahatmas' in recent times was Gandhi, whose title connoted his great spiritual reputation.

rallentando/ritardando/ritenuto
(musical direction to decrease tempo)
The words are Italian, meaning respectively 'abating', 'retarding', and 'restraining'. 'Rallentando' implies a slackening of the tempo, 'ritardando' a gradual slowing down, and 'ritenuto' a holding back, i.e. an immediate slowing, not a gradual one. The usual abbreviated forms of the words, as encountered in musical parts, are 'rall.', 'rit.', and either (confusingly) 'rit.' or 'riten.'.

rambler/rover/ranger (wanderer, or title for member of sports or other organisation)
The words literally mean 'one who

rambles' (wanders in a leisurely or aimless way), 'one who roves' (wanders in search of something), and 'one who ranges' (explores or searches over a wide area). In sporting terms, 'rambler' is usually used by members of walking or cycling clubs, and 'rover' and 'ranger' by members of football clubs, e.g. Blackburn, Bristol, Doncaster and Tranmere 'Rovers' and Queens Park 'Rangers'. 'Ranger' in American usage is a warden or member of the mounted police, and in Britain the keeper of a royal forest or park. In the scout movement, 'Rover' Scouts are now Venture Scouts (senior scouts aged sixteen to twenty), but the guides still have 'Rangers' or 'Ranger Guides' (senior girl guides aged fourteen to eighteen).

ranch/range (type of farm in America for grazing and rearing cattle)
A 'ranch' is, at its loosest, any farm in the west of the USA, or Canada and Australia, especially if a large one. A 'range' is, properly, a region in which cattle or sheep can graze. With 'ranch', however, the association is primarily with the buildings of the establishment; 'range' suggests more the animals and pasture land.

rancid see **rank**

randy/raunchy/rangy (uninhibited, fast and loose)
All three words suggest a type of animal zeal. 'Randy' is most commonly used in the sense 'lustful', 'lecherous', although on a Scottish tongue can mean either **lusty** or **boisterous**. Doubtless this is the preferred sense of males bearing the forename Randy (properly an abbreviated form of Randolph), although the *double entendre* is really no *entendre* at all. 'Raunchy', a word of American origin, has the basic connotation of something that has fallen below standard. The word thus has two main meanings: 'slovenly', 'sloppy' – this in fact is the only sense given in the *Dictionary of Misunderstood, Misused, Mispronounced Words* edited by Laurence Urdang (Nelson, 1972) – and, more commonly, 'earthy', 'lewd', especially of speech or style of writing. 'Rangy' is defined by the *Concise Oxford Dictionary* (1976 edition) as 'tall and slim' (of a person), although *Chambers* prefers 'long-legged and thin', which is perhaps rather closer to the sense of the word as it is commonly used. ('Tall and slim' suggests gracefulness, but a 'rangy' person is actually on the ungainly side.) 'Randy' may be related to 'rant', but 'raunchy' is of uncertain origin: it can hardly be a blend of 'randy' and 'paunchy', say, although the combination certainly conjures up the required degree of coarseness and grossness. 'Rangy' is connected with 'range': the image is of long limbs covering a wide area.

range see **ranch**

ranger see **rambler**

rangy see **randy**

rank/rancid (strong, sour)
'Rank' means 'offensively strong', especially of a smell or taste, as 'rank' cheese or a 'rank' cigar. 'Rancid' has basically the same meaning, but an additional implication that what is producing the smell or taste has gone bad or become stale, as 'rancid' butter or fat.

rapacious/voracious (greedy)
'Rapacious' means 'inordinately greedy', especially with regard to money. Of an animal it means 'feeding on living prey'. 'Voracious' means 'devouring, or inclined to devour, a large amount', as a 'voracious' appetite or a 'voracious' reader.

raunchy see **randy**

ravage/ravish (seize violently)
To 'ravage' is to destroy, damage badly or plunder, as a wind that 'ravages' a wood, waves that 'ravage' the shore and an enemy that 'ravages' a town. To 'ravish' is basically 'seize and carry off by force', hence 'carry a woman off by force', hence 'rape'. But 'ravish' also means 'fill with delight', 'enrapture', as a 'ravishing' scene. For more on these lines see **ravishing**.

ravaging see **ravishing**

ravening see **ravishing**

ravenous see **ravishing**

ravish see **ravage**

ravishing/ravenous/famished/ ravening/ravaging (showing pangs of desire)
'My dear, I'm absolutely ravished!' mistakenly exclaimed an elderly maiden lady as she prepared to go out with a friend to lunch. Possibly even 'ravishing' would have been little better. 'Ravishing', apart from its verbal sense (see **ravage**), means 'delightful', 'charming'. 'Ravenous' means 'very hungry', as 'ravenous' beasts in search of prey. (The word has no link with the bird 'raven', in spite of the creature's greedy, predacious nature.) 'Famished' means also 'very hungry', with the strict sense 'suffering from a famine'. 'Ravening' (also not connected with the bird) means 'seizing and devouring', as 'ravening' wolves. The adjective is related to the verb 'to raven' meaning 'plunder'. 'Ravaging' is the adjective of **ravage** and in fact related to 'ravine' – not directly the English word but the Old French *ravine* meaning 'rush of water'.

rayon see **nylon**

razzmatazz/pizzazz (lively activity or display)
These jazzy words with four z's apiece are very much of the twentieth century. 'Razzmatazz', which may be a variant of 'razzle' or 'razzle-dazzle', means 'to-do', 'noisy fuss': 'After all the razzmatazz of last week's visit I'm quite glad to have a quiet evening at home.' 'Pizzazz' (also spelt 'pizazz' and 'pazazz') is an expressive word, of apparently arbitrary origin, used to denote the quality of being exciting or attractive or spirited. It's something of a vogue word among art critics: a new play or production of some kind is said to have – or lack – 'pizzazz', an indefinable 'zap' or 'zing' or 'zip'. (Many words starting with or containing 'z' themselves have 'pizzazz'. See, for example, **jazzy**.)

reach/retch/keck/puke/cat (vomit, or make effort to vomit)
Five colourful if rather nauseating words.

Only 'puke' and 'cat' actually mean 'vomit'; the other three mean 'attempt to vomit'. 'Reach' is a variant of 'retch'. Possibly it is an assimilation to a more acceptable word, with its incidental but apposite suggestion of 'reach over'. 'Retch' itself comes from an Old English verb *hraecan* (to clear the throat). 'Keck', which is related to 'choke', has the same meaning, but also is used in the sense 'be disgusted', 'feel loathing': 'His servile manner makes me keck.' All the verbs are partly or wholly imitative in origin, although 'cat' is directly derived from the phrase 'sick as a cat'.

reap/wreak (endure – or cause)
A writer in the *Times Higher Educational Supplement*, no less, talked of implications that had a 'potential to reap havoc in our universities' (13 February 1976). He meant 'wreak', of course. To 'reap', in its figurative use, is to suffer as a consequence, as in the following two proverbs, which are both of biblical origin, 'As you sow, so shall you reap' and 'Sow the wind, and reap the whirlwind'. Possibly the association with disaster causes the confusion, since 'wreak' – which in common use means simply 'cause' – usually applies to something damaging, as when one 'wreaks' havoc or 'wreaks' one's vengeance on someone.

rebuff see **refute**

rebuke see **reproach**

rebut see **refute**

recall/recollect (remember)
To 'recall' is to remember something specifically, and usually clearly, as one 'recalls' an occasion, someone's face, or a promise made. To 'recollect' is to 'recall' with an effort, the implication being that one has to 'collect' or 'muster' one's thoughts. The two verbs are often used indiscriminately as mock-bookish alternatives for 'remember': 'I don't recall the occasion.'

recant see **retract**

reckless/feckless (irresponsible, careless)
To be 'reckless' is to be quite careless of the consequences of one's actions. To be 'feckless' is literally to be without 'feck', a Scottish variant of 'effect'. The word thus means 'futile', 'ineffective'.

recollect see **recall**

reconcile/conciliate (placate, make agree)
To 'reconcile', of people, is to bring them together after they have disagreed. Of things, it is to make them compatible. Of people and things, it is to make the people come to terms with the things (or person with the thing). All three of these meanings are brought out in: 'She reconciled the friends who had quarrelled'; 'I can't reconcile the two points of view'; 'He reconciled me to accepting his case.' To 'conciliate' somebody is to placate him by soothing or pacifying, to win him over by doing or saying something to please him: 'I conciliated Fred by telling him that his hollyhocks were much taller than mine.' Or it is simply to 'reconcile'. The context or situation should tell which sense is intended.

recourse see **resource**

recreant see **refugee**

redoubted see **undoubted**

redound see **resound**

reflation see **inflation**

Reformation see **Renaissance**

refugee/renegade/runagate/recreant (escaper or deserter)
A 'refugee' is someone seeking refuge by fleeing to another country. A 'renegade' is one who deserts some party or cause for another. The word comes from the Spanish *renegar* (to renounce, renege). A 'runagate' is an archaic word for a fugitive or runaway especially one who has become a vagabond, The word may be influenced by 'renegade' but 'agate' still exists as a northern dialect word meaning 'away'. A 'recreant' – no

doubt falsely influenced by 'miscreant' – is a coward.

refurbished see **refurnished**

refurnished/refurbished (renewed, restored)
'Refurnished', of course, is 'furnished again', 'fitted with new furniture', 'resupplied'. It's the domestic association that supplies the link. 'Refurbished' is thus 'furbished again', with 'furbish' itself meaning 'polish', 'make bright and new again'. One 'refurbishes' much more often than one 'refurnishes', though, since one 'furnishing' lasts a long time but things have to be polished and brightened up repeatedly.

refute/rebut/rebuff (oppose)
To 'refute' – not related to 'refuse', although this suggests it – is to prove someone or something to be in error. One can thus 'refute' a statement or the person who made the statement. To 'rebut' – literally 're-butt' (as if with the head) – is to 'refute' by means of evidence or argument, repel a blow by giving a blow, as it were. To 'rebuff' is to check or snub, usually abruptly: 'She rebuffed his advances.' Here, too, the origin is a 'blow back', but in this case from the Italian *ribuffo* 'reproof' – literally 'puff back'.

regal see **royal**

rehoboam see **jeroboam**

Reichsrat see **Bundeswehr**

Reichstag see **Bundeswehr**

Reichswehr see **Bundeswehr**

reign/rein (control)
The confusion is not so much between what kings and queens do on the one hand and coachmen and cabbies do (or did) on the other, but in turns of phrase such as 'give free rein (?reign) to one's imagination'. Surely, it might be argued, if one gives something its 'reign' one allows it to take charge in some way, have control, hold

sway – in short, reign. The correct confusible in the phrase is in fact 'rein', the metaphor being that of slackening the rein (which basically checks or limits) of a horse and allowing it a free head. In passing, the 'rein' of 'reindeer' is nothing to do with a horse's 'rein': it is the Old Norse *hreinn* (reindeer) (with English 'deer' added).

rein see **reign**

reiterate see **repeat**

relegate see **delegate**

relic/relict (remains of something valuable)
A 'relic' is an interesting or valuable memento of the past, as a 'relic' of the Stone Age, or a custom which is a 'relic' or survival of the past. 'Relics', in a religious sense, are the holy remains of a saint or venerated person. 'Relict' is usually found in the plural in the sense 'remains', 'remnants', as the 'relicts' of a once glorious city. In the singular it can mean 'survivor' in much the same sense as 'relic' although this form of the word has a rarefied aura. In ecology, a 'relict' is a plant or animal species living in an environment that is not typical for it. Such a plant might well be a 'migrant' (see **immigrant**).

relict see **relic**

remonstrate see **demonstrate**

Renaissance/Restoration/Reformation/Risorgimento (historical period and turning point)
Four great 'come-backs' in European history. The 'Renaissance', or 'rebirth', was the revival in the arts, letters and learning generally throughout Europe in the fourteenth to sixteenth centuries, marking the transition from the medieval to the modern world. The movement began in Italy, with the 'rebirth' regarded as that of the classical world. The 'Restoration' was the re-establishing or 'restoring' of the monarchy in England after the Commonwealth (1649–53) and Protectorate (1653–1660) of Cromwell. It was marked by the return of Charles II, and his subsequent reign (1660–85). (The term sometimes extends to the reign (1685–8) of James II.) The name has a cultural significance as well, especially in the field of literature: the period produced such famous writers as Dryden, Congreve, Pepys, Samuel Butler and Sir William Temple. 'Restoration' comedies, or comedies of manners, were a notable feature of the age. Their wit, elegance and stylishness marked a resurgence of theatrical life after the years of Puritanism. The 'Reformation' was the religious sixteenth century movement which had as its aim the 're-forming' of the Roman Catholic church and which led to the establishment of the Protestant churches and to that of the Anglican church in particular. The 'Risorgimento', literally 'resurrection', was the movement for the liberation and reunification of Italy in the nineteenth century after the end of French rule in 1815.

renegade see **refugee**

repeat/reiterate/iterate (say again)
'Repeat' is the general word – 'do or say again'. 'Reiterate' is 'do or say again repeatedly', a word often used for emphasis, and also where 'iterate', which has exactly the same meaning, would do just as well. Possibly it is felt that a word beginning 're-' expresses a repeated action more effectively.

repel/repulse (drive back)
'Repulse' is the stronger word, often implying discourtesy or denial. To 'repel' an attack is to ward it off; to 'repulse' an attack is to drive it back by force. Used figuratively, 'repel' usually means 'cause disgust in' as in 'His appearance repelled me.' 'Repulse' is less frequently used in this sense, although the noun 'repulsion' is common enough. For the shades of meaning of related words, see **repulsive**.

repellant see **repulsive**

repository see **depository**

repress see **suppress**

reproach/reprove/rebuke (censure)
'Reproach' is a fairly neutral word: 'I reproached her for her forgetfulness', i.e. I charged her with it with the aim of slightly shaming her. 'Reprove' is the mildest word, often meaning simply to correct a fault. One might 'reprove' a child who fails to pass the salt and pepper unprompted to granny. 'Rebuke' is the strongest of the three, usually implying a stern or official 'reproof', a real 'telling off'.

reprove see **reproach**

repugnant see **repulsive**

repulse see **repel**

repulsive/repugnant/repellant (causing aversion)
'Repulsive' is the strongest adjective, and can be used of anyone or anything, as a 'repulsive' idea or the 'repulsive' appearance of someone. 'Repugnant', from the Latin *repugnare* (fight against), is simply 'distasteful', 'objectionable', so a fairly mild word. A 'repugnant' appearance is one that puts you off, not one unpleasant enough to make you feel sick. 'Repellant' – very often spelt 'repellent' – has essentially the basic idea of 'off-putting' and is usually applied to people, their faces, expressions, ideas, demands and the like. The word is rather stronger in tone than 'repugnant' but not as strong as 'repulsive'.

**requirement/requisite/perquisite/
prerequisite** (something needed)
'Requirement' is the general word, meaning 'condition', 'essential', as the 'requirements' of military service or compulsory education. A 'requisite' is something that is indispensable, especially a concrete object, as toilet 'requisites' (what one has to have to wash, dress, do one's hair, etc.). A 'perquisite' is something that is regarded as one's due by right, an incidental or 'fringe' benefit or 'perk' (its accepted colloquial abbreviation). A 'prerequisite' is something that it is essential to have before one can have or do something else. 'A' levels are a 'prerequisite' for university entry, and good eyesight for passing a driving test.

requisite see **requirement**

reservation/reserve/preserve (tract of land set apart for special purpose)
The meanings sometimes overlap, although on the whole it's a question of what the tract of land contains. 'Reservation' is particularly associated with Indian tribes in America; 'reserve' with animals, especially wildlife, trees and plants; 'preserve' with game or fish that must be protected and/or propagated, usually for sport. From this last sense comes the idea of poaching or trespassing on someone else's 'preserves', literally or figuratively.

reserve see **reservation**

resin/rosin (substance used in medicine or for making plastics)
'Resin' is the solid or semi-solid substance secreted by most plants, especially pine and fir trees, used chiefly in medicine and for making varnishes, printing ink and plastics. Synthetic 'resin', made by the polymerisation of simple molecules, is essentially used for plastics, but also for varnishes and adhesives. 'Rosin' – related to 'resin' with an unexplained change of vowel – is the hard, brittle 'resin' left after the oil of turpentine has been distilled off from the crude oleo-resin of the pine tree. It is also used for making varnish, but a more direct application is its use for rubbing on violin bows. In non-scientific usage the two words are often interchangeable.

resort see **resource**

resound/redound (indicate fame or success)
To 'resound', literally 're-echo', is to be famed or celebrated: the name of Shakespeare 'resounds' through the ages. To 'redound' is to bring something as a result. The word is usually heard in the phrase 'redound to one's credit', i.e. make a contribution to it, although things can also 'redound' to one's discredit or disadvantage. Crimes, too, can 'redound' on those who commit them, 'fall on their own heads' as it were. The word has an echo of 'rebound', certainly in this last usage, although it is not related to it. The origin

is in Old French *redonder* (to overflow) with the possible influence of 'renown'.

resource/resort/recourse (a turning to, falling back on)
A 'resource' is an action or measure that one can turn to in an emergency. There is no verb 'resource'. A 'resort' is somebody or something actually turned to for help, especially in the phrase 'as a last resort'. The verb 'resort to' means 'turn to', 'use', when all else fails. A 'recourse' has the same meaning as a 'resort', and this is where the confusion lies, together with the corresponding verbal phrase 'have recourse to' and 'resort to'. (Thus there are no forms, 'have resource to' or 'have resort to'.) So 'flight was his only resource' means virtually the same as 'flight was the only thing he could have recourse to.' The confusion is perhaps more in the usage of the words than the meaning.

restive see **restless**

restless/restive (uneasy)
'Restless' means 'showing an inability to remain at rest', as a 'restless' mood or a 'restless' night (one with little sleep). 'Restive' means 'impatient at having to stay at rest', 'uneasy at being restricted', as a 'restive' horse, which usually means a disobedient one. The word is not so much related to 'rest' = 'repose' as to 'rest' = 'remain', a sense apparent in the phrase 'to rest assured'. 'Restive' is not normally the word used in the catch phrase 'The natives are restless.'

Restoration see **Renaissance**

résumé/précis (summary)
A 'résumé' is a summary or concise account of something; a 'précis' is an abstract or abridged account of something. The words are sometimes loosely used interchangeably to mean 'synopsis', although 'précis' is normally restricted to apply to speech or written work. As a literary exercise familiar to school pupils a 'précis' is an attempt at boiling down a long-winded or verbose text to its essence by distilling the basic facts or arguments contained in it.

retch see **reach**

reticle see **graticule**

retire/retreat (withdraw)
In military terms, to 'retire' is to withdraw for tactical or strategic reasons, almost on the lines of the French *reculer pour mieux sauter* (draw back in order to jump better). To 'retreat', on the other hand, implies an obligatory withdrawal.

retort/riposte (sharp reply)
A 'retort' is a sharp reply; a 'riposte' a reply that is sharp. In other words a 'retort' is a quick reply, a 'riposte' a smart or witty one. Both the nouns are used as verbs.

retract/recant (take back)
To 'retract' a statement or opinion or promise is to withdraw it, so that things stand as they were before it was made. To 'recant' a statement is to go back on it, or be forced to go back, i.e. to deny one's own words. The word literally means 'unsing', with the prefix 're-' not meaning 'again' but a negative, as in 'resign' (= 'unsign'). The 'singing' reference is to the Greek palinode, which was an ode or song in which the author 'retracted' something he had said in a former poem. The Greek word literally means 'singing over again'.

retreat see **retire**

revenge see **avenge**

revolve/rotate (turn, go round)
The basic difference is that 'rotate' implies the turning of something around its own centre. Thus the moon 'revolves' round the earth, and the earth 'rotates' on its axis. 'Rotate' is derived from Latin *rota* (wheel). However, 'revolve' is frequently used where 'rotate' should properly be.

reward/award (prize)
A 'reward' is given in recognition of merit, as a recompense. In other words it gives something in return. 'Rewards' are almost always for something good – only rarely is a 'reward' given for something evil. An exception might be an ironic use, as: 'The gallows was his reward for desertion.' An

'award' is something assigned or ordered, as by a judge, for both good and evil, as, respectively, a payment or a penalty. In practice a 'reward' is usually given for a single, specific action and an 'award' for a more general, continuous service or contribution.

rhomboid see **rhombus**

rhombus/rhomboid (mathematical figure in the form of an oblique-angled parallelogram)
A 'rhombus' must be equilateral. The figure has the basic shape of a lozenge. A 'rhomboid' – the '-oid' suffix means 'resembling' – has oblique angles but unequal adjacent sides. The figure is often shown with upper and lower sides longer than the others, i.e. (in unmathematical terms) as an obliquely but uniformly half-squashed cardboard box.

rick see **wrench**

rigid/turgid/turbid/tumid/torrid
(swollen)
'Rigid' means 'stiff', 'hard', 'strict', as a 'rigid' branch or 'rigid' discipline. 'Turgid' means 'swollen', 'distended', as the 'turgid' udder of an unmilked cow. 'Turbid' means 'opaque', 'muddy', especially of liquids, as a 'turbid' river. 'Tumid' means 'swollen', as a 'tumid' stomach. 'Torrid' means 'oppressively hot', 'passionate', as a 'torrid' climate or a 'torrid' kiss. Both 'turgid' and (to a lesser degree) 'tumid' can be used of speech or written work, as verse, to mean 'pompous', 'bombastic'. Moreover, 'turbid', applied to running water, is often wrongly associated – although correctly etymologically – with 'turbulent' and even 'tumultuous'. No doubt, too, an overall Freudian link sometimes inhibits the precise distinguishing of the meanings.

rigorous see **vigorous**

riposte see **retort**

rise/arise/raise (move, or be moved, into an upright or higher position)
The verb 'rise' never has a direct object, i.e. you cannot 'rise' something. The verb is used of something or someone moving up, so that hot air 'rises', an audience 'rises' to its feet and on a hill the land 'rises'. 'Arise' also has no object. Its use is largely figurative, meaning 'come into being', 'turn up', as a question that 'arises' or doubts that 'arise'. In a literal sense it is normally used poetically or archaically, as a cloud that 'arises' over the horizon or the pseudo-historical 'Arise, Sir Galahad!' 'Raise', by contrast, must always be followed by an object, that is, it does not mean 'rise'. So one can 'raise' an anchor, one's hat, a question, a child and a thousand and one other things. The verbs sometimes present problems in their different tenses, present and past:

rise:	I rise	I rose	I have risen
arise:	I arise	I arose	I have arisen
raise:	I raise	I raised	I have raised

Risorgimento see **Renaissance**

ritardando see **rallentando**

ritenuto see **rallentando**

rococo see **baroque**

rosin see **resin**

roster see **rota**

rota/roster (list of persons on duty)
The two words are almost interchangeable. Strictly speaking, though, a 'rota' – the word is Latin for 'wheel' – is the actual round, as the early 'rota', and a 'roster' is the list which shows who does what and when. The original 'Rota' was a political club, founded in 1659 by the English political theorist James Harrington, which advocated rotation in the offices of government. 'Roster' is in fact from the Dutch *rooster*, originally 'gridiron' (i.e. 'roaster') and later 'list'. The reference is to the ruled paper used for lists. The word was first recorded in English in 1727.

rotate see **revolve**

rotund/orotund (round)
'Rotund' is wider in meaning, with the general sense 'round' or 'circular' but also

with two specific senses: 'plump' or 'podgy', of a person, and 'sonorous', 'grandiloquent', of speech or literary style. 'Orotund' applies only to speech, or more precisely, to utterance, where it means either 'imposing' or 'dignified', or else 'pompous' or 'pretentious' – 'magniloquent', in fact, rather than 'grandiloquent'. The word derives from the Latin phrase *ore rotundo* (with round mouth), found in Horace's *Ars Poetica*:

Grais ingenium, Grais dedit ore rotundo
Musa loqui.

('It was the Greeks who had at the Muse's hand the native gift, the Greeks who had the utterance of finished grace.')

rouse/arouse (stir)
To 'rouse' is to waken or stir, as strong indignation. To 'arouse' – from 'rouse' on the lines of 'arise' and 'rise' – is to excite to action or put into motion. The difference is a fine one. 'Arouse' is more common with emotions and feelings, as 'arousing' someone's curiosity or suspicion. The implication is that 'rousing' stirs from basic inactivity to activity, and that 'arousing' excites something latent or known to be present. Compare 'The sight aroused my pity' (which I had anyway) and 'The sight roused my interest' (which earlier was non-existent).

rover see **rambler**

royal/regal (of or like a king or queen)
The basic difference is that 'royal' pertains to the person of a monarch and 'regal' to the office of a monarch. Thus one talks of the 'royal' family or a 'royal' salute (for an actual member of the 'royal' family), but 'regal' splendour (like that of a king or queen) or a 'regal' bearing. There are certain phrases, however, where 'royal' equals 'regal', as a 'right royal welcome' and 'to have a right royal time', and similar turns of phrase where 'royal' simply means 'magnificent', 'splendid', 'first-rate'.

rucksack/knapsack/haversack (bag carried on the back)
The three words are ultimately German for, respectively, 'back sack', 'oat sack' and 'eat sack'. 'Rucksacks' are mainly used by hikers and ramblers; 'haversacks' by soldiers for provisions; 'knapsacks' also by soldiers but not so much for food as for clothes. A 'haversack', moreover, is usually slung over one shoulder rather than carried on the back.

ruckus see **rumpus**

ruction see **rumpus**

rude see **coarse**

rumba see **tango**

rumple see **crumple**

rumpus/ruction/ruckus (row, disturbance)
All the terms are colloquial. A 'rumpus' is a disturbing noise or commotion or uproar. A 'ruction' is usually a quarrel: 'There'll be ructions soon, shouldn't wonder.' A 'ruckus', more an American word, is a violent disagreement. 'Rumpus' is of unknown origin – could it be related fancifully to 'rumbustious'? 'Ruction' relates to 'eructation', i.e. belching. 'Ruckus' seems to be a blend of both words.

runagate see **refugee**

rural/rustic (pertaining to the country)
'Rural' is a straightforward adjective meaning 'of the country' (as opposed to the town or 'urban') or 'of country people and their life', as a 'rural' setting or 'rural' studies. 'Rustic' has the overtone of 'unsophisticated', even 'uncouth', as the 'rustic' charm of a country cottage (with few mod cons) or 'rustic' manners or speech (uneducated, coarse). 'Rustic' suggests 'rusty', i.e. behind the times, but this is fortuitous since both words derive from Latin *rus, ruris* (country).

rush/dash (hurry)
'I must rush!' 'I must dash!' 'Rush' usually implies both haste and clumsiness, as when one 'rushes' down the stairs (quickly and noisily) or 'rushes' out of the house (tempestuously). 'Dash' implies enthusiasm or 'go' and a short distance, as when one 'dashes' to the shops (keen to get there

before they close) or 'dashes' across the road (impatient to get over).

rustic see **rural**

Sabaoth see **Sabbath**

Sabbath/Sabaoth (religious name mentioned in the Bible)
The 'Sabbath' was, and is, the seventh day of the week (modern Saturday) as a day of rest and religious observance among Jews – 'remember the Sabbath day to keep it holy'. The name came subsequently to be given to the Christian equivalent, Sunday, in commemoration of the Resurrection, which occurred three days (counting inclusively) after the Crucifixion on the Friday (the day before the 'sabbath', when killing was forbidden). A witches' 'sabbath' was a midnight meeting held in medieval times as a kind of orgy or festival supposedly presided over by the Devil. The name refers not so much to the day on which such orgies took place as to the fact that they were alleged to be held by Jews. 'Sabbath' ultimately goes back to the Hebrew *shabat* (to rest). 'Sabaoth' actually means 'armies' or 'hosts' but is left untranslated in the Bible, the *Te Deum* in the *Book of Common Prayer* and some hymns, in the phrase 'Lord (God) of Sabaoth'. The words are classic confusibles: Spenser got them entangled in *The Faerie Queene* where he has the line:
O that great Sabbaoth God, grant me
that Sabbaoth's sight.
The confusion is reinforced by the chain association: 'Sabbath Day' = 'Lord's Day' = day of the 'Lord of Sabaoth'.

sacristan see **sexton**

sadism/masochism/machismo
(sexually-motivated show of strength)
'Sadism' and 'masochism' are virtually opposites: the sexual gratification of 'sadism' is derived by causing pain and humiliation to others, and that of 'masochism' obtained from the pain and suffering inflicted on oneself. The terms derive respectively from the names of two novelists who described the phenomena: the Comte Donatien Alphonse François de Sade, otherwise the 'Marquis' de Sade, an eighteenth century Frenchman, and the Austrian writer Leopold von Sacher Masoch, who lived in the nineteenth century. 'Machismo' is a word unrelated to either. It describes the quality of being manly and virile, especially when overtly expressed, as in 'tough guy' sports and he-man roles. The word originates from the Mexican-Spanish *macho* (male, masuline). In a feature (10 July 1977) entitled 'Summer of the machismonauts' the *Sunday Times* described the sport of sailing on 'one of the new breed of fun boats' as 'one which caters for machismo and masochism in equal parts'.

sally see **sortie**

salon see **saloon**

saloon/salon (public room set aside for a specific purpose)
The general image behind the words is that of masculinity (drinking, driving) for 'saloon' and femininity (hairdressing, hostessing) for 'salon'. 'Saloon' is the term for the better class bar in a pub, the dining-hall (and certain other public cabins) on a ship, and, in the USA, a bar in general. A 'saloon' car is one with a solid roof with seats for four or more (including the driver). 'Salon' – the French word (hall) from which the solid English 'saloon' derives – was primarily the word for a reception or drawing room in a large house, and, by extension, the assembly of guests in such a room, especially of leaders in the world of art, fashion and politics, during the seventeenth and eighteenth centuries. Today the word is used either for the gallery or place where art exhibitions are

held, or, more extensively, for a fashionable shop, such as a beauty 'salon'. The male/female distinction is also evident in hairdressing: barbers or hairdressers have – or had – 'saloons', but hairdressers (the word is ambisexual) or stylists have 'salons'.

salubrious see **sanitary**

salutary see **sanitary**

samba see **tango**

sample see **example**

sanitary/salutary/salubrious (healthy)
'Sanitary' means 'pertaining to health', especially with reference to cleanliness and precautions against disease, as 'sanitary' ware (porcelain for lavatories) and a 'sanitary' engineer (expert on water supply, sewage disposal and the like). 'Salutary' means 'conducive to health', both literally and figuratively, as a 'salutary' swim in the sea or a 'salutary' reminder (one that has a good effect). 'Salubrious' means 'favourable to health', as a 'salubrious' climate. One still hears, though: 'She gave him a good, sanitary warning.'

sapajou see **cockatoo**

sarcastic/sardonic (bitterly ironical)
'Sarcastic' has the implication of making a sneering or cutting remark. It has its origin in Greek *sarkasmos* (flesh-tearing). 'Sardonic' has basically the same meaning of 'scornful' but is usually applied more to a person's nature or features – a 'sardonic' wit or 'sardonic' smile – than to the actual ironical remark. The origin is in Greek *sardanios* (bitter) from the name of a Sardinian plant which, when eaten, was said to bring on convulsions resembling bitter laughter.

sardine see **onyx**

sardius see **onyx**

sardonic see **sarcastic**

sardonyx see **onyx**

sari/sarong (oriental garment)
The 'sari' or 'saree' is the outer garment worn by Hindu women, consisting of a lengthy piece of cotton or silk worn loosely round the body with one end over the shoulder. The 'sarong' is a loose skirt-like garment made of a long strip of cloth wrapped round the body and held or tucked in at the waist, as worn mainly by men and women in the Malay Archipelago and Pacific islands. Both garments have to some degree become fashionable with Western women, with the 'sarong' being an outer garment usually draped in front.

sarong see **sari**

sat see **sitting**

sated/satiated/saturated (fully supplied or satisfied)
'Sated' means 'satisfied to the full', with particular reference to appetites and desires. 'Satiated' means 'supplied to excess', now – but not originally – with the implication that the recipient is sickened or weary of the abundance. One can be 'satiated' with anything from a strawberry ice-cream to sensational journalism. 'Saturated' means 'thoroughly soaked', 'charged to the utmost', as a tablecloth 'saturated' with spilled tea or a literary style 'saturated' with affectation. The noun of 'satiated' is 'satiety' (rhyming with 'sobriety') or 'satiation'; of 'saturated' it is 'saturation' and of 'sated' – 'satedness'.

satiated see **sated**

saturated see **sated**

savour see **flavour**

sawfish see **swordfish**

scamp/skimp/scrimp/stint (do or act sparingly or less than fully)
Take breakfast, for example. If you 'scamp' your cornflakes you eat them hurriedly or carelessly. If you 'skimp' them you eat them inattentively – reading the paper, say. If you 'scrimp' them you are niggardly with them. If you 'stint' the flakes you unduly restrict the amount you

take. 'Scrimp' may be related to 'shrimp', and 'stint' to 'stunt'. 'Skimp' seems to be a blend of 'scamp' and 'scrimp'. English has a generous supply of words beginning with 's' and another consonant to denote meagreness: see, for example, **scarce.**

scant see **scarce**

scanty see **scarce**

scarce/scant/scanty/sparse (not abundant, meagre)
'Scarce' has the suggestion of not being enough: 'Many foodstuffs were scarce in wartime.' A 'scarce' book is one that perhaps ought to be more readily available. 'Scant' means 'barely sufficient'. It tends to be used more with abstract nouns, as 'scant' praise or 'scant' justice. 'Scanty' means 'very small' with a hint of not being enough, as a 'scanty' crop of barley or a 'scanty' dress (so short or revealing as to be considered immodest by some). 'Sparse' means 'thinly distributed or scattered' as 'sparse' hair or a 'sparse' population.

sceptical see **cynical**

schedule see **scheme**

scheme/schedule (plan)
The words overlap, although 'scheme' is more the actual plan as drawn, displayed or written out, and 'schedule' is often the time-table for the procedure or order of operations of a project. One might thus have the 'scheme' of a town's bus routes but the 'schedule' for a conference. Significantly one has a colour 'scheme' but one is behind, or ahead of, 'schedule'. The two words are quite unrelated in origin. 'Scheme' comes from the Greek *schema* (form), and 'schedule' from Latin *scedula* (small strip of papyrus). Whether one pronounces 'schedule' with 'shed' or 'sked' is a matter of choice. Americans say 'sked'.

scorn/spurn/shun (reject, avoid)
To 'scorn' is to treat with contempt, especially when rejecting or refusing. To 'spurn' *is* to reject, but with disdain. To 'shun' is to keep away from someone or

something out of dislike or caution, or to take pains in general to avoid him/it.

Scotch see **Scottish**

Scots see **Scottish**

Scottish/Scotch/Scots (pertaining to Scotland or its people or language)
A much-discussed and tricky trio. When does one use which? It's worth quoting *Chambers*, itself a Scottish (?Scotch) dictionary, on the subject: '**Scotch**, adj. a form of **Scottish** or **Scots,** in common use even among Scottish dialect speakers, though disliked or resented by many Scotsmen: applied esp. to products or supposed products of Scotland: having the character popularly attributed to a Scotsman – an excessive leaning towards defence of oneself and one's property.' That is just 'Scotch', of course. What about the other two? Broadly speaking, 'Scottish' and 'Scots' are applied to both people and things, but 'Scotch' is usually used of things rather than people. It's largely, too, a matter of convention. One traditionally has 'Scotch' broth, 'Scotch' eggs, a 'Scotch' mist, 'Scotch' tape (a proprietary brand of adhesive tape made by 3M), 'Scotch' whisky (otherwise just 'Scotch'), 'Scotch' woodcock (egg and anchovies on toast), a 'Scotch' bonnet, a 'Scotch' fir (which, teasingly, is the same as a 'Scots' pine), a 'Scotch' – also 'Scottish' – terrier and a 'Scotch' thistle, Scotland's national emblem – '(not native)', snaps *Chambers*. Apart from such fixed terms, it seems more correct to use 'Scottish' when referring to the country of Scotland and what is native to it, as the 'Scottish' Highlands and the 'Scottish' character, and 'Scots' for an individual person, as a 'Scots' girl. But 'Scotch' is a frequent alternative to 'Scots' in such cases. Thus one can distinguish between a 'Scots' miner, who is a native Scot, and a 'Scottish' miner, who is one working in Scotland and who may or may not actually be a Scot. To the Romans the *Scotti* were a Gaelic race of northern Ireland: it was only around AD 500 that this people came to what was then the Pictish kingdom of Caledonia to give it its present name.

scowl see **frown**

scrimp see **scamp**

scrub see **bush**

scupper see **scuttle**

scurry/scuttle (move hastily)
Both words suggest the rapid movement of something small, as mice or ants. 'Scurry' refers more to the movement, which is hurried; 'scuttle' to the steps taken, which are rapid and hasty. Further, 'scurry' is perhaps, under the influence of 'flurry', used of a light, flittering movement, as of snow, leaves or birds.

scuttle see **scurry**

scuttle/scupper (sink a ship)
To 'scuttle' a ship is to cut holes through the bottom and/or sides for any purpose, but usually in order to sink it, or, alternatively, to do this by cutting holes below the water line or opening the seacocks. A 'scuttle' is more familiar to most land-lubbers as a porthole. To 'scupper' a ship is to sink it deliberately in any way. As a noun, a 'scupper' is an opening in the side of a ship or just below the level of the deck to allow water to run off. As a slang verb, which may be connected with it, to 'scupper' is to ruin or 'do for': 'That scuppered all my plans.' This is not the same as to 'scapa' or 'scarper' which is to leave without notice. (This verb is more likely to derive from Italian *scappare* than be rhyming slang – Scapa Flow/go.)

seasonable see **seasonal**

seasonal/seasonable (pertaining to a season)
'Seasonal' means 'dependent on a season', as 'seasonal' work, e.g. work done only in the summer. 'Seasonable' means 'suitable for a season', as 'seasonable' weather, i.e. weather one would expect for a particular season. 'Seasonable' also means 'timely', as a 'seasonable' reminder.

seated see **sitting**

secure/procure (obtain, get)
To 'secure' something is to obtain it for certain, as when one 'secures' seats for a particular performance. To 'procure' something is to obtain it by care or effort, as a book that is difficult to 'procure'.

sedate see **solid**

sedulous see **assiduous**

self-deprecation/self-depreciation (the understating of one's worth)
'Self-deprecation' is modesty, expressed by saying or doing something that makes one-self seem less important, talented or whatever, than one really is. 'Self-depreciation' is the act of humiliating or debasing one-self, usually for the wrong reason.

self-depreciation see **self-deprecation**

Semitic/Hamitic (family of languages spoken in North Africa and the Mediterranean region)
As applied to languages, 'Semitic' is the family that includes, among others, Hebrew and Arabic. Applied to people, 'Semitic' usually means 'Jewish'. 'Hamitic' is a family of languages, related to 'Semitic', that includes ancient Egyptian and modern Berber. The names are those of the peoples who are supposed to be descended from the sons of Noah – Shem, Ham and Japheth, who, with their families (listed in Genesis 10), lived before Babel, when 'the whole earth was of one language, and of one speech'.

señor see **signor**

señora see **signor**

señorita see **signor**

sensibility see **sensitivity**

sensitivity/sensibility/susceptibility (capacity for being affected or touched)
'Sensitivity' relates to being sensitive, either of people, as someone who lacks 'sensitivity' or awareness, or of things, as the 'sensitivity' of a nerve or radio receiver. 'Sensibility' relates to 'sensible' – not in the

sense 'having good judgment' but 'having delicate feelings'. A man of 'sensibility' would thus feel pity or some other emotion where another man would not. In Jane Austen's *Sense and Sensibility*, Elinor Dashwood represents the 'sense', and her sister Marianne the 'sensibility'. Both sisters have been deserted by their young men; Elinor bears her disappointment with restraint, but Marianne expresses her grief violently. 'Sensibility' also means 'delicacy of emotional or intellectual perception', as a painter of great 'sensibility'. 'Susceptibility' is close in meaning, but the emphasis is on the degree of impressionability. To offend a person's 'susceptibilities' is to upset or disturb his feelings, which by implication are delicate and easily affected.

sensual/sensuous (giving pleasure to the senses)
'Sensual' has an unfavourable connotation. Referring to the enjoyments of physical sensations it usually suggests grossness or lewdness, as a 'sensual' pleasure in eating or taking cold showers. 'Sensuous', by contrast, has a favourable overtone – that of experiencing and enjoying through the senses, as 'sensuous' poetry or the 'sensuous' music of Wagner. The suggestion of 'sexual' in 'sensual' is apt, although the similarity of the words is a chance one.

sensuous see **sensual**

sentiment/sentimentality (refined sensibility)
'Sentiment' is sincere, refined sensibility (see **sensitivity**), or a tendency to be influenced more by the heart than the head. One can thus appeal to someone's loyal or other 'sentiments'. (The word also, of course, means 'opinions' as in 'Them's my sentiments.') 'Sentimentality' is affected or mawkish 'sentiment', as displayed by someone in a 'sentimental' manner: 'I can't stand his weak sentimentality.'

sentimentality see **sentiment**

sentinel see **sentry**

sentry/sentinel (soldier or person on watch)

Both are stationed to keep watch and challenge or prevent the passage of unauthorised persons. A 'sentinel' is, however, more of a watchdog, in both a literal and a figurative sense. A 'sentry' is essentially a military man, and the word is rarely used outside a military context. Possibly by association with 'citadel', 'sentinel' has in addition the suggestion of someone not merely watching but defending or protecting. The words are related, deriving ultimately from Latin *sentire* (to perceive).

sepia/sienna (brown pigment)
'Sepia' is a brown pigment from the ink-like secretion of the cuttlefish, or a drawing done in it. 'Sienna' is an earth used as a yellowish-brown pigment (raw 'sienna') or, after roasting in a furnace, a reddish-brown one (burnt 'sienna'). 'Sepia' comes from the Greek for 'cuttlefish', 'sienna' is Italian *terra di Sienna* (earth of Siena).

Septuagesima/Sexagesima (Sunday in church calendar)
'Septuagesima' is the third Sunday before Lent, 'Sexagesima' the second before. The names derive from Latin *septuaginta* (seventy) and *sexaginta* (sixty). This cannot refer to the number of days before Easter, since 'Septuagesima' is sixty-three days before Easter. Possibly the words were formed on an analogy with **Quinquagesima**. Or, as the *SOED* points out, perhaps the reference is to the seventy days between 'Septuagesima' Sunday and the octave of Easter – the Sunday next after it. But that would throw 'Sexagesima' out. . . .

seraphic see **chubby**

sewage/sewerage (waste matter – or the system that removes it)
The stuff itself is 'sewage', which passes through sewers. A 'sewage' farm is thus one that treats the matter so as to be used as manure – or that uses it itself as fertiliser. 'Sewerage' is the system by which 'sewage' is removed, including the actual sewers. 'Sewerage' is sometimes used to mean 'sewage', but never the other way round.

sewerage see **sewage**

Sexagesima see **Septuagesima**

sexton/sacristan (church officer)
Both words are from Latin *sacrista* (sacristan), though 'sexton' less obviously so. A 'sexton' is, or was, more of an all-rounder, since in addition to looking after the sacred vessels in the sacristy, which is the responsibility proper of the 'sacristan', he takes general care of the church, its contents and graveyard, and also rings the bell, digs graves and the like. 'Sexton', however, is today found more frequently as a surname than a title of office, since his tasks are often performed by others.

shaft/haft (handle of long implement)
'Shaft' is used to apply to the pole or 'body' of a long weapon such as a spear, lance or arrow; to the handle of a hammer, axe, golf club or other long implement; to one of the two bars of wood between which a horse is placed for drawing a cart. A 'haft' is the handle of a shorter implement such as a knife, sword or dagger.

shallow/callow (trivial)
As applied to people 'shallow' means 'superficial', as a 'shallow' mind or character. 'Callow' means 'immature', 'inexperienced', as a 'callow' youth. Oddly, it derives from Latin *calvus* (bald). The sense is that of 'unfledged', and the word is still used in this literal sense of young birds that are not yet covered with feathers.

shilly-shally see **delay**

shindig see **shindy**

shindy/shindig (row, commotion)
There is a slight but discernible difference. A 'shindy' is a 'rumpus', with the hint of people having a rowdy but enjoyable time. A 'shindig' can also mean 'noisy party' but, as well, 'disturbance', 'quarrel': 'There was a real shindig when I said I wanted my money back.' One kicks up a 'shindy', however. 'Shindy' may derive from the kind of hockey known as 'shinty'; 'shindig' may, possibly, derive from a 'shin dig' – a dig on the shin. For further clamorous confusion see **rumpus**.

shrub see **bush**

shun see **scorn**

sibyl see **nymph**

sienna see **sepia**

sieve see **sift**

sift/sieve (as verb: sort out smaller things from larger)
Used figuratively, to 'sift' is to examine closely, as when one 'sifts' the evidence, i.e. analyses it minutely. The idea is that what is being examined has been scattered into fine particles by means of a sieve. To 'sieve', used figuratively, is to search for something smaller among something larger, as when one 'sieves' for clues by looking for them against the much wider background of the scene or circumstances of the incident.

signor/signore/señor/signora/señora/signorina/señorita (title or form of address of Italian or Spanish man or woman)
The ones with 'gn' are Italian, and those with the tilde (˜) Spanish. 'Señor' and 'signore' mean 'gentleman', 'Mr' or 'sir', with, however, the shorter form 'signor' used in Italian before a name, e.g. 'il signor Lavatelli'. 'Señora' and 'signora' are used for married women, i.e. correspond to 'lady', 'Mrs' or 'madam', and 'signorina' and 'señorita' for unmarried, usually young, women ('young lady' or 'Miss'). Note that 'señorita' is the only one to have a 't' – there is no word 'señorina'. It is worth remembering that 'signore' is also the plural of 'signora' (i.e. could mean 'ladies'). The plural of 'signore' is 'signori'. There exists a 'signorino' as the male equivalent of 'signorina', approximating to English 'Master' as applied to a boy.

signora see **signor**

signore see **signor**

signorina see **signor**

simoom see **monsoon**

simulating see **dissembling**

sinecure/cynosure (something attractive or desirable)
A 'sinecure' is a position or office that requires little or no work, especially a profitable one – a 'doddle'. A 'cynosure' is something or someone that attracts attention by its brilliance or 'aura' in any sense. Brigitte Bardot (or your own particular favourite star) would be a 'cynosure' if she walked down the local High Street. The words have unexpected origins. Latin *beneficium sine cura* was a 'benefice without cure' (cure of souls), i.e. the ecclesiastical equivalent of a 'rotten borough'. 'Cynosure' derives from Greek *kynosoura* literally 'dog's tail'. This was the name of the Polar Star, which forms the 'dog's tail' of the constellation Ursa Minor and was used for guiding or directing.

Sinn Féin/Fianna Fáil/Fine Gael/ Fenians (Irish political party)
'Sinn Féin' means 'we ourselves' and is the name of the left-wing political organisation formed in Ireland in 1902 that today is most widely known for its association with the IRA. Basically it advocates nationalist rule for the country and complete political separation from Great Britain. 'Fianna Fáil', meaning 'soldiers of destiny', is another nationalist but more conservative party founded in 1926 by De Valera and advocating the establishment of an Irish Republic. 'Fine Gael', or 'United Ireland', is a party formed in 1933 in opposition to 'Fianna Fáil'. The 'Fenians' were members of a revolutionary organisation (the Irish Republic Brotherhood) founded in New York in 1858 with the aim of establishing an independent Irish republic. The name apparently derives either from Old Irish *fen* (Irishman) or *fiann* – the title of a legendary band of warriors in the service of Finn MacCool (or Fionn Mac Cumhail). The first three names are pronounced, approximately, 'Shin Fain', 'Feeana Foil' and 'Finna Gail'.

sirocco see **monsoon**

sissy see **prim**

sitting/sat/seated (position of person on or in a chair)
'Sat' is increasingly widely used for 'sitting', much as 'stood' is for 'standing': 'There she was, sat in the corner as usual.' There is no ambiguity here, but the usage is one that some find grating. However, since the verb 'to sit' can take an object, as in 'The mother sat the child on her knee', as can 'to seat', there can be no real objection to it on grammatical grounds. Past participles of transitive verbs are often used as a so-called statal passive, i.e. a verb form that expresses a state or condition that remains unchanged, as in 'The table was laid', 'A task has been set', 'We will be put'. 'Sitting', after all, is very much a passive state. So to say 'She was sat' cannot be regarded as 'bad' English – at the most it is colloquial. Possibly the additional fact that the simple past of the verb and the past participle are the same ('I sat', 'I have sat') causes further reluctance for the form to gain general acceptance. 'Seated', which expresses 'sat' in this way, is now used more as a regular adjective, as a 'seated' model.

skewbald see **dapple**

skimp see **scamp**

skulk see **sneak**

slatternly see **slovenly**

slaw see **coleslaw**

sled see **sleigh**

sledge see **sleigh**

sleigh/sledge/sled (vehicle travelling over ice or snow on runners)
The 'sleigh', the largest of the three, is usually drawn by horses or dogs and can carry passengers or goods. In the USA and Canada a 'sleigh' can be quite a comfortable conveyance, such as the 'one-horse open sleigh' that features in the Christmas song 'Jingle bells'. A 'sledge' is generally used for conveying loads, but can also take passengers. It usually has to have some kind of motive power, either drawn by

horses or dogs or reindeer or pushed or pulled by one or more persons. A 'sled' is either a 'sledge', especially a small one, or an alternative word for 'toboggan', a name more common in Britain than the other side of the Atlantic. A 'sled' (or toboggan) is the one popular for downhill runs, under its own power – or rather that of gravity – as a sport. A 'bobsleigh' or 'bobsled' is used either for sport, as a toboggan, or for hauling loads, particularly logs. Having said this, many people use two or all of the words interchangeably. The distinctions given are the dictionary ones. All three words have a phonaesthetic 'sl-' (see Introduction, p. 4).

slink see **sneak**

slit/slot (narrow opening)
A 'slit' is a straight, narrow opening or aperture as a 'slit' in a fence or a 'slit' in a skirt. A 'slot' is also this, but is usually designed for something to be inserted, as a 'slot' machine or the 'slot' of a letterbox. The words appear not to be related. 'Slot' in its original Old French form *esclot* meant 'hollow between the breasts'.

slot see **slit**

slovenly/slatternly/sluttish (dirty, slip-shod)
'Slovenly' means 'untidy', 'negligent', as 'slovenly' habits or dress. 'Slatternly' means 'like a slovenly woman or girl', so is normally used only of females. 'Sluttish', too, has only a feminine application, since it means 'like a slut', i.e. like a dirty, 'slovenly' or immoral woman.

sluggard see **lag**

sluttish see **slovenly**

snazzy see **jazzy**

sneak/slink/skulk (move or behave furtively)
To 'sneak' is to go stealthily or furtively, to leave quietly and quickly, or, as every schoolchild knows, to let out secrets. It has acquired a jocular past tense: 'There was a space, so I snuck in.' This may have been

prompted by verbs such as 'slink' which have a vowel change to 'u' in the simple past: 'The dog slunk away with its tail between its legs.' 'Slink' itself means to move abjectly, as well as furtively, especially from fear, cowardice or shame. To 'skulk' is either to move slyly or to lie low, in particular for an evil or cowardly reason. All three words are nicely evocative, and conjure up other 'sly' words such as 'snake', 'skull' and 'lurk'.

sociable see **social**

social/sociable (pertaining to society)
'Social' is the general word, so that one has 'social' laws and 'social' conduct, as well as the 'social' services. 'Sociable' means 'fond of society', that is, 'enjoying the company of others', so a 'sociable' person likes people to talk to, parties to go to, and is good in company. Confusion is particularly likely between such things as a 'social evening' and a 'sociable evening'. The first is a more or less formal evening spent in company; the second is one spent companionably with one or more friends. However, many 'social evenings', or simply 'socials', such as those run by clubs, churches and the like, are 'sociable evenings' as well.

solder/weld (join together with melted metal)
One normally 'solders' small objects, such as wires, but 'welds' large ones, such as steel plates. For 'soldering', moreover, one actually needs 'solder' – a fusible alloy applied in its melted state to the metal surfaces, wires or joints to be united. 'Welding' normally also involves the application of heat, but usually directly to the two pieces to be joined, not by means of an agent. There are other forms of 'welding' without using heat. The chief of these are: resistance 'welding' using a heavy electric current; arc 'welding' using an electric arc and then applying pressure; cold 'welding', by pressure alone.

solecism see **sophism**

solfeggio/arpeggio (series of ascending or descending musical notes)
A 'solfeggio' is an exercise for the voice

must be the latter. So similarly one has 'strait-laced', since a person who has strict or prudish morals was originally a lady who was tightly laced. Confusibles like these can drive one to desperate 'straits'.

strained/sprained (of muscles and tendons – stretched or wrenched)
A 'strained' muscle is one stretched too far or overexerted, as when one has a 'strained' back or a 'strained' ham. 'Sprained' is especially applied to the muscles and tendons of the ankle and wrist, with the sense 'excessively strained', usually as the result of a sudden twist or wrench. For similar confusible discomforts see **wrench**.

strait see **straight**

stratagem see **strategy** (plan)

strategy/stratagem (plan)
Both words ultimately derive from Greek *strategos* (a general), so that 'strategy' is literally generalship, or the art of conducting wars and managing armies. (For more on this see **strategy** below.) A 'stratagem', in war or peace, is a trick or ruse for deceiving somebody. *The Beaux' Stratagem*, an early eighteenth century comedy by George Farquhar, recounts how two beaux, Aimwell and Archer, adopt a variety of disguises and devices in order to marry the women they love.

strategy/tactics/logistics (science of warfare)
'Strategy' deals with the planning and directing of projects or manoeuvres that involve the movement of troops, ships, aircraft, etc. The objective is to have the forces moved in such a way that one has the advantage or superiority in conditions, place and time. 'Tactics' deals with the actual process of disposing one's forces, especially when in contact with the enemy. 'Logistics', from the French *loger* (to lodge), deals with the essential but necessarily secondary business of transporting, lodging and supplying troops and equipment – what goes on, in fact, behind the scenes of the actual theatre of war. Thus of aircraft 'strategic' means 'designed to disorganise the enemy's internal

economy and destroy his morale', while 'tactical' means 'operating in the immediate support of a local engagement or manoeuvre'. Both 'strategic' and 'tactical' aircraft therefore fire missiles and drop bombs, but for different reasons.

stratosphere see **atmosphere**

strepitous see **sonorous**

stultify see **stunt**

stunt/stultify (impede)
The association is a false one. To 'stunt' is to check the growth or impede the progress of, as to 'stunt' the growth of the economy. To 'stultify' is to make seem foolish or ridiculous, to render inefficient through frustration. One can thus 'stultify' someone's efforts by deliberately undermining his confidence in his ability to succeed. If one does so by belittling his chances of success one is, in effect, also 'stunting' him by cramping his style. However, the words are unrelated: 'stultify' derives from Latin *stultus* (stupid), and 'stunt' is akin to 'stint' and, probably, 'stump'.

stupor/torpor (dulled or numbed state)
A 'stupor' is the state of being almost unconscious because of disease, drugs or shock: a typical 'stupor' is that of a drunk. 'Torpor' is the state of having one's physical powers suspended, as a hibernating animal. Thus 'stupor' relates more to the mind and the senses, and 'torpor' to the body. Used figuratively, 'stupor' implies a mental dullness or even stupidity, while 'torpor' suggests a lethargic or indifferent state. 'Stupor' is related to 'stupid' and 'torpor' to 'torpid'.

stutter see **stammer**

subconsciously see **unconsciously**

subject see **object**

submerged/immersed (in or under water)
'Submerged' is 'situated under the water', often with the implication that the object itself should not naturally be so, or that it is

using the so-called 'sol-fa' syllables representing the notes of the scale – do, re, mi, fa, sol, la, ti, do (as familiar from the song in the film *The Sound of Music*). 'Solfeggio' is simply the Italian equivalent of 'sol-fa'. An 'arpeggio' is the sounding of the notes of a chord separately but quickly, often up to the treble or down to the bass – a 'spread' chord, in fact, as heard on the harp. The Italian word for this instrument, *arpa*, forms the root of the term.

solid/stolid/staid/sedate (firm, reliable, not excitable)
As applied to character, 'solid' means 'reliable', 'genuine', as a 'solid' worker, or a man of 'solid' sense. 'Stolid' means 'impassive', 'not easily stirred', either in a favourable sense, as a 'stolid' friendship being a detached, unemotional one, or unfavourably as a 'stolid' stare being a dull, stupid one. 'Staid' denotes a settled or 'sedate' character, as, again, favourably as in a 'staid' companion, or unfavourably as in a 'staid' old maid. 'Sedate' means 'calm and composed': 'She's a most sedate young lady.'

solipsism see **sophism**

sonorous/stertorous/strepitous/ stentorian (loud, noisy)
'Sonorous' means 'giving out a resonant sound', especially a deep one, as a 'sonorous' bass voice or a 'sonorous' roar. 'Stertorous' is really a medical term – 'snoring heavily', as of the laboured breathing of someone in an apoplectic fit. 'Strepitous' just means 'noisy'. As the *SOED* points out, its use is mainly in musical criticism. The word's discordant consonants are just right for the purpose, and music critics are not slow to take advantage of a word's phonaesthetic properties (see Introduction p. 4). 'Stentorian', which is almost always used of the voice, means 'very loud or powerful' – literally, 'like the voice of Stentor', the Greek herald in Homer's *Iliad* 'whose voice was as powerful as fifty voices of other men.'

sophism/solecism/solipsism (questionable type of speech or argument)

A 'sophism' is an apparently good but actually false argument, used to display ingenuity or to deceive. (An unintentionally false argument is called a 'paralogism'.) A 'solecism' is a rather grand word to mean simply a lapse of standard speech, as 'We was not going to see no one', (instead of 'We were not going to see anyone'), or otherwise a breach of good manners or etiquette – a sophisticated 'clanger'. 'Solipsism' is the theory that nothing but the self exists, or that nothing but the self can be the object of real knowledge. The term derives from Latin *solus ipse* (only self). The other two words are from Greek, respectively 'clever device' and 'incorrectness of speech'.

sortie/sally (outburst or outrush of someone or something)
'Sortie' is usually confined to military usage: the outrush of troops from a besieged place to attack those besieging, or a particular mission carried out by a group of aircraft, as a bombing raid. A 'sally' can also be used in a military sense (though not of aircraft), but it is mainly found in some figurative sense, as a 'sally' of wit (a sudden outburst of it) or, of one engaged in a conversation or discussion, a brilliant 'sally'. In this sense it applies to a lively remark which is often made by way of a verbal attack. Like several English military terms ('grenade', 'redoubt', 'bombard'), 'sortie' and 'sally' are French words – 'a going out' and 'a leaping out'.

sostenuto/tenuto (musical terms meaning 'sustained')
The words, like the majority of musical directions, are Italian, meaning 'sustained' and 'held'. 'Sostenuto' directs that a note must be sustained to its full nominal value, or even longer than this. 'Tenuto' directs that a note or chord must be held firmly to its full value, or possibly slightly more (as if to be on the safe side). The term is usually used after a staccato passage, or where a staccato passage might be expected, so has the implied contrast, 'not staccato'. The difference is thus very fine.

soufflé see **mousse**

sparse see **scarce**

spasmodically see **sporadically**

specially/especially (particularly)
A very common pair of confusibles. 'Specially' means 'for a particular purpose', 'in a particular way', and is often found with a verb: 'I did this specially for you', 'He came early specially'. 'Especially' means 'exceptionally', 'to a high degree', 'most', and is usually used with an adjective: 'This is an especially difficult question' or 'This point is especially important.' But the difference often needs careful (or special) distinguishing: if you are 'specially careful' you take care in a particular way; if you are 'especially careful' you are very careful. In the nature of things 'especially' is the much more frequent word – but usually turns up as 'specially', which is of course easier to say.

specimen see **example**

spire/steeple (tapering tower on top of a church)
Strictly speaking, a 'spire' is on a tower or roof, or else forms the upper, tapering part of a 'steeple'. This means that a 'steeple' (related to 'steep') is the whole structure – normally a tower with bells and a 'spire' on top. However, the words are up to a point interchangeable. Ordnance Survey maps have special symbols for 'church with tower' and 'church with spire' as well as 'church without tower or spire'.

spleen see **bile**

splutter/sputter (scatter explosively)
Someone talking hastily and confusedly, as when excited or embarrassed, usually 'splutters'; a person almost incoherent with rage or shock may well 'sputter'. 'Splutter' refers more to the actual sound – it is a blend of 'splash' and 'sputter' – and 'sputter', related to 'spout', to the explosive nature of the action. For this reason fat cooking may 'splutter' or 'sputter', but a firework usually just 'sputters'.

sporadically/spasmodically (intermittently)
'Sporadically' means 'appearing or happening at intervals'; if you sleep 'sporadically' you have a fitful or disturbed night. The image is that of seeds being sown, from Greek *spora* (seed, sowing). 'Spasmodically' is, in its literal sense, 'characterised by spasms', so basically means 'by fits and starts'. 'He worked spasmodically' means he worked for a while, then stopped suddenly, then started up again, and so on. 'He worked sporadically' means simply that he worked from time to time, rather than continuously.

sprained see **strained**

spray/spume (moving droplets of water)
'Spray' is water that is blown through the air, or falls through the air, as from waves, a fountain or a waterfall. 'Spume' is the foaming or frothing water found on an agitated surface, as the 'white horses' that form the crests of waves on a rough sea.

sprint see **spurt**

spume see **spray**

spurn see **scorn**

spurt/sprint (short stretch of fast running)
A 'spurt' is a sudden increase in speed of a runner, usually or typically put on at the end of a long race. A 'sprint' is a running race at full speed, especially over a short distance, hence also a separate fast stretch of running before the finish of a long race – differing in this sense from a 'spurt' in that it is not a sudden burst but a reasonably prolonged and premeditated manoeuvre.

sputter see **splutter**

squeamish see **queasy**

SS see **Gestapo**

stable/staple (firmly based)
'Stable' means 'firm', 'steady', as a 'stable' government or a person's 'stable' nature, i.e. one that is steadfast and dependable. 'Staple' means 'chief', 'principal', as a 'staple' export or product of a country. Confusion can arise in the phrase 'stable diet': a 'stable' diet is a balanced one; a 'staple' diet is one based on a particular ingredient or food, as a slimmer's 'staple' diet of fish and fruit (or whatever).

staid see **solid**

stalactite/stalagmite (deposit of calcium carbonate in a cave)
Two notorious confusibles. The 'stalactite' is the 'icicle' that hangs from the roof, and the 'stalagmite' the one pointing upwards on the floor of the cave. Both derive, unoriginally, from Greek *stalaktos* or *stalagmos* (dripping). One handy mnemonic for distinguishing the two, based on their inclusion of one letter, is 'C for *c*eiling, G for *g*round'.

stalagmite see **stalactite**

stammer/stutter (utter words hesitantly or with difficulty)
To 'stammer' is to speak with difficulty owing to a 'block', when the words seem to stick, especially at the beginning. It can happen to anyone in a moment of excitement, embarrassment, confusion or similar heightened emotion, as well as be a congenital defect. To 'stutter' is normally understood as 'to repeat involuntarily the initial letter of a word', as 'B-b-b-b-but you s-s-s-seem t-t-t-tired'. The condition is more likely to be an inherent speech defect than the result of an emotional state.

staple see **stable**

steeple see **spire**

Sten gun see **Bren gun**

stentorian see **sonorous**

stertorous see **sonorous**

stimulant see **stimulus**

stimulus/stimulant (something that stimulates or excites)
A 'stimulus' is the general term for anything, especially an incentive of some kind, that incites to action or exertion or quickens action. The thought of a coming holiday may act as a 'stimulus' in dealing with that job or piece of work you had b off indefinitely. A 'stimulant' is food or drink, that quickens som mental process. Common 'stim coffee and alcohol. Both words d Latin *stimulus* (spur, goad).

stint see **scamp**

stipulate/postulate (demand spec
To 'stipulate' is to make a pa demand or arrangement for someth require it as being essential, as whe 'stipulates' a condition or a pric 'postulate' is to claim the existen something or take it for granted, as w to demand it as necessary. One can 'stipulate' a condition or 'postulate' f condition. The meaning is the sa 'Stipulate' is much more commonly us however.

stolid see **solid**

straight/strait (confined or narrow)
The occasional confusion is something lik that of 'plane/plain' – two words strongly suggesting each other. After all, what is 'straight' is often narrow, and a 'strait' is usually narrow as well. And while 'strait' is usually a noun – 'narrow stretch of water open at both ends' – it can also be an adjective, as a 'strait'-jacket (or is it a 'straight'-jacket?). Conversely, 'straight' is more common as an adjective – 'not curved or bent', 'true' – but is also found as a noun, as the 'straight' of a race-course and the proverbial 'straight and narrow'. In origin, 'straight' derives from 'stretch', while 'strait' is related to 'strict'. But this helps only a little with the 'strait'- or 'straight'-jacket. Which is correct? Dictionaries differ. The *SOED* and *Concise Oxford Dictionary*, sixth edition (1976) recognise only 'strait'. Longman's *English Larousse* recognises both, but comments that 'straight' is an American alternative. *Chambers* prefers 'strait' but adds 'formerly also, and still erroneously, **straight**'. The decision must lie in the definition: is the jacket one designed to keep a person's arms and body 'straight' or is it intended to confine or restrain him, which is the sense of 'strait'? The answer

hidden, as a 'submerged' tree-trunk or, figuratively, 'submerged' fears. Of submarines, of course, 'submerged' is the accepted state. 'Immersed' means 'having been plunged into or under liquid', as false teeth in a glass of water or, in a transferred sense, someone engrossed in work or a book – 'immersed' in it.

subsequent see **consequent**

subtopia see **suburbia**

suburbia/subtopia (residential district outside a city or town)
'Suburbia' was the quasi-proper name first applied in 1896 to the suburbs of London. The word was intended to apply to the characteristic life of those who lived in the suburbs, especially from the point of view of their supposed narrowmindedness. The term now applies to the suburban district of any city or town. 'Subtopia' is a similar name first appearing in 1955 for a '*suburban Utopia*'. The appellation was, and is, an ironic one, since it applied to a country area that had been built up by means of tasteless buildings and dreary streets to create the impression of an ideal suburb, a supposed optimum blend of town and country. Surbiton, south London, is an example of 'suburbia' rather than 'subtopia', yet, it, too, was once in the country as its name reveals: 'southern barley town'.

supermarket/hypermarket (large self-service store)
A 'supermarket', originally rather a grand conception – a large self-service store with a wide range of freely accessible goods – is now simply any self-service store or shop, though usually one selling food products. The 'hypermarket' is a French innovation, the word itself modelled on 'supermarket' with 'hyper-' used to suggest something that was better or superior or 'more so'. The word is a new one to English (first recorded 1970), and opinions still differ, even at professional level, as to what precisely distinguishes a 'hypermarket' from a 'supermarket'. Basically, a 'hypermarket' or 'superstore' is an extra large 'supermarket' that is almost always situated outside a town, and that has a number

of features not always found in a conventional 'supermarket', such as an extensive car park, late opening nights, large non-food sections and, frequently, special ranges of discount prices. There were four 'hypermarkets' in Britain in 1966, then known only by their French commercial name of 'Carrefour'. By 1972 the number had grown to 144.

supernatural/preternatural (transcending the laws of nature)
'Supernatural' suggests divine or superhuman properties, as 'supernatural' power or strength. 'Preternatural' implies the possession of supernormal gifts or qualities even to an abnormal degree, as the 'preternatural' silence of the desert or the 'preternatural' sense of hearing of bats.

supersede see **surpass**

supine see **prostrate**

supplement/complement (additional part)
The two are more frequently confused than they should be. A 'supplement' is something additional to what is regarded as a whole, as a 'supplement' to a newspaper or a 'supplementary' ticket. A 'complement' is an integral second part or portion that makes, with the first part, a whole unit. That is, it is the apparently 'additional' part that makes something complete. A ship will not be complete without its 'complement', or crew of officers and men. 'Complementary' colours are those which, when mixed together, produce white light, e.g. blue and yellow. The confusion between 'complement' and 'compliment' is normally sorted out at the school desk.

suppress/repress (restrain)
The two words are very close, but a distinction can be made. To 'suppress' is to abolish, stop or restrain something that actually or potentially exists, as when one 'suppresses' a riot, an evil practice or the truth. To 'repress' is to check, control, but not necessarily abolish, something – usually something undesirable – as when one 'represses' a thought so that it seems not to exist. To 'repress' a desire is to check

it so that it is as little in evidence as possible; hence to 'suppress' a desire is virtually to eliminate it.

surpass/supersede (go further)
To 'surpass' is to be better than, to exceed or excel: 'The results surpassed my wildest hopes.' To 'supersede' (sometimes spelt, possibly wrongly, 'supercede') is to take the place of: 'John Black superseded Bill White, who had retired, as chairman.' No doubt the confusion, where it occurs, is due to the fact that when one thing supersedes another, it is often superior to it, as: 'The car superseded the horse', or: 'Few Victorians could foresee that planes would largely supersede trains for travelling long distances.'

susceptibility see **sensitivity**

swordfish/sawfish (fish with sharp, elongated snout)
The 'swordfish' is, on the whole, not as large as the 'sawfish' – although large enough – with a length of up to fourteen feet. Its 'sword' is its elongated upper jaw which it uses as a weapon for killing its prey. The 'sawfish', which can be anything from ten to twenty feet in length, has a bladelike snout with strong teeth on *both* sides. Its saws are used mainly for feeding, either by digging out animals from the sea bottom, or, like the 'swordfish', by maiming or killing smaller fish.

sybarite see **sycophant**

sycophant/sybarite (disagreeably selfish person)
A 'sycophant', pronounced 'sickerfant', is a servile, fawning person, one who flatters in order to be praised or rewarded, a 'toady' or 'bootlicker'. A 'sybarite' devotes himself to the pursuit of luxury and pleasure, especially of the voluptuous or sensual. The original 'sybarites' were the inhabitants of Sybaris, an ancient Greek city noted for its wealth and luxury. Greek *sykophantes* means literally 'fig-shower'. 'Showing a fig' was, as it still is in many countries, the classical equivalent of the V-sign (the thumb thrust between two fingers) and a gesture used when denouncing a culprit.

sylph see **nymph**

sympathy/empathy (feeling with or for a person)
'Sympathy' is literally 'feeling with' – a compassion for or commiseration with a person, a feeling of understanding towards him. 'Empathy' is literally 'feeling into'. The term originated in psychology in 1912, as a Greek-type translation of the German *Einfühlung*, to describe the ability to project one's personality into someone and so more fully understand him. The word has subsequently come to mean little more than 'appreciative understanding'.

synchrocyclotron see **cyclotron**

synchrotron see **cyclotron**

tack see **track**

tactics see **strategy** (science of warfare)

taiga see **tundra**

tamper see **tinker**

Tang see **Ming**

tangerine/mandarin (small type of orange)
The 'tangerine', originally from Tangier, Morocco, is a small, loose-skinned variety of 'mandarin', which itself is a native of south-west Asia. 'Mandarins' probably owe their name to the particular shade of yellow of their skins, which is that of the costume of the former Chinese mandarins – the public officials, organised in nine grades, who also gave their name to 'Mandarin' or 'Putunghua', the form of Chinese based on the Peking dialect.

tango/conga/rumba/samba/mambo
(Latin-American dance)
The 'tango' is the ballroom dance of Argentine origin with varied steps, figures and poses that became all the rage in fashionable European circles before the First World War. Its music has a characteristic four beats to the bar rhythm, with the first beat strongly accented. The 'conga' is essentially the street dance, of Afro-Cuban origin, that became popular in America and subsequently Britain in the late 1930s. It is performed by a single column of people, each clasping the waist of the person in front, with a 'three-steps-forward-*kick*' progression. There is a slightly jerkier ballroom version. The 'rumba', also of Afro-Cuban origin, is danced with a basic pattern of two quick side steps followed by a slow forward step and is best known for the horizontal 'hip wiggle' of the dancers. The 'samba' is of Brazilian origin, and caught on in western Europe and the USA in the 1940s. It is danced to a four beats to the bar rhythm with a simple forward and backward step and tilting, rocking body movements. The 'mambo' is in effect an offbeat version of the 'rumba', with the slow forward step held through to the first beat of the following bar and dancers not in standard ballroom embrace but holding one hand only or not touching at all. The cha-cha-cha of the 1950s was a development of it. (The 'mamb*a*' is a poisonous snake of the cobra family, and 'Samb*o*' a derogatory nickname for a negro as well as a judo-style sport popular in the Soviet Union. The 'Cong*o*' is the name of two central African countries, one of which is now Zaire.)

tarsus/metatarsus/metacarpus/carpus
(group of bones in the hand or foot)
The 'tarsus' is a collection of bones in the foot between the **tibia** and the 'metatarsus', which is comprised of five longish bones between the 'tarsus' and the toes. The arrangement of the 'metacarpus' *vis-à-vis* the 'carpus' in the hand is similar: the 'carpus' consists of eight bones that comprise the wrist, and the 'metacarpus' is the group of bones between the wrist and the fingers. 'Meta-' in each case means 'beyond'.

task/tax (as verb: make serious or excessive demands on)
To 'task' something, as one's strength or resources, is to put a strain on it or subject it to severe or unreasonable exertion. To 'tax' a thing, as one's brain or someone's patience, is to make serious but not impossible demands on it. The implication is that to 'task' a person's strength, say, is to subject him to exertion to such an extent that he can barely do what is required of him, whereas to 'tax' someone's strength is to submit him to a heavy strain but not to such a degree that he cannot perform the act.

tax see **task**

teeter see **totter**

temerity/timidity (state sometimes caused by fear)
'Temerity' is a reckless boldness, a foolhardiness, which may or may not be engendered by fear. 'He had the temerity to tell me I drove too fast.' 'Timidity', seen by comparison with 'temerity', is either fear itself or shyness, and the more common of the two. Possibly the confusion springs not only from the resemblance of the words to each other but also from the tendency of frightened people to perform rash acts. There is no common adjective for 'temerity' – a bookish word 'temerarious' exists – but 'timidity', of course, has **'timid'**.

tenacity see **persistence**

tendency see **trend**

tense/terse (brief)
'Tense', literally 'drawn taut', means 'characterised by strain', as a 'tense' moment or 'tense' anxiety. To say something in a 'tense' manner or voice might well be to say it abruptly or snappily. 'Terse' has the basic meaning 'brief and pithy' but, similarly, a 'terse' remark could easily be one made at a 'tense' moment.

tenuto see **sostenuto**

tepid/insipid/vapid (lacking warmth, interest or flavour)
The confusion lies not in the basic meanings, as respectively given in the 'common factor' definition, but in the extended uses of the words. A 'tepid' remark, for example, would be one made without enthusiasm, while an 'insipid' remark would be an uninteresting one and a 'vapid' remark a dull – in fact 'insipid' – one. A possible further influence, especially on 'vapid', is 'sapid', which actually means the opposite of 'vapid', i.e. 'having flavour'.

terraced house/terrace house (house with a terrace)
'Terraced house = terrace house', says the *Concise Oxford Dictionary*. And yet. . . . A 'terraced house' is really a house with its own terrace, while a 'terrace house' is a house (one of a row) on a terrace, now often called a 'town house'. Strictly speaking, therefore, one could have a 'terrace house' which was also a 'terraced house' – a terraced terrace house! The distinction seems, *pace* the *COD*, a useful one.

terrace house see **terraced house**

terse see **tense**

Terylene see **poplin**

testify/attest (bear witness)
The words are close in meaning. 'Testify', however, is more simply 'give evidence', while 'attest' is 'affirm that something is true', i.e. something previously mentioned or known about. Thus one witness can 'testify' that he left the door locked, and another can 'attest' that this was the case since he had been with him at the time.

testy see **touchy**

tetchy see **touchy**

theism see **deism**

thesis see **treatise**

thrilled/enthralled (highly delighted)
To be 'thrilled' by someone's performance is to be very excited or stirred by it. To be 'enthralled' by someone's performance is to be captivated or spellbound by it, literally 'held in thrall' or 'held captive'. Put another way, to be 'enthralled' is to be so 'thrilled' that one is unaware of anything else.

thymus see **thyroid**

thyroid/thymus (gland in the neck)
The 'thyroid' is the large ductless gland that lies near the larynx and trachea and secretes a hormone that regulates growth and development through the rate of metabolism. The 'thymus', also ductless, is situated at the level of the heart near the base of the neck and in man becomes much smaller with the approach of puberty, continuing to shrink with increasing age. Its functions relate chiefly to the newborn, in particular with regard to the production of lymphocytes. The names of the glands indicate their shape: the 'thyroid', from Greek *thureos*, is shield-shaped; the 'thymus' has a shape resembling that of a thyme leaf.

tibia/fibula (bone in lower half of the leg)
The 'tibia' is the shinbone, the inner of the two bones of the leg that extend from the knee to the ankle. The 'fibula' is the other, outer and thinner of the two. A kick or dig on the shinbone is more likely, in fact, to be a kick on the 'fibula'.

timid/timorous (shy, easily frightened)
The words are from the same Latin root, *timere* (to fear), but there is a slight but distinct difference. 'Timorous' has a connotation of 'shrinking back', 'hesitating because afraid', as a 'timorous' remark, one made nervously and apprehensively. A 'timid' remark is simply a shy *or* frightened one. For more about 'timid' see **temerity**.

timidity see **temerity**

timorous see **timid**

tinged/tinted (slightly or lightly coloured)
'Tinged' means 'with a trace or slight degree of colour', as an evening sky 'tinged' with pink. 'Tinted' means 'with a delicate

or pale colour', as 'tinted' glasses (delicately darkened) or 'tinted' lines (faint or feint ones). However, 'tint' also means just 'shade', 'hue', as the 'tints' of autumn, with no special suggestion of delicacy and certainly no implication of paleness. Used figuratively, both words mean 'shaded', 'coloured', 'slightly having', as a voice 'tinged' with regret, although 'tinted' is, for some reason, rarely used in a non-literal sense.

tinker/tamper (botch, spoil by poor workmanship)
To 'tinker' with something is to work on it unskilfully or clumsily or at any rate amateurishly, as when one 'tinkers' with the car or a radio. The word is related to 'tinker', the mender of pots and pans who was originally, according to one theory, a worker in tin. To 'tamper' with a thing is to meddle with it deliberately so as to alter or damage it, as someone who 'tampers' with a lock or the works of a clock. The verb is a variation of 'temper'.

tinted see **tinged**

titillate/titivate (touch up)
To 'titillate' is literally to excite a tingling or itching sensation by touching or stroking lightly, and, figuratively, to excite pleasantly – in both senses 'tickle', in fact (although 'tickle' does not always have the implication of a deliberate excitation). To 'titivate', sometimes spelt 'tittivate', is a colloquial word meaning 'smarten up', 'make spruce'. The verb is not used figuratively. It seems to derive from 'tidy' with a modelling on some word like 'cultivate'. 'Titillate' comes from the Latin word of the same meaning.

titivate see **titillate**

to-do/ado (fuss)
'What a to-do!' The word implies fuss and excitement, pleasant or unpleasant. It derives from the phrase 'What's to do?' meaning 'What's the matter?' 'Ado' used also to mean 'fuss' but now has the meaning of 'activity' or 'doing', as in the phrase 'without further ado'. Shakespeare's *Much Ado . . .* has the old sense of 'noisy fuss', with 'much ado' itself a northcountry phrase meaning originally 'much to do'.

Tony see **Emmy**

toreador see **matador**

tornado/typhoon (violent storm)
The essential feature of a 'tornado' is that it is a whirlwind. The derivation is in Spanish *tornar* (to turn) with the influence of *tronada* (thunderstorm) – an apt blend of senses. A 'typhoon' is a violent tropical storm or hurricane occurring in the China seas and adjacent regions in the months July to October. 'Tornadoes' are mainly associated with the USA, but they can in fact occur virtually anywhere in the world. 'Typhoon' derives from Chinese *tai fung* (great wind) under the influence of Greek *typhon* (violent wind). In Greek mythology Typhon was the grisly monster with a hundred dragons' heads who was conquered and banished to the Underworld by Zeus. He was the personification of volcanic forces and father of dangerous winds.

torpor see **stupor**

torrid see **rigid**

tortuous/torturous (painful, twisting)
'Tortuous' means 'full of twists and turns or bends' as a 'tortuous' road or a 'tortuous' argument (a complex and involved one). 'Torturous' means 'characterised by torture', as a 'torturous' ordeal. In many cases what is 'tortuous' will also be 'torturous', as 'tortuous' exercises or a 'tortuous' journey.

torturous see **tortuous**

totter/teeter (sway or rock, balance unsteadily)
To 'totter' is to walk with faltering steps, as if very weak and about to fall, or to sway or rock unsteadily – also as if about to fall. 'Teeter', a variation of 'titter', itself a dialect form of 'totter', is a word more common in American English to mean 'move or sway from side to side or up and down', not necessarily with a suggestion of being about to fall. (A specific American

meaning of the verb is 'seesaw', so that children go to a playground to 'teeter'.) Both verbs are often used figuratively.

touchy/tetchy/testy (irritable)
A 'touchy' person is one apt or quick to take offence on only slight provocation: 'He's very touchy about his pay'. The word is a variant, by association with 'touch', of 'tetchy', which basically means 'irritable' or 'crotchety', as a 'tetchy' old man or a 'tetchy' answer. 'Testy' has the implication of being impatient as well as 'tetchy' or crusty. A 'testy' reply is a hot, angry and intolerant one. The verb has its origin in Old French *testif* (heady, headstrong) from *teste* (modern *tête*) (head).

track/tack/trail (line of motion or direction)
A 'track' is a line of travel or motion, as marked by, say, a road, path or 'trail'. If you are 'on the wrong track' you are (figuratively) moving in the wrong direction. A 'tack' relates to ships and is either the direction or course of a ship in relation to the position of her sails, as the starboard 'tack', or one of a series of straight runs made by the ship on a zigzag course into the wind. This second sense has given the phrase 'on the wrong (right) tack', where one's course of action or conduct is right or wrong – and differs noticeably from the preceding one. A 'trail' is a path or 'track' made usually by men or animals, especially one across wild country or as followed by a hunter. It is the 'hunting' sense that lies behind 'on the right (wrong) trail' or simply 'on the trail', with the actual objective possibly more in mind than 'on the right (wrong) track' where what is important is the course itself.

trail see **track**

traitorous see **treacherous**

tramp/vamp (seductive woman)
'The lady is a tramp', as Lorenz Hart immortalised her in *Pal Joey* (1937). As applied to a female, 'tramp' has greater currency in the USA than in Britain. It means 'prostitute', or at the least 'dissolute woman'. (The word would not be readily taken to mean 'vagabond', since in the USA a 'tramp' in this sense is usually called a 'hobo' or a 'bum'.) A 'vamp' is a woman who uses her charms to seduce and exploit men. The word is a shortened form of 'vampire', and dates from 1918, liberation year.

transient see **transitional**

transitional/transitory/transient (passing, short-lived)
'Transitional' means 'passing from one position, state or stage to another', 'intermediate', as a 'transitional' phase of government. The stage itself may be quite lengthy. 'Transitory' means 'lasting only a short time', as 'this transitory life'. 'Transient' means 'passing, and therefore short-lived', as the 'transient' beauty of spring or a 'transient' smile.

transitory see **transitional**

treacherous/traitorous (betraying)
'Treacherous' relates to 'treachery', of course, and 'traitorous' to 'traitor', who is a 'treacherous' person. The difference is a fine one: 'treacherous' implies the abstract quality of 'treachery', as a 'treacherous' action (one that betrays) or 'treacherous' ice (liable to break under pressure); 'traitorous' suggests the personal act of one who betrays or commits treason, 'traitor-like', and therefore can apply only to a person or to a deed, manner, attribute etc. of a person, as a 'traitorous' thought or a 'traitorous' letter. Rather surprisingly, the words are not related in origin. 'Treacherous' (and 'treachery') derive from Old French *trechier* (modern *tricher*) (to trick); 'traitorous' (and 'traitor' and 'treason') come from Latin *traditor* (betrayer), which, also a little unexpectedly, gives 'tradition', the common theme being the 'handing over'.

treatise/thesis (formal account on a particular subject)
A 'treatise' is a book or written account on some particular subject, especially one that explains it or sets out its principles as, for example, Hume's *Treatise of Human Nature*. A 'thesis' is basically a subject or

proposition laid down or stated, especially one to be discussed or defended. The word is commonly used, especially academically, to apply to the dissertation itself, as 'Jane's working on her thesis on the influence of moonlight on earthworms'.

trend/tendency (drift in a particular direction)
'Trend' is the general word to apply to an actual drift of some kind, a gradual moving towards, as the increasing 'trend' towards football hooliganism. A 'tendency' is an inclination or disposition to move, proceed or act in some direction or in a particular way, as the increasing 'tendency' towards football hooliganism, i.e. the likelihood, but not certainty, that football hooliganism will increase.

triumphal see **triumphant**

triumphant/triumphal (celebrating a victory or success)
'Triumphant' means 'having triumphed', as a 'triumphant' gesture or look. 'Triumphal' means 'pertaining to a triumph', as a 'triumphal' procession or speech. Whether something that is 'triumphal' is also 'triumphant' will depend on the manner of its performance: a 'triumphal' speech could be a dull and boring one, but if made exultantly it would also be 'triumphant'.

troop/troupe (band, company)
Two standard confusibles, but ones that still turn up fairly often. 'Troop' is the more general word, so that one has a 'troop' of soldiers or (boy) Scouts and of animals such as monkeys or giraffes. 'Troupe' is more specialised, and usually confined to performers such as actors, singers and acrobats. 'Troupe' came into English from French (for 'troop') in the first half of the nineteenth century.

tropopause see **atmosphere**

troposphere see **atmosphere**

troupe see **troop**

tumid see **rigid**

tumult/turmoil (commotion, disturbance)
A 'tumult' is almost always a noisy affair; a 'turmoil' is a state of disorder or agitation or disquiet, not necessarily a noisy one. Moreover, 'tumult', except in the sense 'mental disturbance', implies a large multitude of people or things, whereas a 'turmoil' is basically just 'agitation', 'confusion'. The etymology of the word is not certain: even *Webster*, who usually comes up with something, has to admit 'origin unknown'.

tundra/taiga (vast stretch of land in the Arctic regions of Europe and Asia)
Both words are chiefly associated with Russia. The 'tundra' is one of a number of treeless plains in the Arctic where permafrost conditions prevail. The 'taiga', by contrast, is a large, coniferous, evergreen forest in the sub-Arctic, especially in Siberia, where it lies between the 'tundra' and the steppe.

turbid see **rigid**

turgid see **rigid**

turmoil see **tumult**

twat see **twerp**

twerp/twit/twat (contemptible person)
The terms of abuse are in ascending order of strength. 'Twerp' (or 'twirp') is used to apply to a stupid, objectionable or merely insignificant person: 'silly little twerp!'. 'Twit', often preceded by an adjective such as 'stupid' or 'silly', applies to a foolish or, again, insignificant person. 'Twat' is a far stronger word, although often used by speakers who are not aware of its basic meaning – 'female genitals'. It can be applied, as and if desired, to both males and females. The four-letter word has caused trouble in the past. It appears in its basic sense in the seventeenth century *Vanity of Vanities*:

His ambition is getting a Cardinal's hat;
They'd send him as soon an old nun's twat.

This is said to have led Browning to believe that a 'twat' was an article of religious

venturous see **adventurous**

verve see **vim**

veteran car/vintage car (old model of motor car)
The exact years appropriate to each category of car vary from source to source. The Veteran Car Club of Great Britain, however, states that all cars built before 31 December 1916 are 'veterans' and that cars manufactured before 31 December 1904 are 'true veterans' and are eligible for the annual Brighton Run. 'Vintage cars', sometimes called 'classic cars', are those built between 1916 and 1930, with some of the best cars of the 1930s classed as 'post-vintage thoroughbreds'.

vice/pace (term referring to a particular person or persons)
Both words are Latin, pronounced respectively 'vicey' and 'pacey'. 'Vice' means 'instead of', 'in the place of' and appears mostly in official reports and military orders to denote that one person is being substituted for another: 'Capt J F Williams is appointed OC Applied Skills Section wef 19 June 1978 vice Capt A L Sanders (sick in quarters)'. The word is much more common as a prefix, e.g. 'vice-chairman', 'vice-captain'. 'Pace', usually printed in italics, means 'with the permission of', 'with due deference to', as a polite term of disagreement: 'I would suggest, *pace* Mr Wilson, that we would do better to defer this project no longer' (Mr Wilson had wanted to defer it).

vicegerent see **vice-regent**

vice-regent/vicegerent (one acting in place of a ruler)
Perfect anagrams. A 'vice-regent' is one who acts in place of a ruler, governor or sovereign, i.e. a substitute for a 'regent'. As *Chambers* points out, the word is 'often blunderingly' used for 'vicegerent' (no hyphen), who is an officer having delegated authority acting in place of another, or any deputy acting for a superior. The pope, for example, is sometimes referred to as the 'Vicegerent' of Christ. The term comes from the Latin *vicem gerens* (wielding office). There is a rare noun 'gerent'.

Vietcong/Vietminh (Vietnamese political organisation)
The 'Vietcong' were the Vietnamese Communists in South Vietnam who were opposed to the successive American-sponsored South Vietnamese governments in the country and who provoked a civil war which led to the Vietnamese War. As a nationalist movement they had the aim of reuniting North and South Vietnam. The 'Vietminh' – the name is an abbreviated version of the full title meaning 'League for the Struggle for the Independence of Vietnam' – was a resistance movement working originally against the Japanese occupying forces. After the Second World War the movement, which had been founded by Ho Chi Minh in Annam, gained control of North Vietnam with strong support in the South (then under British occupation). In 1951 it was succeeded by a new organisation, the Lien Viet, or Vietnamese National People's Front. North and South Vietnam were finally officially reunited in July 1976 as the Socialist Republic of Vietnam.

Vietminh see **Vietcong**

vigorous/rigorous (forcible)
'Vigorous' means 'full of vigour', 'energetic', 'powerful', as the 'vigorous' growth of a plant or 'vigorous' measures (firm ones). 'Rigorous' means 'full of rigour', 'rigidly strict', 'harsh'. 'Rigorous' measures are strict or severe ones – which might or might not also be 'vigorous'.

vim/verve (energy, vigour)
'Vim', a slang word of American origin, means 'force', 'vigour in action', 'go': 'Put some vim in it!' The word is said to derive from Latin *vis* (strength). 'Verve' is 'energetic enthusiasm', especially in something artistic: 'Sarah played Miss Prism with tremendous verve.' The ultimate origin is in Latin *verba* (words).

viniculture/viticulture (cultivation of the vine)
'Viniculture' is basically the science or

study of wine-making (by cultivating the vine). 'Viticulture' is the cultivation of the vine itself, i.e. grape-growing. The derivations are from Latin *vinum* (wine) and *vitis* (vine).

vintage car see **veteran car**

violent/virulent/vehement   (forceful, intense, powerful)
'Violent' is the general word, often meaning little more than 'very great', as a 'violent' storm or a 'violent' dislike. 'Virulent' means 'actively poisonous' – the word is related to 'virus' – hence, of a disease, 'violent', in the sense 'malignant', 'evil'. Of people 'virulent' means 'bitter', 'spiteful', as a 'virulent' speech. 'Vehement' means basically 'strong', 'passionate', 'impetuous', especially of a person or his feelings. The connotation is not necessarily evil: a 'vehement' desire is simply a strong or intense one. Less often the adjective is applied to things, as a 'vehement' wind (a strong or even 'violent' one), or the 'vehement' onset of a disease.

virulent see **violent**

viticulture see **viniculture**

voodoo see **hoodoo**

voracious see **rapacious**

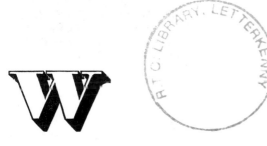

wake/awake/waken/awaken (rouse, or be roused, from sleep)
One can both 'wake' a person or simply 'wake', as 'I'll wake you up early' and 'I always wake early'. 'Awake' can be used similarly with or without an object, but the application is often figurative: 'Only then

did he awake to the reality of what he had done', 'The book awoke his interest in the subject' (roused it). 'Waken', with an object, often has the meaning 'rouse from inactivity', 'arouse', 'excite': 'The letter wakened his hopes of getting the job.' Used without an object, 'waken' means exactly the same as 'wake' or 'awaken', but again, is found more in figurative than literal speech. Finally, 'awaken', with or without an object, is simply a stylish or bookish alternative to 'waken'. Usage is thus fairly blurred. On the whole, the shorter verbs are used in a literal sense, and the longer in a figurative. The past and present forms of the different verbs are also not firmly fixed, but the following are reasonably well established and grammatically acceptable:

	Present
wake	I wake
awake	I awake
waken	I waken
awaken	I awaken

Past

I woke	I have woken
I awoke	I have woken/awaked
I wakened	I have wakened
I awakened	I have awakened*

(*increasingly heard, rightly or wrongly, 'I have awoken')

waken see **wake**

walrus/grampus (large sea creature)
The 'walrus', from the Dutch *walrus* (whale-horse), is the Arctic creature related to the seal, with flippers and a pair of large tusks. A 'walrus' moustache is one hanging loosely at both ends. The 'grampus', from the Latin, via French, *crassus piscis* (fat fish), is otherwise the killer whale – a member of the dolphin family found in all seas famous for its blowing and spouting – 'puffing like a grampus'.

wander/meander   (go aimlessly or casually)
To 'wander' is to go, roam, rove, stray or generally proceed idly, aimlessly or casually. To 'meander' is much more specific: used literally of a river, it means 'proceed by a winding course'. Figuratively

it has the sense 'wander aimlessly', 'stroll around'. One cannot therefore 'meander' down to the shops, only 'wander', but one can 'meander' along the street (with no objective in mind). 'Meander' comes from Greek *maiandros* (winding), originally the name of a winding river, now the Menderes, in Turkey.

warden/warder (administrative head or officer)
'Warden' is fairly common as the title of the head of some body or organisation, as 'Warden' of the Cinque Ports, 'Warden' of the Royal Mint, and the like. The word is also found as the name of a member of a guild or governing body, especially the 'Great' London Livery Companies, and as the title of the head of an educational establishment, as a college or school. (Six Oxford colleges are headed by a 'warden'.) The most common use of the word, of course, is as a short form for traffic 'warden', church 'warden', air raid 'warden' and similar administrative posts. Confusion is perhaps most likely in the matter of prison officials: the head of a prison in the USA is a 'warden', but in Britain a 'governor'. On the other hand a 'warder' is an unofficial and now dated term for a British 'prison officer', who in American prisons is a 'jailer' or, more properly, 'prison guard'. In Britain detention centres are in the care of a 'warden', but borstals are under the charge of a 'governor'.

warder see **warden**

warp/woof/weft (yarns in a spinning loom)
'Warp' is the term for the yarns placed lengthwise in the loom, i.e. across the 'weft' or 'woof'. The 'woof', which rhymes with 'hoof' (not like the 'woof' of a dog), is the name for the yarns that travel across from one selvage (edge of the fabric) to the other, interlacing with the 'warp'. This 'woof' provides the thread for the 'weft', which is basically the 'woof' in woven form. 'Woof' was originally 'oof', but 'w' was added by association with 'warp' which, like 'weft', is related to 'weave'.

wary/chary (cautious)
'Wary', related to 'beware', means 'watchful', especially habitually. 'I'm very wary of people who say that.' 'Chary', related to 'care', means 'careful'. 'I'm chary about letting her go on her own.' It has the additional sense 'sparing', 'careful about giving', as one who is 'chary' of praise (ungenerous with it).

weald see **wold**

weft see **warp**

weigh anchor/raise the anchor (raise – or lower – the anchor)
To 'raise the anchor' is obviously to haul it up, so that the ship is ready to sail. Over 'weigh' there is a double confusion: of sense and sound. 'Weigh' suggests heaviness – but to 'weigh the anchor' is not to drop it but, similarly, to raise it. The idea of 'weigh' relates to the heaving up of the anchor – when hauled up it will be 'weighed' or balanced. Confusion over sound is between 'weigh' and 'way', so that both 'under weigh' (by association with the raised anchor) and 'under way' (relating to the course of the ship) are found. Is 'under weigh' incorrect? *Chambers* regards 'weigh' as a misspelling, although the phrase is allowed by most other dictionaries. The *SOED* comments that 'under weigh' is a 'common var. of *under way*, from erron. association with the phr. "to weigh anchor".' The later (1976) *Concise Oxford Dictionary*, however, has simply 'under weigh = under way', which seems the best solution. In the phrase 'anchors aweigh', though, 'away' would be wrong.

weld see **solder**

whim see **fancy**

whimsy see **fancy**

whirl/whorl (something that turns or coils)
'Whirl' applies to something that whirls or has whirled, often in a figurative sense, as thoughts in a 'whirl' or the social 'whirl'. A 'whorl' is more a scientific or technical

term to apply to something having a circular or coiled arrangement of similar parts, as the ring of leaves round the stem of a plant or a drumlike section on the lower part of a spindle in a spinning machine that serves as a pulley for the tape drive. In fingerprinting, a 'whorl' is a complete circle of ridge-shapes (as distinct from a 'loop' or an 'arch'). Both 'whirl' and 'whorl' are pronounced alike.

whorl see **whirl**

who's/whose (relating to 'who')
'Who's' is the colloquial form of 'who is' or 'who has', as 'Who's going first?' and 'Who's been sitting here?' 'Whose' is the form to use for 'belonging to whom' as 'Whose chair is this?' For a similar distinction, see **it's.**

whose see **who's**

wigeon see **pigeon**

wince see **flinch**

winch/windlass (device for hoisting or hauling)
A 'winch' is the crank or handle of a revolving machine, so that a 'windlass', which is the whole lifting or hoisting device, has a 'winch'. However, 'winch' can sometimes apply to a complete hoisting gear, especially when a simple or basic one, such as that over a well. A 'windlass' is often a fairly complex powered device, as that on a ship for raising the anchor. Both are related to 'wind' (turn). Windsor, of castle fame, has a name that may mean 'landing-place with a windlass'.

windlass see **winch**

windward see **leeward**

woebegone see **woeful**

woeful/woebegone (full of, or showing, woe or distress)
'Woeful' means 'full of woe', 'wretched', 'unhappy', as a 'woeful' tale or a 'woeful' sight or 'woeful' ignorance. 'Woebegone'

means 'affected by woe', especially in appearance, as a 'woebegone' expression which is a mournful, miserable one. The 'begone' element derives from a former verbal construction in which the object was governed by a compound tense of 'bego' (meaning 'beset', i.e. 'surround by'). An example would be 'Me is woe begone', literally: 'Woe has beset me'.

wog/wop (abusive term for a foreigner)
'Wog' is mainly used of a dark-skinned foreigner, especially one from the Middle East or North Africa, and in particular an Arab or Egyptian. 'Wop', not so commonly used, is a derogatory epithet for an Italian, or any Italian-looking foreigner. The derivation of the term is perhaps in the Neapolitan dialect word *guappo* (dandy). The origin of 'wog' has been much debated. The most likely candidate would seem to be 'golliwog'. Unlikely candidates are the various acronyms from such words as *w*ily *o*riental *g*entleman, *W*orkers *o*n *G*overnment *S*ervice (in the construction of the Suez Canal), and Egyptians serving as porters and handlers of *W*ar *O*ffice *G*eneral *S*tores. Four-letter terms of abuse often upstage the many three-letter ones, as: oik, erk, yob, git, nig, Nip, nit, Yid, and the two in question. In the main, such words are more racial and social than sexual and scatological.

wold/weald (tract of open or wooded country)
Both words derive from Old English *wald* (wood, forest). In Britain, the 'Wolds' are those elevated tracts of country, especially in Yorkshire and Lincolnshire, that resemble the downs of the southern counties. The word is also found in the 'Cotswolds', whose first element is not, in spite of the association, 'cot' or 'cottage' – picturesque cottages are a feature of the district – but the Old English personal name Cod, pronounced (approximately) 'Code', that is, 'Cod's wood'. The 'Weald' is the name of the former wooded district of south-east England in Kent, Surrey and Sussex, now primarily put to agricultural use. 'Weald' is found in a number of English place names, as Harrow 'Weald' and various villages called 'Weald'. Both

words, in changed form, crop up in such place names as Northwold, Southwold, Waltham and Harrold.

woof see **warp**

wop see **wog**

wraith see **wreath**

wreak see **reap**

wreath/wraith (symbol of death and the dead)
Where 'wraith' is confused with 'wreath' it is usually the association with graves and ghosts that causes the trouble. A 'wreath' is not only a band of flowers left at a grave but also a term to describe a curling mass of smoke or vapour. A 'wraith' is principally an apparition of a dead – or living – person, as well as a word describing something pale, thin and ethereal, as a plume of vapour or smoke. The words are not related: 'wreath' is akin to 'writhe', while 'wraith' may come from an Old Norse word meaning 'guardian'.

wrench/rick (strain or sprain)
To 'wrench' an ankle is to overstrain or injure it by a sudden violent twist. To 'rick' one's neck or back is to sprain or strain it in a similar manner. For further diagnosis, see **strained**.

wyvern see **gryphon**

yang see **yin**

yin/yang (one of two fundamental principles of the universe in Chinese philosophy)
The two are opposite yet complementary.

'Yin' is regarded as the feminine, passive (or negative) and yielding principle, associated with cold and wetness. 'Yang' is the masculine, active (or positive) and assertive principle, associated with height, light, heat and dryness. The two interact and combine to produce all that comes to be in the universe. The basic meanings of the words are respectively 'dark' and 'bright'.

zany/zombie (stupid person)
A 'zany' is a clown or silly person. The word comes through French from the Venetian Italian *zanni* (clown), related to the Italian proper name Giovanni. A 'zombie' (or 'zombi'), of West African origin, is the snake or python god worshipped in voodoo ceremonies in the West Indies and certain parts of the Southern States of the USA. The god has the power of bringing someone who has died back to life, hence the transferred sense of the word to mean 'dead person brought back to life' and its modern extension to refer to a dull or apathetic person, one resembling the walking dead. The term is often wrongly used in such phrases as: 'There I was tearing round like a zombie'; no 'zombie' would do that, but a 'zany' might.

zeal/zest (enthusiasm)
'Zeal' is 'ardour', 'eager desire', 'enthusiasm': 'He attacked his steak with zeal.' 'Zest' is 'keen relish', 'hearty enjoyment', 'gusto': 'He attacked his steak with zest.' The word originally meant 'flavouring', and although of ultimate uncertain origin comes from obsolete French *zest* (now *zeste*) (orange peel).

Zen/Zend (eastern religious philosophy)
'Zen', from the Japanese (ultimately

Sanskrit) for 'meditation', is a Buddhist sect popular in Japan – and now with a certain following in the West – which advocates self-contemplation as the key to the understanding of the universe. The religion was introduced to Japan from China in the twelfth century. The 'Zend' is not itself a religious faith but the traditional translation and exposition of the Avesta – the Books of Wisdom, or sacred scriptures, of Zoroastrianism. This was the dualistic religion of Zoroaster or Zarathustra, its Persian founder in the sixth century. The combined text and commentary is called the Zend-Avesta. 'Zend' derives from Persian *zand* (interpretation).

Zend see **Zen**

zest see **zeal**

zither/cittern (stringed musical instrument played by plucking)

The 'zither' is a folk instrument of the Austrian Tyrol. It consists of a wooden box, acting as a resonator, with about thirty to forty-five strings stretched over it. The instrument is played flat, on a table or the knees, with a plectrum (hard pointed device for plucking the strings) and the fingertips. It became very popular from its association with the 'Harry Lime Theme' played on it in the film *The Third Man* in the early 1950s. The 'cittern' (also rendered as 'cither', 'cithern', 'gittern' and 'zittern') is an old instrument related to the guitar, with a flat, pear-shaped sounding-box and wire strings. 'Zither' derives from Latin *cithara*, the name of a musical instrument of ancient Greece (*kythara*), and it is a blend of this Latin word and 'gittern' that gives 'cittern', which, together with all its variants and 'zither' itself, is related to 'guitar'.

zombie see **zany**

APPENDIX I

Prefixes and suffixes

Many confusibles owe their confusibility to their common prefixes or, to a lesser degree, suffixes. See, for example, the large number of confusibles beginning with 'con-', 'pre-', or 'pro-'. Or take those confusibles whose prefixes differ by only one letter, such as affect/effect, eruption/irruption. Such confusion is increased, in fact, since many prefixes mutate their spelling depending on the letter that follows, so that 'in-', say, can be disguised as 'ill-', 'imm-', 'irr-', 'imb-' or 'imp-'.

Again, some confusibles that seem to start with a prefix do not actually have one at all.

Words that begin with the same group of letters must therefore be distinguished, and the question decided: 'Do these letters represent a prefix or not?' Often only a fairly detailed analysis will reveal the presence or absence of a prefix, and a dictionary the meaning of a particular prefix. Consider the words 'astatic', 'astern', 'astonish', 'astray', 'astringent', 'astrology' and 'astute', all picked at random from a standard dictionary (see the *Concise Oxford Dictionary*, 1976 edition, pp. 57–8). They all have 'ast-' in common. But analysis shows a more or less complete disparity of meaning between the words and a wide range of prefixes:

Word	prefix	meaning of prefix	literal sense of word
astatic	a-	not (Gr)	not static
astern	a-	to (OE)*	to the stern
astonish	ex-	out (L)	thunder out (Latin *extonare*)
astray	extra-	out of bounds (L)	wander out of bounds
astringent	ad-	to (L)	binding to (Latin *adstringere*)
astrology	astro-†	star (Gr)	study of the stars
astute	(none)		crafty (Latin *astutus*)

* OE is Old English
† strictly speaking not a prefix but a combining form or element

In an attempt, therefore, to sort out some of the chief English prefixes and suffixes, three tables follow. Table 1 is that of basic prefixes, with their meanings and language of origin (usually Latin or Greek). Table 2 contains some common suffixes, many of which are found in scientific words. Table 3 gives the variant spellings that prefixes can assume. Examples of words containing the relevant prefix or suffix are also given. The meaning of any unfamiliar or uncertain words can be checked, of course, in any standard dictionary.

TABLE I   *Prefixes*

prefix	meaning	language of origin	examples
a-	not, without	Gr	agnostic, amoral
ab-	away, from	L	abduct, abuse
ad-	to, into	L	addition, adhere
ante-	before	L	antenatal, antedate
anti-	against	Gr	antiseptic, antipathy
bi-	two	L	bilateral, biennial
cata-	down	Gr	catastrophe, catapult
com-	with	Gr	combine, compare
de-	down, away, off	L	descend, deduct, decapitate
di-	twice	Gr	dioxide, diphthong
dia-	through, across	Gr	dialogue, diameter
dis-	apart, away, not	L	distinct, dispose, disused
dys-	bad, difficult	Gr	dysentery, dyslexic
en-	in (same as in-)	L	engulf, enfold
epi-	upon, above	Gr	epigram, epidemic
ex-	out, away	L	exclude, exonerate
for-	away, not	OE	forgo, forbid
fore-	before	OE	foresee, forebode
hyper-	above, greater	Gr	hypercritical, hypermarket
hypo-	below, lesser	Gr	hypodermic, hypothermia
in-	1 in	L	intrude, inflame
	2 not (same as un-)	L	inedible, inattentive
inter-	between	L	intervene, international
intra-	inside	L	intravenous, intramural
mal-	bad	L	malpractice, malevolent
mis-	1 bad, wrong	OE	mislead, mistrust
	2 bad, not	L	misadventure, mischief
non-	not	L	nonsense, nondescript
ob-	1 exposed, open	L	object, obtrude
	2 meeting, facing	L	obviate, obvious
	3 opposition	L	obstreperous, obdurate
	4 hindrance, blocking	L	obsess, obfuscate
	5 finality	L	obsolete, obtain
para-†	1 beside	Gr	parameter, paramilitary
	2 beyond	Gr	paranormal, paradox
per-	through, thorough	L	perforate, pervade

TABLE 1   *Prefixes* (cont.)

prefix	meaning	language of origin	examples
prie-†	round, about	Gr	perimeter, periscope
poly-	1 many	Gr	polygamy, polymer
	2 polymerised	Gr	polythene, polyester
post-	after, behind	L	postpone, post-war
pre-	before	L	precede, prerequisite
preter-	beyond, more than	L	preternatural, pretermit
pro-	1 favouring	L	pro-Market, pro-Communist
	2 forwards, downwards	L	proclaim, prostrate
	3 onwards, in front	L	proceed, progress
	4 before	Gr	prognosis, prophetic
pur-	(same as pro- 1–3)	L	purport, pursue, purchase
re-	again, back	L	renovate, repel
se-	apart	L	seclude, secure
sub-	below, close	L	submerge, subsequent
super-	over, beyond	L	supernatural, supervise
sur-	(same as super-)	L	surcharge, surface
syn-	with, together	Gr	synchronise, synagogue
un-	1 not	OE	unselfish, unconscious
	2 opposite of	OE	unlock, untie

† not related to the para- of parachute, parasol, which is from Italian *parare* (to defend)

TABLE 2   *Suffixes*

suffix	meaning	language of origin	example
-algia	pain	Gr	neuralgia
-ane	paraffins	(after -ene)	methane
-asis	disease	Gr	psoriasis
-ate	salt of an acid ending in -ic	L	chlorate
-ee	1 one affected by verbal action	Fr	employee
	2 one concerned with	Fr	absentee
-ene	unsaturated carbons	Gr	benzene
graphy	1 descriptive science	Gr	geography
-ic	higher valence or degree of oxidisation	L/Gr	ferric

TABLE 2   *Suffixes* (cont.)

suffix	meaning	language of origin	example
-ide	binary compound	(after 'acid')	oxide
-ine	derived substance	L	chlorine
-ite	1 fossil or mineral	Gr	ammonite
	2 explosive	Gr	cordite
	3 commercial product	Gr	vulcanite
	4 salt of acid in -ous	Gr	nitrite
-lite	name of mineral	Gr	zeolite
-lith	type of stone	Gr	monolith
-logy	subject of study	Gr	geology
-oid	resembling	Gr	rhomboid
-ol	1 name of an alcohol	(after 'alcoh*ol*')	phenol
	2 name of an oil	L	benzol
-on	elementary particle	(after 'ion')	neutron
-one	compound	Gr	acetone
-ose	name of carbohydrate	(after 'gluc*ose*')	sucrose
-osis	pathological state	Gr	neurosis
-ous	lower valence than -ic	L	ferrous
-phil(e)	one who is fond of	Gr	Francophile
-phobe	one who hates	Gr	xenophobe
-phone	instrument using sound	Gr	xylophone
-phore	bearer	Gr	semaphore
-phyte	vegetable or plantlike organism	Gr	zoophyte
-scope	thing looked through or at	Gr	telescope
-stasis	slowing or stopping of flow	Gr	haemostasis
-stat	keeping fixed	Gr	thermostat

TABLE 3   *Variant spellings of prefixes*

prefix	variants	when occurring	examples
ad-	1 ac-	before c, (k), q	accept, acquire
	2 af-	before f	affix
	3 ag-	before g	aggressive
	4 al-	before l	ally
	5 an-	before n	annex
	6 ap-	before p	appeal
	7 ar-	before r	arrive
	8 as-	before s	assail
	9 at-	before t	attend
	10 a-	before sc, sp, st	ascend, aspire, astringent
com-	1 co-	a before vowels	coerce
		b before gn, h	cognate, coherent
	2 col-	before l	collect
	3 cor-	before r	correspond
	4 con-	before all other consonants	conceal, confer, connect
dis-	di-	before vowels	diaphanous
ex-	1 e-	before consonants	edict, egress, elect, erupt
	2 ef-	before f	effect
in-	1 il-	before l	illegible
	2 im-	before b, m, p	imbibe, immigrant, impel
	3 ir-	before r	irresistible
ob-	1 oc-	before c	occupy
	2 of-	before f	offend
	3 op-	before p	oppose
re-	red-	before vowels (sometimes)	redeem, redound
sub-	1 suc-	before c	succour
	2 suf-	before f	suffer
	3 sug-	before g	suggest
	4 sup-	before p	suppose
	5 sur-	before r	surrender
	6 sus-	before c, p, t	susceptible, suspend, sustain
syn-	1 syl-	before l	syllable
	2 sym-	before b, m, p	symbol, symmetry, symphony
	3 sy-	a before s + consonant	system
		b before z (rare)	syzygy

Warning! Some of these variant spellings assume the forms of other prefixes. Thus a- (variant 10 of ad-) should be distinguished from the prefix a-, di- (variant of dis-) from prefix di-, and sur- (variant 5 of sub-) from prefix sur-.

APPENDIX II

Six suggestibles

absinthe, absent – One might well become 'absent' or 'out' on absinthe, a green liqueur made originally from wine and wormwood. 'Absinthe' is related to 'absent' in the same way that 'wormwood' is to 'worm' and 'wood' – not in the least!

brackish, bracken – Dead, damp ferns by the sea? 'Brackish' means that the water is salty. The words are unrelated: 'brackish' comes from an old Dutch word and 'bracken' is derived from a conjectured word in Old Norse.

brunt, blunt – It may help, of course, to be 'blunt' if one is to bear the 'brunt' of an attack. 'Blunt' may be related to 'blind' or 'blunder'; the origin of 'brunt' is unknown.

Calvary, cavalry – The image is probably that of a religious painting showing mounted soldiers. 'Calvary', or Golgotha (meaning 'skull'), was the name of the hill near Jerusalem on which Christ was crucified.

hallow, halo – Both have an odour of sanctity, and 'hallow' is indeed related to 'holy'. 'Halo', however, derives from Greek *halos*, which had the basic meaning 'threshing-floor' (on which oxen walked in a circle) and the subsequent meaning 'disc of sun or moon'.

shrift, shift – To give a person 'short shrift' is to treat him curtly. 'Shrift' means 'shriving' (related to 'Shrove' Tuesday): to 'shrive' a person was, of a priest, to hear his confession, assign him a penance, and absolve him. Criminals being 'shriven' often had little time for this between their sentence and execution or punishment – they had 'short shrift' and, in a way, had to 'shift' for themselves. . . .